Praise for

NOBODY'S WOMEN

"Miller took the time to tell each and every victim's story, from how they began their lives with the same hope we all have to their drug addiction downfalls. But, more important, he *humanized* them."   —True Crime Zine

GIRL, WANTED:
THE CHASE FOR SARAH PENDER

"Wanted: more from this author . . . [A] classic example of fine journalistic reporting . . . Simply put, *Girl, Wanted* is a fantastic read."   —True Crime Book Reviews

A SLAYING IN THE SUBURBS:
THE TARA GRANT MURDER

by Steve Miller and Andrea Billups

"Much more than true crime or another update of *An American Tragedy*. It's an unflinching look inside a marriage and what led to murder."   —*Creative Loafing*

"Very interesting . . . Very fast paced, intriguing, well written . . . Once you pick it up, you won't be able to put it down."   —True Crime Book Reviews

"An eventful tale of deceit, jealousy, and the ultimate betrayal."   —True Crime Books Examiner

MURDER IN GROSSE POINTE PARK

Privilege, Adultery, and the Killing of Jane Bashara

STEVE MILLER

BERKLEY BOOKS, NEW YORK

BERKLEY

An imprint of Penguin Random House LLC
375 Hudson Street, New York, New York 10014

MURDER IN GROSSE POINTE PARK

A Berkley Book / published by arrangement with the author

ISBN: 978-0-425-27242-8

PUBLISHING HISTORY
Berkley premium edition / December 2015

PRINTED IN THE UNITED STATES OF AMERICA

10 9 8 7 6 5 4 3 2

Interior text design by Kelly Lipovich.

Penguin
Random
House

TABLE OF CONTENTS

INTRODUCTION

Daniel Defoe, the author of the eighteenth-century classic *Robinson Crusoe*, is, some claim, the father of the true crime genre for his coverage of Jack Sheppard, a habitual burglar and incorrigible jail breaker who told Defoe his story before his execution in London in 1724.

Defoe's stories on Sheppard's deeds were blared across the pages of a local newspaper. The public was duly titillated, and papers were sold.

Realizing he was onto something, Defoe next wrote the tale of a guy named Jonathan Wild, a crime fighter turned racketeer who was also executed. Wild's tale was one of duplicity; he befriended thieves then turned them over to law enforcement for the reward, a real rat fink. Even the public didn't dig that kind of deceit, and when he was headed to the gallows, he was pilloried with rocks.

It's tame stuff compared to today's sordid crimes,

including the one you are about to read. But it proved that people like to read about bad guys.

Murder, while many find it compelling to read of, is never easy to write about. It's heavy to be in the middle of a project like this and realize that just for a second, you forgot that someone died. That takes you down for a bit.

Crime is almost impossible to understand, and it comes like a tornado to innocent people who think, "It can't happen to me." I notice it over and over, and it truly blindsides survivors.

On the more technical end, true crime books are usually eighty-thousand-word crime stories. The writing draws a writer deeper into a story than any five-thousand-word Sunday feature, but it's the same exercise in many ways.

For *Murder in Grosse Pointe Park: Privilege, Adultery, and the Killing of Jane Bashara*, I found myself from the beginning talking with Bob Bashara, the man who was ultimately convicted of the murder of his wife.

We exchanged emails and phone calls, which began shortly after his initial arrest on charges of solicitation of murder. I would explain this book to people unfamiliar with the case as a situation in which a guy hired someone to murder his wife and then tried to hire someone to murder the guy who murdered his wife.

"You could get rid of the whole human race that way," one friend told me. "We could just keep paying people to kill off everyone."

When you toss in Bob's acknowledged embrace of BDSM—an expansive acronym folding in bondage, dominance, submission, sadism, and masochism—a sexual fetish world that is probably followed by more people than would acknowledge it, the story becomes even more fascinating.

The book *Fifty Shades of Grey*, a novel by British author E. L. James about young lovers immersed in their devotion to the practice of BDSM, was released to the mass market in June 2011. It was less scary reading about the practice while sitting front and center at the local Barnes & Noble just a few feet from the Starbucks counter. Nothing can be intimidating in that scenario. The popularity of the book speaks of the practice, though, and some people are fascinated by it, even if they don't practice it.

Jane Bashara's body was found January 25, 2012, and word of Bob's other world was quickly revealed. It included a basement room outfitted for bondage and other sexual mischief in a commercial rental strip along a main street in Grosse Pointe Park. The media called it a dungeon and did whatever it could to draw readers with lurid headlines and broadcast teasers.

Lester Holt, introducing an episode of *Dateline* in May 2012, called it "one of the most unusual cases we've ever had."

I never thought it was all that odd. People live their lives in accordance with the wishes of others far too often; lives of quiet conformity, following the leader into a trap of sameness that is hard to recover from. It's a set path and a trap ripe for revolt—graduate high school, go to college, decide what to do for the rest of your life, get married, have children, retire, die.

Bob Bashara started this way, walking the trail of so many before him, groomed to be upstanding and to follow the rules. His dad, George Bashara Jr., was a state appellate judge, an esteemed legal mediator and corporate counsel for Federal-Mogul, an international mechanical parts manufacturer.

Bob got married once, briefly, then again. He had the kids, the house. He was a community leader. He worked a solid job selling chemicals for a fine company. His wife, Jane, was an outgoing, generous soul who people naturally liked.

"My whole life is dedicated to giving back," Bob told a local reporter from the *Grosse Pointe News* in 1993. "Like Rotary's motto: 'Service above self.' I like that. Everyone in Grosse Pointe should appreciate Grosse Pointe and southeastern Michigan. Parents should be involved with their children and with their children's education."

He believed that, I am sure.

But the mind is a slippery thing and can get away from you if you're not careful. Somewhere, Bob's wires got crossed; a little short circuit, perhaps.

He began to find himself attracted to things that were rather out of the ordinary while living out an antiquated notion of the American Dream.

He liked the idea of dominating someone in a sexual way. While working on this book, sometimes after conversations with Bob, I tried to think how his mind must have fucked with him as he lay in bed in his four-bed, four-bath, 3,400-square-footer in that upscale neighborhood, the kids sleeping down the hall, Jane blissfully unaware of her husband's proclivities. Jane, by the way, was clearly the dominant in the Bashara marriage. There's nothing wrong with that, unless your spouse feels stifled and takes action.

You want to think his course of action, which felt so good, scared him, but maybe it didn't. Many people believe he is a sociopath. If so, it would allow him to rationalize his thoughts away, much like you can try to explain a scary noise in the forest off of a lonely, dark, wooded path.

That couldn't be a bear thrashing in those woods. They don't even come out this time of year, right?

For Bob, they came out all the time, and his sexual proclivities slowly started to rule him. He created an alternate identity, Master Bob. He went online to the websites that cater to "the lifestyle," as it is politely described. That term applies broadly, from your common swingers to the BDSM games that Bob gravitated to.

Bob was into it. Really into it. Later on in this book, you'll read about his games and the women he scared nearly to death. They tell me they didn't like it, that Bob became crazed once he was given that power, once he had them bound and helpless.

Hollywood does movies that lampoon and ridicule the suburban life and for good reason. Drive down a soulless, treeless street pocked with boxes that masquerade as homes, all outfitted with seventy channels, central air on seventy degrees, windows and doors shut, and you should be afraid. These seem to me to be petri dishes of mayhem, if not in deed then at least in thought. I understand that contentment can be found under the rooftops. But if you are huddling under there for the wrong reason, well, that could very well flick the switch of weird and send someone looking for something to scratch a whole different itch.

American Beauty, *The Truman Show*, and *Revolutionary Road* all paint these benign streets as the hovels of victims, turmoil, and potential dissent.

Bob became a secretive, X-rated version of Lester Burnham, Kevin Spacey's character in *American Beauty*. Instead of outright defying his circumstances, he decided to keep them and create a second universe.

He found girlfriends who shared his affinity for the lifestyle. And that wasn't enough. The whole escapade into BDSM became a psychological mind-fuck that drove him crazy, this conflict of obsession and addiction to a scene and the synapses that fire in the throes of arousal.

After he was arrested for solicitation of murder, Bob and I began to email each other. He was certain he was a victim, and I suppose he was, in a way.

On February 5, 2013, he wrote to me from prison:

I love my family and try to reach out as often as I can . . . As for my wonderful son, i am soo very proud of him, his work ethic and just the man he is becoming . . . Jane and I worked very hard with both kids, giving them every advantage possible in their young lives.. my daughter is also a wonderful lady, and can debate with the best . . . i see her as a Senator, someday . . . I was shocked to read an article wrought with outright lies and misconceptions, as they need to continue to debase me and drag me thru the muddy waters of life . . . I must go, but know it is not press

or fame I seek, but only to get back to a life interrupted by
a senseless act, by a man I was trying to help. Had I know
how sick he was, i would have never associated with him.
Finally, if you do happen to reach out to my son, tell him
how much I love him and I hope he is well . . . and did he
get my letter, sent also for jessica . . .

I've met a number of killers and other bad folks. Some were just like Bob, living in nice houses, raising fine children until—snap—the thing came crashing down by their own hand.

Today, Bob still maintains he never hired anyone to kill his wife.

"I've talked to a number of people in here," he told me one day in a jailhouse phone conversation. "And they all said they could understand how I would hire someone to kill the guy who killed my wife."

One gorgeous fall day in 2013, October 21, I went to the jail in Wayne County, downtown Detroit, for a visit. As government buildings in Detroit go, it was nicer than average. No scowling guards barking orders, no rush to get in as there is across the street at the county courthouse. I simply filled out my information on a clipboard, was verified as being on Bashara's visitor list, and entered the jail, walking into an elevator that took me to the seventh floor. I walked into a booth with a piece of glass and a phone, just like in the movies. There he was, dressed in jailhouse green scrubs, a clear plastic ID bracelet on his right hand. He was tall and unshaven. "They never got me my razor today," he explained right away, aware he was looking grizzled. He said the lack of a shave was part of being in county custody rather than state. He had recently been moved back to the county from the state in order to be closer to his legal counsel.

"At the state they let us keep them, but here, I mean, can you imagine? This is short term. Who's gonna kill themselves?"

We talked about the news and something that had recently come out that I found to be one more ratings grab: Bob had been accused of molesting a young female relative in 1995. The *Detroit News* had obtained a police report that stated Bashara faced second-degree criminal sexual conduct charges after the five-year-old told her parents that Bashara had twice caused her hand to touch his genitals, one time while wrestling in his bed and one time while she was being spanked in his home.

I was dubious when I read the story, which stated he had passed a lie detector test.

"Two tests," Bob corrected, his face ashen. I did believe him, right? I actually did. If it's a big deal when one fails the polygraph, it should also be a big deal when they pass.

During a lull in our conversation, which we were both aware was being taped by the county, he held up a yellow pad with a short yellow pencil and a message that he did not want recorded: it read there was a "conspiracy" to get him, and "we have 12 examples."

"There were reports that my car was seen backing out of my driveway that night of Jane's death," he said. But those reports all disappeared.

"What happened to those?" he asked me. I shrugged.

He had an answer.

"The police put that out there to see if it would get me to confess. But there was no way I was there at the time they claim Jane was killed," he said.

To the end, Bob wants to be understood as a good man who had bad things happen to him. It just doesn't work that way, though.

You just can't explain it away like that. The justice system, such as it is, found him guilty. He is guilty.

As I worked on this book, I made the acquaintance of Rachel Gillett, the mistress that Bob was wooing when Jane was murdered.

She was reluctant but willing to tell her side of the story. We met on the patio of a Starbucks and talked about her ordeal.

"I have trust issues," she told me almost as soon as I sat down with my iced coffee. She wanted nothing, only to talk and ensure that her story is fairly represented.

The bottom line, she said, is that she was completely hoodwinked by Bob. She thought throughout her entire three and a half years with Bob that he was estranged from Jane, as he represented himself first as widowed, then separated, on the brink of divorce, and finally divorced.

She was believable and kind, naïve to say the least, and completely embarrassed by the entire debacle. You'll meet her in these pages, and her story is presented, her life described. A lost soul looking for something that she thought she'd found in Bob.

And she never asked me, as so many people do, for a dime. I wish I could say that about others.

There is an ugliness that these books bring out in people, and it's no doubt partially attributable to the macabre circumstances.

Bashara's longtime connection to the pillars of Grosse Pointe high society made it sometimes comical to watch the "get away quickly" sentiment.

"I am NOT allowing any use of any photo/image on that URL you sent in the below email," came a response from a fellow who had taken a number of shots of a grinning Bob Bashara for the Rotary Club. I had inquired about using one for this book. I was impressed with the yelling of the word "NOT."

Then there were the in-laws from long ago. Bob was married at a young age to a young lady named Priscilla Langs, in 1981, when she was twenty-one and he was twenty-three. The union lasted about a year.

I called Beverly Langs, Priscilla's mother, as part of the reporting. She was as ugly as I've had to deal with.

"I don't say a word without money," she said, portraying the bottom rung of greedy America, where a home run ball is not handed back to the hitter as its own reward but instead shows up on eBay.

Journalists can't pay for information, interviews, or time. It is simply unethical, a situation in which the subject becomes an employee and can then say anything, or at least the interviewer can make the story fit any scenario that he or she would like. Besides, what kind of journalist has to pay for information? May as well hang it up if that's your game. Or move to England, where such a practice is in keeping with the gossipy flavor of the reporting.

But Beverly assured me that several media groups had paid her—$1,500, to be exact.

"I'm sorry to hear that things have gotten so bad for you," I said.

"Yes, they really have," she replied. "Now, are you going to pay me?"

"No," I said, and I restated why I could not pay her.

"Good-bye, then," and she hung up.

This is the mind-set we have wrought in the age of greed.

The family of Jane Bashara also refused to speak to me. I am particularly respectful of a surviving family.

In a previous book, *A Slaying in the Suburbs*, I worked hard to get the cooperation of the family of Tara Grant, who was slain in another Detroit suburb by her husband. The family had proclaimed they would live their lives to ensure the memory of Tara was kept alive and that she always had a voice. But when I asked to get some insight into Tara's life, I was told not just no but hell no.

"I'm going to do my own book," her sister, Alicia Standerfer, told me. The book never appeared.

Of course. In every book I've ever done I've encountered such notions. Everyone is going to do a book. They're just waiting for . . . what?

In the case of Jane Bashara, I reached out to her family via a family friend. They declined, and, yes, one of the sisters was—cue it up—going to do a book.

And one last thing: I've outlined before that I listen to music as I write these crime books. Rarely do I do that for any other bit of writing, but the music soothes as I tackle what could break my heart if I let it in.

For this one, I listened, inexplicably, to a lot of Wynn Stewart, Merle Haggard, Buck Owens. I got into Brian Eno's recent works, and when I was hitting the brutal scenes, Monster Magnet, Easy Action, and Human Eye came to the rescue.

Thanks for being here. Let's take a walk past the benign conformity and into a side of suburbia that some might find even scarier.

Steve
Avalanche50@hotmail.com
@penvengeance
Avalanche50.com

1

"Holy Shit, You Have the Mercedes"

The body was lying across the backseat, facedown just a foot from the passenger side door of the Mercedes SUV, her legs pushed down on the floor. It looked as if she were kneeling, and her legs were pushed together by the driver's side seat, which was pushed all the way back.

The woman's windpipe was crushed underneath her thin gold necklace, and her face was a battered mask, covered with welts, wounds, and bruises. Across the left ear and down to her neck was a gash, the blood just turning to scab. Her mouth was slightly open.

Her fingernails, manicured just days before, were torn off in a battle with her assailant.

She wore black stretch pants, a dark purple sleeveless blouse, a gold earring in her right ear, and black socks, with a few small leaves, autumn colored, stuck to the sock of the left foot. A pair of tan bedroom slippers was tucked, formally, under the driver's seat. Her arms were half clad in a black nylon jacket, and the jacket was put on from the front facing backward, creating a straitjacket effect.

The faux fur hood of the jacket was unzipped from the jacket and rested on the back passenger side floor.

The woman, married for twenty-six years, wore no wedding ring.

On the front passenger side floor, her beige purse and various items—a compact, lipstick, Kleenex, Dentyne Ice gum, cell phone, credit cards—lay strewn about. Her checkbook was slightly open at the top of the purse. A prescription bottle for hormone pills, prescribed for women going through menopause, sat on the passenger seat.

Twelve hours before, about 4 P.M., she had been a very vibrant, alive woman, talking on the phone with her nineteen-year-old daughter.

"I need to get home where I can write something down while we're talking," she told Jessica, the daughter. It wasn't cryptic or weird. It was the plan of a woman with a life to live. It was a note she wanted to write to herself to refer to in the future.

She was fifty-six years old and had started a post-retirement job in the fall with KEMA Services, a public utility consultancy.

She had come home, dropped her cell phone and purse down, and turned on the TV. Her husband, Bob, was not there.

Just after 6 P.M. the previous evening, the woman had been beaten and strangled in her own garage by a large man, a stranger. It took at least four minutes for her to die with her larynx crushed under a large Red Wing work boot. A parting thought—"that's it, I'm dead"—it was a quick realization before the darkness, no doubt a relief after those endless minutes of being mutilated. After she was dead, her killer made a final stomp on her neck, smudging it around as one would put out a cigarette.

Now, in the darkness, four hours before daylight, it was Midwest chilly out, thirty degrees with a wind that made it feel like twenty-three. A broken chunk of moon was fading to the east. The locals didn't know it, but the worst of winter was over even at this early date, January 25. It would be one of the warmest winters on record, but right now, the starkness of bare trees and dead grass was still a reminder that winter always paints Detroit a little darker with the brush of bleak that envelops the Midwest.

The neighborhood was still. It was among the worst neighborhoods in the city of Detroit, a shell of a town that has decrepit blocks by the acre.

The black 2004 Mercedes ML350 sport-utility vehicle was the only touch of luxury for many blocks, eight miles and another world from Grosse Pointe Park, where the woman lived. The 3,400-square-foot house where she was killed sat two blocks from Lake St. Clair, which is sometimes counted as part of the Great Lakes, its shores lined by some of Detroit's wealthiest suburbs.

Around her now were ghetto scraps, long boarded-up wooden-framed houses surrounded by heaps of garbage, some of it in torn-open black plastic garbage bags. The back doors of some of the empty houses were torn off, leaving black holes leading to darker basements. Just outside the

SUV was a pile of old clothes, and a few feet past that, a cheap, discarded wooden kitchen table with one leg missing.

Much national attention has been given the idea that a house in some parts of Detroit can be purchased for $1. Median price in this two-square-mile area was $21,000. Needless to say, schools in the area performed solidly below the state average and even below that of the lowly, beleaguered Detroit school district.

"Chav WTA Van Dyke" was scrawled in black spray paint on the side of a dirty white garage just down the alley from where the SUV sat. More graffiti was scattered around the area, on the sidewalk, on abandoned homes, on other garages, on light poles that hadn't worked for a decade.

In a previous six-month period, the area in which the SUV sat reported twenty-six shootings, eight assaults, and five robberies.

In the darkness, Franco Leone was driving his tow truck through the streets of Detroit. He was a driver for H & B Land and Elite Towing, one of several tow truck companies to have a contract with the city of Detroit. It was a typical weeknight, a Tuesday night into Wednesday morning, and even the scofflaws were down for the evening. Leone was working the 8 P.M. to 8 A.M. shift and had seen some action that night. A drunk had parked in a thoroughfare, and another driver had taken a reserved spot in a condo complex. Both warranted a tow. A couple accidents.

But now, it was getting toward dawn, and Leone moved his attention over to an area between Seven Mile Road and

Hoover Street in East Detroit. He cruised slowly down Pinewood Street, between Bradford Street and Annott Avenue, looking for stolen cars.

It was a good spot to dump a vehicle after a night of joyriding, and Leone could sometimes find a heisted car dumped in a sketchy area. Some nights, he could find a couple of them, although cars weren't getting stolen like they used to.

"They make them better now, tougher to steal," he was thinking to himself, when all of a sudden, pay dirt. What would a nice luxury SUV be doing in a place like this?

"I seen a Mercedes amongst a bunch of abandoned houses," Leone says. It sat behind a sad-looking, empty redbrick house on the corner.

He stopped behind the SUV, blocking the alley it sat in. Leone wrote down the plate number and got out to have a look. It was now closing in on 6 A.M., and he called dispatch. He'd have to call it in before he could haul it. Hopefully, the cops would be quick about it.

He read the license and make of the vehicle to his dispatcher at H & B.

"Holy shit, you have the Mercedes," she told him. "Frank, stay right there."

The Mercedes had been called in around 11:30 P.M., almost seven hours ago. A worried husband and a missing wife.

The first cop car arrived within minutes. One officer stood with Leone, making small talk, as the other officer approached the car in the darkened alley. It was quiet and cold, and he could tell it wasn't okay to be here. He took his flashlight and peered in. The back of a head of bloody hair lit up in the light beam.

More cops arrived shortly. In a city where the response time to an emergency call is an hour, the discovery of a body motivates even the most jaded cop. The city had 344 homicides in 2011. This would be number 26 for 2012 if it turned out to have been committed inside the Detroit city limits.

Leone stood by his tow truck fielding questions from a parade of investigators. By 8 A.M., the news was out and being broadcast around the city. But Leone was still talking to cops, waiting to go home.

As he wrapped up the last round of interviews, the investigator had to ask: "Did you kill her?"

"No, I didn't. I just found the car." And with that, Leone was allowed to leave.

The police decided quickly to tow the vehicle to the Wayne County Medical Examiner's Office with the body still inside in order to preserve the entire crime scene.

Within three hours, the story of the dead woman from the Pointes found over by Seven Mile Road was dominating first the local news, then the national airwaves. The story's heft was inevitable. A rich white woman with no enemies and a gracious and considerable influence among her wealthy peers was found dead in the back of her luxury car in the middle of Detroit.

Around midday on Wednesday, January 25, the woman's employer issued a press release.

"KEMA is deeply shocked and saddened to learn about the death of Jane Bashara today," the release read. "She has been an employee of KEMA for over 2 years. She was very well respected and has many close colleagues here. We are doing everything we can to help Detroit police in the investigation and to support her family during this tragedy."

Today's rapid-fire news mélange that mixes authoritative media with the generally misinformed public and false punditry swung into full bloom, accusing and defending anyone within a blood test of Jane Bashara, wife and mother of two from the tony village of Grosse Pointe Park.

Most obviously, the attention swung to her husband, Bob Bashara, the son of a once esteemed state judge, George Bashara Jr., who died in 2002, leaving Bob and his sister an inheritance of $100,000 to split with the rest going into a trust for his wife, Suzanne. In the event of Suzanne's death, the trust was to be divided among four parties, Bob included. Several times over the years Bob would ask Suzanne for an advance on a portion of his share. He was always denied.

Despite his dubious fiscal skills, Bob considered himself a stalwart community leader—"I give it all back," he was frequently heard to say—and served as head of the local Rotary Club, a deacon at his Episcopal church, and a member of the Lochmoor Club, a local country club.

He was a landlord, holding both residential and commercial properties. The residential places were what some might see as poorly located, in run-down areas, making him fair game for cries of "slumlord," warranted or not.

But he kept them rented and most of the time did so with few beefs on either side of the transaction. In the right hands, these could have been moneymakers.

Rather than pay a management company, Bob handled them himself.

"I liked renting to people. Sometimes they needed a break and I could help them," he says. "It also gives me time to do my other charity work, to make my own schedule."

Bob Bashara spent the evening of January 24, 2012, sweeping, which was weird. His tenants said Bob never did his own cleanup work, preferring to use his network of handymen and helpers, who often performed menial labor in exchange for a break on rent.

On that evening, though, Bob was sweeping and working behind his property on Mack Avenue, his prime real estate, which housed a tavern, the Hard Luck Lounge, and an oyster bar, Dylan's Raw Bar & Grille.

There were some other storefronts where tenants and businesses came and went: Paul Engstrom Fine Art, a storefront for a photographer who divided his time between Detroit, Chicago, and San Francisco. An office unit that sat mostly empty. Above the commercial spaces, two apartments that were usually occupied.

It was a typical Detroit area piece of real estate; across the street, a liquor store drew street denizens and shady characters. A walk on one side of Mack was safe, the other dicey.

That chilly evening of January 24, Bob decided he would sweep and tidy up the place.

"I'd usually clean the place in the day when no one was around," Bashara says. "People smoked out back, and the tenants never cleaned. It just happened that I was out there that night."

Regardless, beyond the anomaly of cleaning in the evening, Bashara acted strange in the eyes of his tenant that evening.

"Bob was in and out of the bar that night," says Mike Mouyianis, who ran the Hard Luck Lounge. He'd been there since 2008 and had also hatched a line of liquor, Hard Luck Candy Vodka, during that time. The Hard Luck was a smoky misplaced hipster joint, cool amidst privilege, with dark lights and a fifties' dive vibe. A couple of pool tables, some locals out for a walk on the wild side. Cops liked to drink there sometimes, or would sit in their cars out front on Mack Avenue and check Facebook on their laptops while on duty, poaching the bar's Wi-Fi.

Mike's beefy biker character called for a certain clientele, younger, cooler, and more into music than the general population of the moneyed Pointes.

Mouyianis was introduced to Bashara by a friend at a bachelor party in 2008. The party was at the Crazy Horse, a strip joint on Michigan Avenue favored by out-of-town athletes and rappers. Into that mix came Bob Bashara, wearing a pastel golf shirt.

In the men's room, Mouyianis stood at a urinal and Bob took the one next to him.

Bashara pulled a small baggie out of his pocket, tapped some cocaine onto the web of his thumb, and took a hefty snort.

"Want some?" Bob asked gamely.

If the sight of a fifty-something man in a golf shirt snorting cocaine fairly openly wasn't enough to deter Mouyianis from indulging, nothing was. He passed.

"Bob walked out of that bathroom, sat down at a table, and paid two dancers to give him a lap dance almost immediately," Mouyianis says.

Mouyianis ran with all kinds of people, and he is a born businessman, looking for a way to make some money doing what he loves, which includes running a bar. So when he learned that Bashara had some space in a fairly trafficked area, the two got together.

"He owned dozens of properties in the area, and I thought the one we were looking at was pretty good," Mouyianis says. He noticed Bashara was a strange guy who had a lot of things going on, a fellow who took pride in the fact that he was a local working for his community.

"We'd go over to the city offices and he's telling me how he knew everyone and he was pals with everyone, but when we got there it was clear that they didn't really like him at all. They'd kind of say, 'Okay, what do you want now, Bob?'"

The Hard Luck's location was perfect. Business was fine, and the new line of liquor was selling and getting popular enough for Mouyianis and a couple other guys to make more and sell it elsewhere.

The building, though, was a drama.

Every year Mouyianis would get a notice saying the building was going to be seized for tax arrears. Bashara would tell him it was a misunderstanding and he'd fix it.

When he was first moving in, Mouyianis was cleaning, moving some things, and he noticed a door in the basement of the building. It could have led to storage, maybe an office, but the sturdy wooden door was always locked. It was odd; he never saw anyone going in or out of this room, even when Bashara was around.

One day he was moving some stock around in the basement—the Hard Luck had its own storage area—and Mouyianis saw a female friend of Bashara's. She was dropping something off for Bashara, who wasn't around.

"How's it going?" she asked.

"Just working down here in the dungeon," Mouyianis said.

Within five minutes, Mouyianis's cell phone rang. It was Bashara.

"What do you mean by dungeon?" he asked.

Perplexed, Mouyianis said, "I was just using a term, Bob."

Mike was working behind the bar on January 24 around 6 P.M.

"I'm working out here in back, just working on some stuff," Bob went in and told him. That evening, Bob would have a beer then head back out.

"He was real chatty, uncharacteristically," Mouyianis says.

Around 7 P.M., though, Mouyianis felt sick—he chalked

it up to food poisoning—and seeing as it was a slow night, he left his regular bartender, Kristy, in charge and went home.

Bob continued the pattern, in and out, with Kristy behind the bar.

Around the same time Mouyianis left, Michael Carmody walked in to meet Bob, who was at a table having a beer.

Carmody was a longtime friend and fellow Rotarian. They sat for one round, talking about football, talking about the Rotary, easy conversations about things they had in common. Carmody left after forty-five minutes, happy to have Bob as a friend. It would be the last time he felt that way.

A couple hours after Carmody and Bashara parted ways, a man who had been in the Hard Luck a few times came by. He was a big guy, six feet four inches, 250 pounds, barrel-chested with a broad back and thick legs. He looked like a guy who made a living working, a tough, as someone might have called him in the fifties. He had a silver brush cut, a loud mouth, and a limited vocabulary.

"Not all there," is how some put it.

Kristy told Mouyianis the next day of this man coming in around 10 P.M. The man would later match a description of Joe Gentz, a slow-talking fellow in his forties who had moved into an upper flat a few blocks down the street. But no one ever mentioned it, and there would be plenty of discussion about this Gentz fellow and his actions on that evening.

There was one other thing that was strange that night.

As Kristy closed up the Hard Luck, she exited through the back, as always, locking the door. She noticed the area that Bob had been intently cleaning.

"It was this little three-foot-square area. That was it. He had really done nothing," Kristy later told Mouyianis.

The next morning, Mouyianis felt better, and his wife, Natalie, was preparing to go to work at the Greektown Casino. It was around 9 A.M., and she watched the local news on television while he puttered in the kitchen.

"Mike, oh my God, look at this," she said, a little loudly, startling Mouyianis.

On the screen of the local NBC affiliate was a shot of a black Mercedes SUV, sitting in an alley in one of the city's many slums. "Missing Mom's Body Found," the bold lettering on the screen read.

There was Franco Leone talking about finding the SUV in an alley.

"He killed Jane and we're his alibi," Mouyianis said quietly.

The cops were working from scratch at the murder scene of Jane Bashara, and no one even needed an alibi yet. Sure, the husband is the first suspect, but Bob Bashara's pedigree didn't scream murderer.

Just a little over a month before, on December 16, Bob and Jane Bashara delivered $28,000 in a fund-raiser for their church, St. Michael's Episcopal in Grosse Pointe Woods.

And there was legacy to their devotion to their community. Readers of the *Grosse Pointe News* could see a

Bashara photo routinely, be it Jane or Bob. The family took a copy of the local newspaper along to a family reunion in Ocho Rios, Jamaica, in January 2009, then posed for a photo of themselves reading it: Bob and Jane; their daughter, Jessica; their son, Robert; and Bob's mom, Nancy. The Bashara name was golden in the Pointes.

Sure, Bob had some weirdness to him, and he was a big man with a loud voice and a lot to say, a hail-fellow-well-met who came across as sometimes absentminded.

But the idea of a guy who had a twenty-four-year record of perfect attendance at the local Rotary Club being a wife killer was unthinkable.

He had come home, he told police, at 8 P.M. to find the TV and the lights on, but no Jane. He later told police he had called her around 7 and told her he would be home shortly. He also told a television reporter that the two had touched base via phone around 5 P.M., and she said she was on her way home.

Around 9 P.M., he called Patricia Matthews, one of Jane's closest friends, and asked if Jane was there.

"I think Jane is missing or something is wrong," Bob said. "It's late, and she always leaves a note."

Matthews didn't find it odd and wasn't even concerned. She'd called over to the house for Jane a number of times, and no one knew where she was, and there was no note. Why would Bob be so convinced something was wrong?

"I got home and she wasn't around, and I relaxed and figured she was out running an errand," Bashara told one of the news crews that began to camp outside his home. "As nine o'clock and nine thirty approached, I became much more concerned, and I got more people involved. I called my kids to see if they had heard from her, and they hadn't. I had been calling her cell phone to find out, and then as time got on, I involved the police, because I was concerned there might be something wrong."

After he contacted them around 11:30 and officers came by, police felt that Jane had been in a struggle at the house.

Since the crime took place in Grosse Pointe Park, the case was being handled by the local police, for whom "murder" is a word rarely heard.

When the Mercedes was found several hours later, the department was handed its first murder case since January 16, 1992, when Grosse Pointe Park resident Phyllis Ann Lenart was shot and killed in a robbery at a bus stop at Wayburn and Jefferson. The perp, Raynell Hampton, had been out of prison for less than two months on a drug charge.

At a candlelight vigil on the evening of January 25, Bashara, clad in a blue baseball cap, black gloves, and beige raincoat, received hugs and blessings of condolence from many of his and Jane's friends.

"God bless you all," he said.

The next day, he headed over to the police department for questioning.

"I'm doing what I need to do to cooperate with the authorities to find who did this to my wife," he told reporters outside the station.

The next day, he took a polygraph. He failed. While he was at the police department, the cops executed a search warrant on his house, complete with dogs searching for God-knows-what. They took computers and some documents. He went back to the house minutes after they left. It was set up that way. There was evidence to be sifted through. And there was a single small drop of blood on the garage floor. It contained DNA from two people: Jane Bashara and Joe Gentz.

2

Growing up Wealthy and Healthy in Detroit

Bob Bashara grew up in a family of letters, law, and geographical consistency. His grandfather and father, George Sr. and Jr., were lawyers and hard-charging intellectual minds walking paths padded by ambition.

The Bashara family line traced to Lebanon in the late 1800s, part of a wave of Lebanese Christians who came to the U.S., first basing themselves peddling in the sidewalk trades of New York City but quickly broadening into the Midwest, where the living was cheaper, the spaces wider.

George Sr. was born in Hartford City, Indiana, in 1901. The family moved to Grand Rapids, Michigan, briefly, before George went back to Lebanon for a few years, and returned for good a few years later. He was eight years old when he returned, still knowing little English. Within years he won a national oratorical award for his mastering of English and he had landed in Detroit with his family.

Middle Eastern immigrants eschewed even temporary work in the auto factories of Detroit to pursue an education, George among them. He enrolled first at the University of Pennsylvania, then moved to the University of Michigan Law School, plowing his way through to a degree.

Perhaps his biggest contribution to the culture of Detroit was his work: counsel to the waves of Arab immigrants that began to really hit in the 1940s following World War II.

As honorary counsel for the Republic of Lebanon in the Midwest, "he was partly responsible for the large Arab population in Detroit," Bob says.

His specialty became immigration law, particularly helping newly arrived immigrants navigate U.S. immigration rules.

"He knew the language, he was willing to help his community, and this was his real skill at that time," says Edward Deeb, who fraternized with both George Sr. and George Jr. as a businessman and a resident of the Pointes.

Setting the tone for his family, George Sr. was a joiner, enlisting in community causes that included bar associations, the Syria Lodge, and the Cedars of Lebanon. He moved the family to Grosse Pointe Park into a large home on Balfour Street.

George took an office in the downtown Cadillac Tower for many of his years, and for a few years in the sixties, he and his only son, George Jr., who also became a lawyer, opened Bashara & Bashara.

The elder Bashara's landmark case was the defeat of the UAW on behalf of Arab grocers, who were being pressured, sometimes menaced, in a move to unionize them. In particular, the merchants were harassed when they drove their trucks to pick up produce and other goods at a central distribution facility.

"George took the case when the grocers asked him, and he won," Deeb says. "He was a hero after that, although it probably didn't help his political ambitions."

He was running up against a well-established legal fortress of steely union entrenchment and winning on occasion.

Bashara took a case in 1969 representing a plaintiff against another grocery union. The plaintiff claimed his union did not fairly represent him in a squabble with Kroger.

The union emerged victorious, thanks in part to the legal work of a young lawyer named Jimmy Hoffa, already a political presence behind the scenes.

But, yes, while his passion was the law, George Sr. was also a hopeful politician, albeit an unsuccessful one. At age forty, he ran for judge in the local circuit court, which hears a range of cases both civil and criminal. He lost but was unbowed. He ran again in 1947, 1948, 1953, and 1959. In 1959, he ran for U.S. representative against an entrenched incumbent, Democratic lawyer Louis Rabaut, and lost. In 1966, George ran for the state senate seat against George Fitzgerald, an Irish Catholic Democrat who had the backing of the Detroit political machine. Bashara, the Republican from Lebanon, never had a chance, and it was the last time he ran for office.

In his later years, George and his wife, Josephine,

bought a condo in Pompano Beach, Florida, where Bob and other family members would visit during winter breaks at school.

But he always kept his home in Grosse Pointe Woods, living a solid, community-based life that set the stage for his kids, and their kids, where life was lived to improve, not move.

"He helped me pay for college, and he helped my dad in his practice when money was short," Bob says.

George died on the second Friday of September 1980 of heart problems. He left behind George Jr., four daughters, and a wife.

He fell not far from the tree, did George Jr. He was born in 1934, at the end of the Great Depression, but he knew little hardship. A chatty boy from the start, George Jr. fell in love with words early on. He was inspired by a guy in his neighborhood, Toby David, a local entertainer and radio personality on WJR, then later Canadian station CKLW across the bridge in Windsor, Ontario. David, also of Lebanese descent, was a national figure who had started in Detroit, moved to New York and Washington, D.C., then returned.

George Jr. accompanied David to the studio when he could, watching him work his words over the air with magic, sometimes using dialects and imitations to entertain. It was a gift George Jr. knew he had to have to accomplish what he wanted. He needed an ability to lead people, and words, he realized, were a tremendous asset in a crusade to motivate.

It was a given early on that he would attend the esteemed University of Michigan, as his father had, giving George Jr. an edge over other applicants.

While at U of M in 1957, he met and married Nancy Brinker. It was also a natural move on to law school, and George Jr. chose the Detroit College of Law.

Nancy was the daughter of Harold and Grace Brinker, lifelong residents of Grosse Pointe and high on the social ladder that George was destined to climb with ease. Harold headed his own prospering company, Grosse Pointe Research Corp., and had also spent time with a lucrative catering operation that provided meals to, among other places, the Uniroyal Plant on Jefferson Avenue.

George Jr. and Nancy quickly had children, first a son, Robert Michael, then a daughter, Laura Ann.

As a freshly minted lawyer and family man, in 1960, George Jr. set about making a name for himself, ideally the same esteemed sort of name his father had made.

His ambition was through the roof. He spent time learning the craft of law while a partner at Bashara & Bashara, but he moved fast. He became a member of the appeals board of the state's employment security commission—an important body in economically booming Michigan—then was named chair of the entire commission. By 1969, George Jr. had become a probate judge, appointed midterm seat to what was generally an elected position by Governor William Milliken, a Republican who saw promise in the striving barrister. The next year, George Jr. was reelected in an election that gave the family some consolation. His opponent was John Patrick O'Brien, a politically popular, union-backed Irish Catholic. George Jr. won by 95,000 votes, showing a political mettle that his father lacked.

"My grandfather was political, but my father was even more so," Bob says.

George Jr. was a law and order man, and he felt the existing structure for dealing with nonviolent offenders was not working. He was a Republican in a heavily Democratic region and state, and his approach to handling small crime was to limit the system's direct involvement.

He believed in second chances for nonviolent offenders and was especially concerned about kids who were getting involved with drugs. When his schedule allowed, and when he determined that he needed a boost in profile, he would visit area schools with a recovering addict in tow, who would then tell his or her story to kids.

"Stay off drugs" was the message, of course, delivered at a time when even a marijuana smoker was considered an outlaw with a drug problem.

George Jr. also implemented a self-designed program that allowed teenagers to come to his courtroom to watch the sentencing for drug offenders, one more stab at a "scared straight" effort by authorities that no doubt got more kids into drugs than off them.

If the kids were really interested, George Jr. arranged for them to visit the Wayne County Jail, to see what life behind bars was like.

So set against the evils of drugs was he that he sought out and received an appointment to the State Advisory

Commission on Drug Abuse and Alcoholism, a now defunct panel.

All of this was excellent resume padding, for George Jr. in 1972 became the youngest judge to sit on the bench of the Michigan Court of Appeals, the last stop for legally entangled parties before the state's supreme court. It was created only seven years before, and Bashara became one of its nine members, a young man compared to his court colleagues, some of whom were in their seventies.

He was elected twice following his appointment, in 1974 and in 1980, before he stepped down in 1982 to join the Dykema Gossett law firm.

In late 1978, he and his wife, Nancy, with whom he had raised two children, Robert and Laura, divorced. By 1980, he married a worker at his law firm, Suzanne.

It happened a lot in the Pointes.

While he had always been involved in his community, by the early eighties, George found himself with some time to give back to that community. He phoned friends with an idea.

"We live in this beautiful community, but the town doesn't have the funds to do everything we'd like," he said in a number of calls to colleagues and neighbors. "We should do something to help."

George helped found the Grosse Pointe Shores Improvement Foundation in 1984, raising money for basic quality of life improvements like landscaping and park development and maintenance.

In his spare time he played some classical piano, and

played well. He was active in the local theater, winning an award for his portrayal of Robish in *The Desperate Hours*, the tale of three escaped convicts taking a family hostage in their own home.

Meantime, George Jr. was also pulling down some serious cash. His judgeships and hard work as a lawyer had paid well, and he also became vice president and general counsel for Federal-Mogul Corporation, then a high-performing auto aftermarket parts supplier. In 1993, he was paid $243,000 plus 16,000 shares in options and $42,000 in supplemental benefits.

"George was this huge presence, a real talker and joking kind of guy," says Lonnie Ross, who worked in public relations at Federal-Mogul. "And he had a lot of respect around the office because of his past work as a judge."

He retired in 1995, spending even more time with his church, St. Michael's, and doing some mediation and arbitration.

By the time his health began failing in the late nineties, George was worth a lot of money, but poor investments had hobbled his riches.

"My dad wasn't that good with money," Bob says, the same thing others would say of him in his later years.

George Jr. died in April 2002 at the age of sixty-seven of a heart ailment, similar to the malady that had taken his father's life.

The wealthy always seem to get that prime real estate.

Such a blanket statement is shakily true today, but it also

dates back to the 1800s, when Grosse Pointe was settled by a cavalcade of enterprising Europeans who hit the swampy patch of land on Lake St. Clair, first establishing orchards, then seasonal homes.

The properties evolved into an area simply referred to as "the Pointes" by locals, and today there are five of them: Grosse Pointe Farms, Grosse Pointe Park, Grosse Pointe Woods, Grosse Pointe Shores, and the city of Grosse Pointe, all wrapped up tidy and shiny.

As the years passed, a fine golf course, a country club, a yacht club, and a couple of private schools were built to serve the residents of all the Pointes.

Grosse Pointe Park, established in 1907, is neither the largest nor the newest of them, a "just right" medium of these wealthy enclaves that sit just north of the city of Detroit.

Today its boundaries contain a lot of money sitting inside a little over three square miles, with a population of 12,000.

Rather than police departments, each of the Pointes have Departments of Public Safety, which provide police, fire, and emergency services rolled into one unit.

There's so little crime that it makes perfect sense, and a number of other communities around the nation have found that the municipal good is best served and money saved in doing so.

Crime, in fact, has never been a problem in the Pointes, in part due to the privileged demographic, but also for the same reason that New York City's Italian areas were never afflicted by street crime: there was a built in "enforcement" division referred to commonly as the Mafia.

Starting in the early thirties, La Cosa Nostra operated with great success throughout the Detroit area, making huge sums of money. That money liked mansions and hated street crime, of which there was little anywhere in the city up until the sixties.

The syndicate members lived quiet lives with their money, using upright establishments as a front, from flower shops and restaurants to dry cleaners. Their children went to the fine public schools, many graduating with honors from Grosse Pointe South High School and, later, when demand for another high school in the Pointes was called for, Grosse Pointe North High School.

Oh, there were bumps that included congressional hearings in the sixties in which testimony alleged there were sixty-three Detroiters who were Mafia members.

There were more whispers and allegations as the decades passed: The Detroit mob operated the Aladdin Hotel and Casino and the New Frontier Hotel in Las Vegas. Teamster leader Jimmy Hoffa was killed in a mob hit.

While Hoffa's body was never found, it is indisputable that the mob loved living in Grosse Pointe.

More specifically, Grosse Pointe Park. Even more specifically, Middlesex, which later became the title of a 2002 novel by Grosse Pointe Park native Jeffrey Eugenides that won the Pulitzer Prize for Fiction. There were rumors of an underground tunnel system connecting Middlesex homes and secret hiding rooms tucked away in the catacombs of the houses.

Its infamous residents included Anthony Zerilli, aka "Tony Z," an alleged mob underboss who was sentenced to prison in 1974 for skimming profits and hiding his interest in the Frontier in Las Vegas.

His cousin, Giacomo William Tocco, known as "Jack" or "Black Jack" to the cops, was a mobster, according to the feds.

Tocco spent his childhood in the ritzy Windmill Pointe section of Grosse Pointe Park, a waterfront slice of heaven set in an already ritzy place. He grew up and began investing in real estate, legit concerns that made him quite a tidy sum, lending credence to the truism that "money makes money."

In 1979, Tocco became the boss of a group the cops called the Detroit Partnership, a kinder way of saying the Detroit Mafia. In 1996, he was convicted on two counts of conspiracy under the Racketeer Influenced and Corrupt Organizations Act, better known as RICO.

Tocco served two years and went home to the place he had lived for many years: 560 Middlesex. He died in 2014. For most of the last two decades of his life, his neighbors were Bob and Jane Bashara.

"We would take great vacations, quite a bit, up to Northern Michigan to Disneyland in California," Bashara says. "Both sets of my grandparents lived on the east coast of Florida at least part-time, in Pompano Beach and Boca Raton, and we would visit them. My dad made a good living, and he also lived beyond his means, which was great for me and my sister. We had everything we needed."

His is a fond recollection of childhood, a time of riding

his bike under a canopy of branches extending from sturdy oak and maple trees that graced his neighborhood in the Pointes. Snow in the winter meant snowmen and festive holidays with the large extended family. There were few worries. The Basharas led a life insulated from the sixties' and seventies' street crime and violence that was infecting Detroit, as they were living in an area that had very little crime or reason for concern for the safety of its residents.

Summers for Bob were idyllic months of childhood in Michigan that he still dreams of. When he talks of it, his eyes look upward as if he could will back something carefree, before he took on the responsibility of being an adult.

Bob dabbled in sports, with little inspiration or interest. He was physically big but doughy and hardly the type who wanted to push and shove.

Every summer, George, Nancy, Bob, and Laura would stay at the Indian Trail Lodge, a mom-and-pop motel on the Grand Traverse Bay, one of the tourist areas of Northern Michigan.

The area is now desecrated woodland, where condos and chain eateries trump simple pleasures. But back then, in the late sixties, there was nothing but thick forest and uncultivated beach opening onto clear blue waters. In the evenings, entertainment was shuffleboard—and not just for the old folks.

"This was before anyone had Jet Skis or anything like that. We would go out and walk into the woods. I could go out there alone and catch frogs, just roam, with no worries," Bob says. "We were all really into hiking, the whole family, and we could spend whole days walking up the coastline and back to the motel."

He loved high school, although it was more for the social opportunities rather than the activities.

"I played some baseball in Little League, then some soccer and football in high school," Bob says. He was growing toward the six feet four inches he would be as an adult, making him a recruitment target at Grosse Pointe North High School. "I was fairly athletic, but I wasn't crazy about it."

By his junior year in 1975, Bob was emerging as a chip off the old block of sorts. He came from a class that never had to clean up after itself, and it showed. There was a built-in immunity to the more minor of life's problems when you grew up in the Pointes, and Bashara dug that.

At the same time, the family was steeped in structure and protocol, where everyone was taught and expected to maintain manners and courteousness. Napkins were in laps at the dinner table, and thrift was considered wise.

Bob was smart, but not too smart. He also enjoyed seeing the kids that were supposedly from the so-called Mafia families. As a rule they were cultured and smart, but they had a streetwise edge that he most certainly didn't have but craved.

"I was into reading books on political science, and I was interested in how communities worked and who made them work," Bob says. "I really didn't want to be a politician, and I knew I didn't want to be a lawyer. I wanted to be a businessman."

He left for college after graduating high school in 1976, with a stop in Colorado for a few months. He considered a life as a ski bum—his family had been to Aspen on ski trips when he was in high school—but opted out.

Instead, he enrolled at Albion College, one of the few schools that would accept his mediocre academic performance. He was certainly not University of Michigan material. Albion was a tiny private mid-Michigan school with around eight hundred students.

Bob was a character at the college, although he wasn't necessarily popular. By the end of his freshman year, he had pledged to the Sigma Chi Fraternity. He moved into the frat house his sophomore year, and his elected task was to be head of maintenance.

"He talked all the time, and he got in your space when he talked, real close," says one former roommate, who switched rooms midyear his sophomore year to get away from Bob's loud garrulousness. Bob was also pushing three hundred pounds, drank like a college kid, and was a passionate pot smoker, like so many in those days.

"I smoked, everyone smoked," said another former Albion classmate, now a lawyer. "But he took it to another level. He made terrible grades, and that's because he was more into smoking pot than anything else."

Bob also lost part of the middle finger on his right hand in an accident at the college.

He was playing keep-away with some girls. The front door to the frat house was steel with a broken hydraulic hinge at the top. As head of maintenance, it would fall on Bob to see that it was fixed, but he hadn't gotten to it.

On that day, Bob was trying to run into the house and close the door behind him. As it wouldn't shut automatically with the hinge broken, he pulled it shut behind him, on his hand, and severed the tip of the finger.

The tip was sewed on but didn't last long.

"It grew into this disgusting black thing, just kind of dangling from the end of his finger, and he'd tap it when we were in the cafeteria eating," says one former classmate. "Tap, tap, tap, like a rock hitting the table. Thank God it finally fell off."

One of the perks of having a lawyer for a father is the connection in the legal field. The college quickly settled damages for $19,000, found money for Bob, who would go through life with the three middle fingers on his right hand the same length.

Halfway through Albion, he began to date Priscilla Langs, a Grosse Pointe girl two years younger who was also attending Albion. Her father, Richard, was, like Bob's, a well-known legal mind.

Richard was a corporate lawyer who had attended law school at the University of Michigan, class of 1958, and Priscilla was his only daughter. The Langs lived in a 6,000-square-foot, six-bedroom, six-bath home not far from the Basharas, and although Bob and Priscilla were young, their social class was a perfect match. One of the Langs, Priscilla's grandfather, had been part of the team that formed Michigan National Bank, a large grouping of six regional banks.

Priscilla was Alpha Xi Delta, and while they had seen each other around in Grosse Pointe, it was usually in passing at the country club or the grocery store. At Albion, they were introduced formally by one of Bob's frat brothers.

They dated and stuck together after Bob graduated in 1980 with a degree in economics and speech communication.

He was back in Detroit, where he held a day job as a sales rep with Michigan First Aid and Safety while he dreamed of having a business of his own.

Bob and Priscilla were engaged in January and married at Grosse Pointe Memorial Church on Saturday, July 11, 1981. There was Schiffli lace and chiffon, carnations, daisies, and mums. The bride wore white, of course.

Priscilla was twenty-one; Bob was twenty-three. He called her "Cil," which she dug.

They moved to a small house on Elkhart Street in nearby Harper Woods, a less upscale version of the Pointes but a decent area anyway.

"Priscilla married me to get out of her parents' house," Bob says. "She was sweet, and she came from a good family, but we were so young.

"I was in love with her. And her mother, Beverly, loved me. But Priscilla wanted to get a divorce within a year, and they supported her on that. We had talked about having kids, and I didn't want to be divorced. But she hadn't sown her wild oats, and she didn't want to be married anymore, so she made excuses about me that I was into this and that."

The marriage ended after a year, in mid-1982.

Shortly after the divorce, Bob got his first taste of being his own boss.

His uncle owned a little eatery on Mack Avenue, the Wooden Nickel, that the family thought might be a good start for Bob's fledgling interest in entrepreneurship.

Bob was twenty-six years old and eager to jump into something new. He opened a new, second outlet of the Wooden Nickel.

"My dad was all about the Lebanese thing of having your own business," Bob says. "He had paid for the Wooden Nickel, like part of a franchise, that my uncle owned, which meant there was that one Wooden Nickel down the road. I got permission to copy it."

For a little over three years, Bashara learned the restaurant business.

Being married had sidetracked Bob from his business pursuits.

Soon after taking on the Wooden Nickel, Bob bought his first rental home.

The three-bed, one-bath house on Cadieux Road, not all that far from the family home, was in the middle of a divorce Bob's father was handling. A business friend of George's had bought the small wood-frame home for his daughter and her husband. When the husband left, the wife wanted out of the house, and there was Bob, with George's help, snapping up the place for a song, $10,000 with $1,000 down. The title was held jointly between Bob and his father, so he had some financial backup if things went south on the deal. But they didn't, and Bob learned that property makes money when you fix it up a little and rent it out.

Shortly after Bob and Priscilla had legally split, Bob met a young lady named Jane Engelbrecht.

3

"He Came from an Affluent Family . . . a Life of the Party Kind of Guy"

Every Sunday, Jane Bashara could be found at St. Michael's Episcopal Church in Grosse Pointe Woods. Her husband, Bob, would be with her, smiling, glad-handing his way through the church's wide entryway. Jane, her smile wide and sincere, did her own hobnobbing.

"They rarely missed a Sunday," says Drew McSkimming, whose wife and three children were among the St. Michael's faithful.

Their faith was imbued in both of them, but Jane was going the distance. By the end of 2011, she was taking classes at the church to broaden her knowledge of the faith, an affirmation of her belief. Jane was soon to be a member of the church's vestry, an esteemed position on a board that takes care of finances and assets and selects church members for leadership positions.

"She was very into the faith," McSkimming said.

Indeed, Jane was a faithful person who had a blessed life.

Her father, John Engelbrecht, was a Korean War veteran, U.S. Army Infantry, and one of the first things he did upon returning to Michigan was to marry Lorraine R. Naeyaert in 1953.

The couple had four children, three girls and a boy, beginning with Jane, who was born on June 22, 1955, in Mount Clemens.

Sitting on the banks of the Clinton River, Mount Clemens is the seat of Macomb County, twenty-five miles north of Detroit, and in the late sixties, it was four square miles of relatively safe streets with even a touch of Andy Griffith, Mayberry-esque homespun flavor.

The Engelbrechts raised their children mostly in a smallish house down the street from the Gowanie Golf Club, the town's private course, which was built in 1910 and soon thereafter named as such by a Scottish immigrant named Dave Millar.

It was that kind of place: predominantly white, pulsing with hard-won European heritage.

Mount Clemens was known for, among other things, its mineral baths in the early twentieth century, and it drew from the ranks of celebrity for its visitors: Babe Ruth, Jack Dempsey, Clark Gable, and Mae West rode the rails to Mount Clemens to enjoy the life-restoring baths.

The Babe, in particular, loved the town, where he could wander from drinking hole to drinking hole, then sleep it off on a bench near the river. Back then, celebrity needed no limo, just a warm place to stretch out.

The Engelbrecht family was both tightly knit and outwardly giving, and Jane had all the confidence in the world, growing up in an American dream, riding her bike in leafy streets, digging into the world of books and sports.

She grew into an athletic, sturdy young woman, climbing trees as well as any of the boys in her neighborhood.

By the time she hit Mount Clemens High School, she was both an accomplished academic as well as an athlete who played on the tennis and volleyball teams. She blossomed into an intense competitor with a good soul.

"She raised the level of everyone's play because she was so diligent," her high school volleyball coach, Linda Petros, says. The team was already strong, she says, and Jane was a presence both athletically and academically. "The other coaches were jealous of me because my kids had such high GPAs," Petros says. "It was expected back then. On the buses back from away games, they would be studying." That Jane played both volleyball and tennis made sense as well. Petros added: "Those were the cool sports to play at the time."

Jane checked out the French club, joined the National Honor Society, and worked shifts at the Miller Brothers Creamery, a Mount Clemens institution, while she went to high school.

She was popular enough that she hung out with the same group that ran with John MacArthur, the president of the class of 1973, Mount Clemens High School.

"We were a combination of kids who tended to be academically strong and pretty much athletic," says MacArthur, who was captain of the men's tennis team. He'd seen Jane on the court and realized quickly that she had natural ability in most things that involved sports.

She was serious, too, but not in an uptight way.

"We all were getting a little less, ah, merriment, than some of the kids, but I also thought we were fun loving," MacArthur says.

In other words, they didn't get stoned every day.

That doesn't mean they didn't dig into some pretty choice parties. Selfridge Air National Guard Base was humming in the early seventies, an active installation dating back to World War I. The base had a radar station and, until 1969, the 94th Fighter Squadron, a collective of hard-flying cowboys that had been around since the 1900s.

The base saw the same transient personnel as any other in the U.S. The conflict in Vietnam was still raging, and the influx kept the local high school populated with interesting kids "who liked to party, and had pretty nice places on the base," MacArthur says. Officers, especially. And their kids tended to enjoy a good time as well, like the guy who set up his drum kit in the living room when his parents would leave, the wife often accompanying the officer to a duty station.

"He'd set up lights to go with his drums, and they'd flash when he hit them, like a DJ, and he had these big speakers."

Jane would be out there once in a while, sometimes on a date ("she tended to go out with jock types," one former classmate says).

Mount Clemens was just the right size for someone like Jane, whose outsized, pleasant personality embraced the hominess and history of the town.

Jane moved on to Central Michigan University after graduating with her high school class of five hundred students in 1973.

Central was small enough to keep from getting lost amidst a sea of strivers. Unlike Bob, she didn't come from heavy bankroll and social prestige—Bob could likely have made a case to attend the University of Michigan, the Harvard of the Midwest, as his daughter, Jessica, would do so many years later—and so Jane satisfied herself with a small-town atmosphere that wasn't all that far from that of her hometown.

College was an emotionally rich time for her, and Jane joined the Alpha Sigma Tau Sorority, giving her a chance to help organize the sorority's events, serving time as secretary, while working on her bachelor's degree in business administration.

"Jane was an organizer," said Connie Folse, a colleague at the sorority. Jane dated plenty of boys at Central, Folse said, but no one in particular, and she loved the usual college life with the parties and friendships.

Jane's younger sister Janet went to Central in 1975 and joined the sorority, "and they were very close," Folse said. "They did a lot of things together."

The year Jane enrolled, the school revived the intercollegiate women's volleyball team. It was serendipitous—she certainly didn't select Central because of sports. But when the team was announced in October 1973, Jane was among the starters on the fifteen-member team.

There was sports—flag football, basketball—and Jane, at five feet eight inches, 140 pounds, a weight that moved up a bit as she aged, excelled even when fun was the main function of the activity. "Competitive" was a word that applied to Jane, over and over.

"And the other things we'd do, sometimes getting together in the summer, one of the sisters in the sorority had a home on Lake Michigan and we all got together for a weekend there, and Jane came to my graduation party in Lansing, where I grew up, at the end of Central."

In February 1976, Jane was brought into the honor society of Phi Kappa Phi, a national group that recognizes academic excellence and requires a minimum grade point average of 3.75 for a member's junior rank. Her 4.0 grade point average made her a shoo-in. Two months later, she was inducted into Mortar Board, another national scholastic honor.

After graduating, Jane moved on to Mercy College of Detroit to pursue her MBA. She wasn't kidding around about life, but at the same time, she was enjoying the ride.

She was a driven success in everything she did, and she accomplished her goals with a smile. It was impossible not to like her, even as she showed a ladder-climbing aggressiveness. Toward the end of getting her master's degree, Jane took an internship at Detroit Edison, the region's largest electric provider.

It was a monster investor-owned utility that provided

electricity to millions of customers. Detroit was in the throes of achieving the dubious title of "Murder City," as a plague of murder and drugs staked its claim. The homicide rate in 1983 was just over 53 per 100,000 residents.

Around the same time, 1983, Jane met Bob Bashara, a very eligible bachelor with a pedigree from the Pointes, at a party. He was glib and poised if not loud and sometimes boisterous. He was in real estate and doing some freelance sales work for whomever would offer some flexibility in his hours. Coming from money helped his chances with a girl like Jane, who was selective with men.

"He came from an affluent family, was educated, a church-goer, family oriented, ambitious, a life of the party kind of guy," is how one member of Jane's family described him.

"I knew pretty quickly that Jane was the one I wanted to spend my life with," Bob says. "I was focused on that. I loved her soon after meeting her."

The couple was married at St. Michael's in a 6 P.M. service on April 26, 1985, a Friday. Jane, who was raised in the Protestant Church, converted to the Episcopalian faith shortly before their wedding.

Jane wore her mother's wedding gown. Bob's father, George, was his best man. The couple took off the next day for a Pacific cruise that hit the high spots of Mexico. They went back and settled into a place on Alger Street in St. Clair Shores.

Bob was hired shortly after they returned from their honeymoon by United Laboratories, a specialty chemical company that sold a number of products including cleaning solutions, pesticides, and lubricants.

He was a sales representative and managed his own hours, while Jane began putting in the hours at Edison.

"I also repped for a coffee company and a packaging company," Bashara says. "What those jobs allowed me to do was have the flexibility to allow Jane to continue her career. I took the pressure off of her for raising the kids, and it gave me the huge pleasure of raising my kids and interacting with them more than 99 percent of men do. It also allowed me the flexibility to manage my rentals."

Jane was hired as a full-time employee after her internship and was now moving through the management ranks, first in marketing, learning about every element of the department.

She loved her job and her blossoming career.

And in turn, her employees liked her. Even though she had a big office and obvious authority, she didn't wield it like a corporate cudgel.

"She kept this open door, even though she was a supervisor," says Peggy Willockx, one of the employees who worked for Jane over the years.

Willockx didn't finish college, while Jane, of course, had enough formal schooling to be considered an academic.

"Of course she was after me to finish my degree, but it sure didn't affect how she respected me and my abilities," Willockx says. The respect for academics would later be part of the gentle persuasion Jane used on her own children.

At work, it didn't matter as long as an employee could do the job.

"It didn't matter to her if you had the degree. She was

doing things to help my career, and she didn't have to do that," Willockx says.

Her family was never far from her mind, even in the midst of fifty-hour work weeks.

"She talked about her kids and what they were doing all the time," another co-worker said. And at corporate outings, Jane was front and center at any of the games.

"She was always in there."

With Bob, Jane played golf, at least nine holes a week and sometimes in a couples league at the local country club. In the winter, they hosted euchre tournaments while Bob talked and talked. They went to social functions year-round as part of an almost dizzying social life.

Bob would dance with any woman who would have him, often leaving Jane tableside to chat with her friends.

"I always knew I would not marry someone boring," Jane once said to a friend, watching Bob two-stepping at one more high-end benefit in the Pointes. "But I never knew I would marry someone like Bob."

Bob had his own friends, and when they met Jane, they were enchanted.

"Jane is a sweetheart," said Jim Wilson, a real estate developer. "She's the salt of the earth."

Jane's father helped Bob on building projects; he was "a great guy," says an old Bashara friend, Jim McCuish. "Jane and her parents were wonderful people."

Bob did well with United, earning a couple of vacations for his performance. One took them to the French Riviera, another to Hawaii.

Jane took to the church, teaching in the worship

center and to youth groups and serving as chair for fundraisers.

Most of all, for Bob and Jane, the family life was satisfying.

"The best thing that happened in our lives was our children," Bob says. "That was what made good into the best."

Robert Jr. came first, in 1988, then Jessica in 1992. Bob and Jane had moved to a home at 552 Middlesex, a prestigious house in a prestigious old neighborhood, the kind made for TV movies, with wide sweeping streets that are gracefully covered under treetops in the heat of the summer, littered with golden leaves in the fall, and swept clean by fastidious snow plows in the winter.

The house was 3,400 square feet with five bedrooms, three full bathrooms, two half baths, a finished basement, and a wine cellar.

Jane had couches—full, cushy sofas with pillows—arranged all over the house, and nothing was too formal but still maintained a *Better Homes*–styled livability.

The kitchen was open, with a large industrial-sized range and hardwood and glass cabinetry. The center of activity was the island, a granite rectangle with four stools. The fireplace was set off by a huge map of the world on the mantel, while the spare bedroom served as an office, and later, Rob's room was turned into a place where fitness equipment—a weight bench, a stair stepper, and a treadmill—was stored.

The master bedroom had a king bed, and the adjacent bathroom included a hot tub. In the basement: a pool table, more couches, and a fireplace. It was truly a fine home done with money.

The place was made larger by 1,300 square feet of living area Bob added to the back of the home, which he had encased in glass to make it feel even roomier, he says, and Jane was always organizing parties that took in three blocks and often used 552 Middlesex as the centerpiece.

"A real estate buddy of mine sold it to me, a real good deal," Bob says. "A great street."

Indeed, it was a great street, once known to locals as "the compound" for its abundance of residents with reported connections to the Detroit Mafia.

The most prominent names from the neighborhood's legacy ended in vowels: Meli, Corrado, Tocco. It was solid upper-class, and Bob was at home, rubbing elbows with the money.

For Robert's first Christmas, Bob went out and bought a spruce tree from a local nursery. It was the season, of course. But when it came time to toss the tree, he couldn't find the heart to do it. This was part of his son's first big holiday, and to simply set the tree by the curbside seemed so crude.

"So I planted it in the front yard," Bob says. When Jessica's first Christmas came around, he did the same thing.

"I brought them into the house first, of course, for the Christmas season, then just took a look at the yard and the trees and realized what I could do," Bob says. "They always meant something to me and I hope to the kids. It was like their youth kept living."

The kids were super achievers, which was predictable given their heritage.

Robert Jr., who went by Rob, was a math and science wizard right off. He was a masterful student, and by high school he was a true brain in a place where such a thing was cool.

It made sense, then, that in high school he joined the FIRST Robotics team, a program that fosters kids with interests in science and technology. They develop projects and socialize with like minds, a place they can explore their geekery. Rob also joined the Boy Scouts and the Interact element of the Rotary Club, where Bob was such a large presence that some of the locals thought he owned it. To ensure he wasn't a complete nerd, Rob also ran cross-country and was part of the Detroit Boat Club as a crew member.

Jessica was also a brain, but her dad had her playing soccer when she was four years old. She loved her studies, but Jessica also grew up tall, like her parents, to five feet eleven inches and with a strong, thin frame, weighing about 140 pounds.

Like her mother, she played volleyball. Jessica, though, took it far and deep, playing four years for an Amateur Athletic Union team. She was named a captain of her high school varsity squad, and her coach said she played "college-level volleyball." It was quite a compliment at the high level she was playing, as Grosse Pointe South was a top-tier school and competed with the best in the region. During her senior year the team was lousy, with three wins, nine losses, two ties, but it was clear Jessica was an A-list player.

Jessica was close to her father, accompanying him to Rotary Club meetings and on occasion leading the Pledge of Allegiance.

"We involved the kids in many of our community events," Bob says. "We'd do golf outings, benefits, and all of us would participate. I was teaching them how to be involved and help your community. We came out very lucky; we were comfortable and our neighbors were kind, good people. That made it easy to want to see people enjoy their lives and try to make that happen."

Rob graduated Grosse Pointe South in 2006 and headed to Purdue for engineering. Jessica graduated in 2010 and elected to go to the University of Michigan. There was a soft cushion of scholarship money and well-heeled parents, coupled with high achievement, to give them a wide choice of schools. They were both can't-lose kids, coming from a can't-lose place, one of the wealthiest enclaves in America.

4

"This Is a Great Guy, I Personally Vouch for Him"

Joe Gentz was just one more misguided, mentally challenged guy, most people figured.

But he was dangerous, that's for sure.

The six-foot-four-inch, 260-pound former merchant marine walked into the Christmas party in December 2011 at the Texas Bar and Grill in Detroit wearing cowboy boots, a Western shirt that would make Roy Rogers proud, and a harsh don't-fuck-with-me frown.

He was accompanied by local woman, Susan, a small blonde in her forties.

The two danced. Gentz was strutting around, talking loud, grabbing at his date, talking up the crowd with a deep voice and diction that could be garbled when he was excited.

The bar is a one-room joint, although it is not by any means small. There are some pool tables, plenty of

aisle space, TVs at both ends of the bar, some tables liberally sprinkled through what turns into a nice dance floor
when the need is there. Which is what was warranted on
that crowded night.

Almost immediately the trouble started when Susan
began to flirt with Miguel, the boyfriend of the bartender,
Ashley.

That didn't sit well with Gentz, who began to move in
on Miguel.

"Tiny, these guys are causing trouble," Ashley whispered
to the joint's de facto bouncer that evening. The place didn't
actually have a bouncer, but saner heads sometimes did
prevail, and Tiny, predictably outsized, often served.

Gentz was angry, and that was never good.

"Who do you think you are?" he bellowed to Miguel,
as Tiny watched.

The two danced the barroom brawl waltz, staring at
each other. Except staring at Gentz created a dilemma: do
you look at his right eye, the one that glances straight at
you, or at the lazy left eye, which aims to the perimeter?

Gentz dropped the matter and headed to the bathroom,
and Tiny followed. Once inside the small space, Gentz took
a few blows to the head, a warning shot of a potential future
beating.

He left humiliated, muttering to himself.

The Texas, which sits on the wrong side of the border
of Detroit and Grosse Pointe, was also a four-minute walk
from the studio apartment on Wayburn Street that Gentz
had been living in since autumn.

It was a good upper flat apartment where he could hit

the town without the need for a ride, walking first to My Dad's Place then down two blocks to the Texas. If things were really cooking, he would hit the Sunrise Sunset Saloon, another fifteen-minute walk away.

Trouble is, Gentz had some time to think about his smacking around at the hands of Tiny before coming back to the Texas a couple days later.

Gentz went in the next night with his buddy, another large man everyone knew as JJ. While the barkeep talked with JJ, Gentz began to talk smack. There were a few people in there, sitting mostly at the bar. They paid him little attention. He wasn't a favorite there.

"That's it, I'm coming back here with a gun. I'm going to take out everyone," Gentz said. No one paid a lot of attention.

The manager, a veteran bar hound handler named Rose Tucker, told him to leave. This kind of promise of retribution was so common that the Texas had put in an electric door.

At certain hours customers had to look in, try the door, and be approved by whoever was working behind the bar before they could be buzzed in.

You could never be sure who was packing there, either. Two years after Gentz's promise of mayhem, Rose's daughter, Brenda, would tragically kill herself at the bar, using a handgun.

Gentz, like the others, never made good on his promise. He wasn't special in any way, except perhaps in his low IQ.

"Joe has disabilities," said his oldest brother, Steven.

"He graduated high school, but his abilities of speech and writing are about third to fifth grade education. He's like a child who needs to be guided and always sort of [looked] after."

"You never got that he was retarded, but he wasn't all there," adds Karyn Brown, a Texas Bar regular. "He was alone a lot, walking in and out of bars. He was always talking, a blowhard."

Gentz looks like actor Ron Perlman on the TV series *Sons of Anarchy* and tells people so—he's into it enough that he has a picture of Perlman on his cell phone to make sure people can observe the likeness.

He has a graying brush cut, a sometimes-beard, sometimes-stubble on a square jaw on a large face, and a bewildered look in his disjointed blue eyes.

His tattoos are puzzles. On his upper left arm, "how it works way of life" is inked in blue. On his upper right arm, an anchor and eagle, also in blue. For several years, off and on, he has worn a silver stud in his left ear.

By that night at the Texas, Gentz had been married three times and had spent his life as an itinerant wanderer.

A Michigan native, Gentz was born to Detroiters and grew up in Warren, one of a string of working-class communities with an auto plant, Chrysler's Warren Truck Assembly, as its root.

The family was, like Gentz, large. His sisters, Lori and Kim, and his brothers, Steven and Kevin, lived in a 900-square-foot redbrick home on Hudson Avenue in a neighborhood full of almost exactly the same houses. One might have an extra half bathroom, and most had two bedrooms upstairs and a basement that was converted into two more. No garages but maybe a carport. They were modest quarters for modest, working-class people.

His dad, Richard, worked in the water department for the city of Warren. He was a large man, like his son, six feet four inches, with a garrulous smile. His mom, Joanne, was a housewife who helped out at school events and took part in church events, as the family was deeply religious.

He went to St. Louis Center in Chelsea, Michigan, starting at seven years old until high school. It was a place for developmentally disabled kids, and it had a boys' school that could help Gentz. It was a residential facility, and Gentz would go home on weekends and over the holidays.

He went home to a family-tilted neighborhood. Most everyone knew one another and if a neighbor needed a hand, be it a stubborn car that wouldn't start or something more serious like an illness in the family, there was sure to be some help from someone on the block.

Every New Year's Eve, each home would have snacks and drinks set out to create a wandering party, where everyone stopped by, had a couple, and moved on.

At midnight, the fireworks came out. Most of the homes also had guns, as this was a heavy hunting culture and the long guns were as much a part of local life as Stroh's, Vernors, and Chevrolet.

One year, Joe got his dad's gun and decided to really celebrate the new year.

"Happy New Year," was barely out of Richard Gentz's mouth before BOOM. Joe had fired his dad's Russian rifle into the winter air, as people moved away, well aware of gravity.

Gentz always aimed to please, and everyone knew it.

"Joe was influenced by everybody," Joanne says. "But he did know right from wrong."

There were dares that got him in trouble nonetheless.

"I bet you won't throw that rock through that window," one bullying local once taunted Gentz.

"Will too," Gentz shot back. He looked at the stone, about half the size of a baseball, in his right hand.

"Naw, you aren't going to do it. You're chicken," his tormentor said.

With that, Gentz flung the rock through a parked car window, shattering it, as Gentz had the strength of a grown man.

His anger issues stemmed from his mental disability. A man forced to reckon with a world that is quick to take advantage of slowness, combined with the confusion of life, has turned the gentlest of giants into pissed-off dudes, and Gentz could be as surly as they come.

Joe got out of high school and began to drift. Joanne, who was divorced from Richard in 1987, would get calls from all over hearing he was in trouble.

"He was doing things that we didn't approve of," she says now. "Drugs, drinking. There were years where we didn't know where he was."

He spent time in Fort Lauderdale in the eighties, racking up a misdemeanor disorderly conduct charge in 1985.

He posted his own meager bond and never went back

to the court. The bench warrant that was issued was useless; Gentz joined the merchant marines and the Seafarers International Union in Houston. He shipped out on the *Overseas Philadelphia*, a midsized shipping tanker built in 1983 with a route that included anywhere and everywhere, from the Florida coast near Miami on up to the Great Lakes. It hauled anything from oil to granite. Gentz worked the deck as a union laborer for five years, earning up to $8,000 a month.

"When I was young, I was playing Russian roulette," Gentz says. "I was drinking, taking drugs. It was the eighties and I just did it hard."

He says he got sober in 1990—a claim refuted by some who later knew him—then moved to Houston that same year to find work. He ended up working as a civilian contractor for the military during the Persian Gulf War. Gentz says he served on supply ships. He came back to the States and stayed in the Gulf region near Louisiana, painting water towers "because that's where the money was at." When that ran out, he worked for a towing company, and by 1992, he was on the East Coast.

Gentz docked in Baltimore and decided to stop working the ships. Richard married a woman named Letty. Joe didn't care so much about the fractured family, but he was close with his dad. They kept in touch the best Joe could ever keep in touch, mostly via collect calls.

Gentz lived with a sister in Washington, D.C., where her husband was in the air force. "Until he got in trouble on the base and they made him leave," Joanne says.

He migrated north to Waldorf, Maryland, and met a local

girl named Lorrie VanMeter. She was a retail worker, trying her best to get by, just as Gentz was. The two got married in 1993 and moved into a small apartment. He did what it took to pay rent, shoveling asphalt, working in a pizza joint.

"I don't want to say he was stupid, but he was slow," said Angela Adelman, VanMeter's sister.

Despite his emotional fragility, his inability to deal with consequences, and his dangerous moods, Gentz figured out a way to get some easy money.

In 1993 he sued the Maritime Overseas Corporation over injuries he suffered while working in the Gulf of Mexico off the coast of Galveston, Texas.

Gentz used a legal provision so common it has its own name, the Jones Act, a ninety-five-year-old federal legal statute that requires shipowners to maintain their crafts. So many workers are injured at sea that complaints such as Gentz's are frequent. Shipping companies fight them, but often it becomes a matter of settling for the lowest amount possible.

Gentz was injured on the deck of the ship, claiming his back had been hurt in a fall during inclement weather.

He asked for unspecified damages over $50,000 and opted to go with a magistrate judge rather than a jury. He was awarded $26,000.

He was supposed to go to Adelman's wedding in 1996 but said his father had called him back to Michigan. VanMeter told him if he left and missed the wedding, it was over.

Gentz, flush with the settlement, left and never came back.

"I came back because I promised my grandmother that I would help out around the house when I was needed, and my dad said, 'I need you here,'" Gentz says. He and his father were close: "He knew every move I made."

Back in Michigan, he worked more jobs: food service, machinery, snow removal.

In 2000, he married a local woman named Donna Lowery, and the couple had a daughter, Brittany. Within five months of her birth, the couple had split. Donna was quickly determined unfit to be a parent, due to neglect of the girl, the court ruled. The ruling sent Brittany into an on-again, off-again dance of foster care and temporary custody of one parent or another.

The divorce was a bitter dispute between a couple that was unequipped to have a child in the first place. They filed mutual personal protection orders on each other. She sued him for child support. Donna says now that despite their acrimonious split, "Joe is not the kind of person to kill someone. I was with him for three years, and he never yelled at me and never put his hands on me in anger."

She blames the divorce on Joe's dad. "He even paid for the divorce. He didn't think anyone was good enough for Joe."

"Richard did not like Donna, and he would take Joe out all night drinking and leave her with the baby," says Joanne Gentz. "Then the county gave the baby to Joe, after the divorce, which never should have happened."

The daughter, Brittany, was deemed developmentally disabled, meaning that she, like Gentz, suffered from a below-average IQ and the accompanying social and behavior problems.

Gentz had increasing issues with drinking, and while he would say he was a handyman, he was a roving party. By the time of the incident at the Texas Bar, Michigan's Department of Human Services was trying to terminate Gentz's parental rights.

In court documents, the agency alleged he began neglecting his daughter several years before by leaving her in the care of a relative who had no business taking care of anyone.

By the requirement of the state, Gentz underwent psychological testing, which indicated he lacked the emotional skills needed to parent his daughter.

While he lacked impulse control during all of his life, in 2003, he was diagnosed as bipolar and as suffering from organic mood disorder. More testing, however dubious the system is, determined that Gentz "lacked the ability to parent his daughter, becomes easily agitated, has difficulty with female authority figures, and can be paranoid," according to court records.

The results also showed he was quick to anger and showed symptoms of clinical paranoia. One report even noted that Gentz at one point threatened to call the president and "feels the world is out to get him."

In Lowery's child custody filing, her lawyer claimed "there was significant violence throughout the relationship on both sides of the relationship, however, the majority of the incidents were situations where (Gentz) was on the offensive side of the arguments."

On one occasion, a Children's Protective Services worker found the house in which Lowery and Gentz were living to be unfit.

"The bathtub was black and moldy," a report states. The washroom was unsafe, according to the assessment, because of exposed wires, the child's bedroom was covered in trash, and the family dog had a festering wound leading to a chronically bleeding mouth, leaving splatter all over the home.

It was the last straw; the child was placed in foster care.

Gentz had been paying child support off and on, sometimes forcing the court to garnish his wages. Now he needed money to fight the court and show he was solvent enough to take care of his daughter.

Gentz was never a good bet to have money for long. Part of his problem was a fondness for casinos. He was the fool with the money, and sure enough, he and the cash soon parted.

His life as a free man stumbled along in the last year or so before Jane's murder. In addition to the custody battle with his ex-wife Donna over ten-year-old Brittany, he was having beefs in the neighborhood and with one more woman he had married in October 2009, Rose Fox.

The two were renting a small frame house on Liberty Street in St. Clair Shores, a mixed area in Macomb County, just north of Grosse Pointe.

Around 7 A.M. on March 9 2010, Gentz called 911. A man who was staying across the street, thirty-five-year-old

Alfonso Lara, had ripped the screen door off Gentz's house and was trying to kick his way inside.

The cops got there and, when Lara resisted, tased him. He was arrested and charged with attempted home invasion, which his court-appointed lawyer bargained down to a misdemeanor illegal entry plea that would get Lara a year of probation.

"I called victim Rose and discussed the plea situation," reads a police report on the case. "Rose didn't completely understand . . ."

It was a small-fry crime among people who didn't have a full grasp of their rights or the law. Lara walked with probation and under $2,600 in costs.

In November 2010, Gentz again called police to the house on Liberty. Fox was now gone from the house, and Gentz was living there with Brittany. He and Fox were separating, he explained to the officers, and she had stolen a number of items belonging to both him and his daughter.

Among the items he alleged she took were three Lake St. Clair Walleye Association jackets, two belonging to him and one to Brittany. She had also stolen three suits from him, he said, and two antique dolls and a Hewlett-Packard laptop from his daughter. To top it off, he claimed Fox took what Gentz described as an Egyptian marble ashtray worth $1,000.

He told the officers that the laptop and dolls were gifts to Brittany from his late father.

Gentz had no idea where Fox was living since she left, and he was in the process of moving to an apartment in St. Clair Shores. It was one more domestic problem for Gentz that was dropped amidst the usual tumult and confusion of his life.

There were shady deals and shadier characters that made up the fabric of Gentz's life. In September 2011, Joe Holland called the police and said the Honda moped he had purchased two weeks ago for $350 from Gentz had been stolen and he suspected Gentz or one of his friends.

After the sale, Gentz had asked for the moped back. Holland upped the price to $400, and Gentz was pissed.

The kicker was that the bike was registered to Steve Virgona, a longtime pal of Gentz's who had been staying with him. Gentz had sold his friend's bike out from under him.

This is how his life had been going. Small problems tinged with money woes and the heartbreaking fight to keep his beloved daughter.

"He really went bad when his father died," Joanne Gentz says. "But then he was acting up pretty much all the time."

The Gentz family had a running joke about his woes.

"It always began with 'it's a long story' and ended up that somehow, it wasn't his fault."

By 2011, Gentz was getting disability payments and sometimes volunteering to load boxes and move things at the St. Vincent de Paul store on Kercheval, not far from his apartment.

In October of 2011, Gentz was being evicted from his apartment at Nine Mile Road and Jefferson Avenue in St. Clair Shores. Saddled with his weak intellect and an uncontrollable temper and fighting a custody dispute on an income of $1,000 a month, Gentz needed an ally. He found it in Bob Bashara, who needed some work done on his places and had met him through a local used furniture salesman named Steve Tibaudo.

Bashara needed a worker; he also had some other, heavier things to take care of, and looking at the bulk of Gentz and what appeared to be a malleable nature, he signed on to take care of him, sort of. He would find him a place to live.

Bashara had helped others do the same. In fact, the mother of Rebecca Forton enjoyed working with Bashara, who found her a tenant for her rental duplex in Grosse Pointe Park earlier in the year.

Now it was October and Forton needed a tenant for the top floor of an upper-lower house at 1224/1226 Wayburn, just a few blocks from her mother's rental. Her father, Richard, was living in the lower flat, and she was looking for a quiet tenant who could afford the $750 a month rent plus utilities.

After describing a few unsuitable prospective tenants—a single mother with two children and a family—Bashara called and told her, "I've got the perfect guy. This is a family man, a single father trying to get custody of his daughter, a hard worker. He'd be sure the place was always in order, because he's going to have case workers checking on him, and he's handy, he can do odd jobs when you need them done. This is a great guy, I personally vouch for him."

A few days later, Forton met Bashara and Gentz at the place on Wayburn. Gentz went with Virgona, who drove him everywhere. It was a strange relationship; the two lived together at times, and Virgona knew a lot of cops for some reason.

Gentz, who was no friend of the cops, was simply a man who lay where he fell. He was easygoing that way.

Forton described Gentz as "a rather large man," in a vast understatement.

During the meeting to lease the apartment, "he did not make eye contact. Bob did all the talking."

Bashara handed her the rental application, which appeared to have been done by a child. Scrawls and unanswered questions throughout the document raised concerns almost immediately, with the writing in two different markers, black and blue, rather than in pen.

Doing the math gave her even more pause; $1,000 a month would give him little to live on after he paid rent and bills. Bashara said he would put the utilities in his name to give her some reassurance. Still, she hedged. She turned to Gentz.

"Do you have any questions?" she asked him. He hadn't said a word since they all met.

Gentz looked at the floor and spoke, slowly, still looking down. Forton had worked with mentally disabled adults in her past. She felt she was looking at one there in the kitchen of her rental.

"He spoke very slow. I used to work with handicapped individuals, and I thought he was either handicapped or that he had a closed head injury," Forton said. Against her better instincts, she went ahead and rented the place to him.

It went alright for a while. Gentz began doing work for Bashara.

He was a handyman, he told people, and he could sometimes be seen driving around a beaten blue Ford van, heading to one maintenance crisis or another, or to move furniture into the worn-out old apartments that Bashara rented out.

Bashara and Gentz became workmates. Between September 2011 and January 2012, there were 472 calls made between the two, some answered, some not. That was over three calls a day, including weekends and the Christmas/ New Year's holidays.

There was no doubt the two were doing business.

He told a number of people as much. And more.

A week or two after moving into the place on Wayburn, Gentz was surfing the dating sites when he came to a woman he fancied. Lorna Riikonen was living near the Detroit Metropolitan Airport in Romulus, a long way from a suitor with no car.

She also worked at the airport as a server at Einstein Bros. Bagels inside the main terminal and had a German shepherd dog for a pet.

Riikonen was a rosy-cheeked, heavy woman with a nicotine rasp and a felony rap in her past, an assault with intent to rob while armed back in 1994. While she was going through the court process for that, she underwent an examination for diminished capacity and a competency hearing. She ended up pleading guilty and got probation.

Riikonen, in her late forties, also had a daughter in foster care, like Gentz.

They talked a few times on the phone, mostly about the foster care system. He told her he had no car and that he was doing some volunteer work while recovering from a hernia surgery. He said he hurt himself while pushing a car out of the snow. She considered Gentz more of a pen pal than anything. That's the thing with these dating sites; you like some of the people you meet, and others can be pals.

"When you get your act together, maybe we can meet," Riikonen told him one night. "You could come over and meet me at work."

She didn't think anything would ever come of it. The two texted each other frequently, talking mostly about their respective hardscrabble lives.

With a woman in the picture, Gentz had ideas. And he wanted to make sure she didn't think he had no prospects. He told her he was going to be getting a Cadillac at some point. He said he was working for someone who was going to give it to him.

She didn't think much of it, but a couple days later they were texting and catching up.

"What have u been doing? Did u get the Cadillac from your buddy?" Riikonen wrote to Gentz.

"No I did not get it but I am working on it."

"Is he really giving it to you?"

Gentz wrote: "Yes. I am get the car."

He was clearly hoping to win her favor, a tech courtship carried out via text message. He upped his game when he heard that Riikonen's oldest daughter had died of a drug overdose in early November.

"Her father said he might hurt somebody," Riikonen

texted Gentz one day, referring to the provider of the fatal drugs.

"I'll help him out," Gentz shot back. "I can do that."

He disregarded her reply that they were waiting for an autopsy to be sure of the cause of death.

"I have fds in high places," Gentz texted. He followed that with "I will not let this go." He inferred that he owned an AK-47, which was untrue.

He then upped his fabrication.

"I can find out something for you," he texted. "I have an FBI friend."

A few weeks later, in December 2011, Riikonen was working at the airport, and toward the end of her shift, she noticed that her cell phone was going off over and over. She didn't answer it and could only hear the buzzing sound, as she had the ringer off.

Riikonen got off work and looked at her phone. It was Gentz. She called him. He was at the airport to see her and had been for a while.

"We can go back to your place," he suggested hopefully. Riikonen, with a daughter at home, didn't even consider it. The last bus had left for the city, though, and he was stranded.

"I'll drive you home if you'll direct me," she said. "But no, you can't come to my place."

They began the drive down Interstate 94 east toward Detroit, past the Uniroyal Giant Tire, which has been a landmark for anyone driving from the airport to a downtown hotel since 1966. They talked, some of the usual chatter about kids and money troubles.

"I'm going to be getting that Cadillac pretty soon," Gentz said proudly.

"Is something wrong with the car?" Riikonen asked. No one just gives someone a working vehicle, let alone a piece of fine Detroit machinery like a Caddy.

"Someone is giving me the Cadillac and money to put a hit out on someone," Gentz replied.

"Who's giving you money for that?" Riikonen asked, skeptically.

The name she remembers is unclear. For Gentz, it had to be clear, as he had just met a man named Bashara, the guy who he was talking to almost every day on the phone.

"Basher, Basher," Gentz said cryptically.

It was all she would remember until January 25, when it was reported that Jane Bashara was murdered.

5

"I Am a True Master, Come to Me"

The last twenty-four months of Jane Bashara's life were the beginning of a new one for her husband, Bob. He had fallen in love with a woman he met cruising websites devoted to practitioners of an alternative view of sex and relationships.

One man's "alternative" view is another one's "aberrant" view.

The world of BDSM—bondage, discipline, submission, sadism, masochism—is much like a sexual version of *Dungeons & Dragons.* There is a heavy element of fantasy and unpredictability, an unreality that ostensibly fulfills yet hurts no one.

Some couples find that world to be the perfect outlet for their yearnings, while some singles hope to enter the world and meet their own version of a perfect mate.

Bob was part of the lifestyle contingent called "weekend warriors," in that he had a straight life—called "vanilla" by die-hard lifestyle practitioners—and enjoyed some kink during his time off.

Sometimes that kink meant sex, and other times it was simply intimate contact. And on occasion, there was contact but it wasn't intimate at all.

"There are situations in which a partner can't provide everything the other wants," says James,* who has been in the lifestyle for thirty years. He knew Bashara for much of that time and watched him engage and interact at BDSM parties.

"Sometimes they get involved away from their partner because he or she can't go there and can't do the things that the partner needs. Either they don't have personality for it or the traits or persona make up to be in the role they need to be in, whatever that role may be."

The partner that wants this, James explains, then looks outside the marriage not because he does not love his spouse.

"Sometimes they can communicate it to the spouse and then are knowingly allowed to seek it out. And just because they do doesn't mean they're having sex with people. Often, they're playing, not getting blow jobs or giving or receiving oral sex or intercourse."

Bob and Jane Bashara had a very traditional life in all senses of the word. The fine neighborhood, the children, the safe community in which they were active, and the church at which they worshipped along with their neighbors

---

* Denotes pseudonym.

made the Basharas part of the Gibraltar-like rock that kept residents of the Pointes firmly attached. The belonging was intoxicating, and Bob and Jane were both part of the attraction and firmly ensconced in its cocoon. If anything, at least in appearance, Bob worked hard to ensure the cocoon was spun tightly.

"Jane and I raised $800,000 for the community," Bob says. "We did wine tastings, bake sales, sporting events, so many things. I was named the honorary mayor of Trombly Elementary School."

Shortly after the death of his father in 2002, Bob went to his first BDSM party. He knew people from all walks of life.

Soon, he began hitting the BDSM websites. He was escaping the tried-and-true, the predictable, that he professed to love so much.

In early 2008, Bob began to create profiles on a series of websites, calling his new alter ego "Master Bob" while establishing his preference as a "dom," as in dominator.

On May 22, 2008, Bob had established a profile on the sites, calling himself MasterBob1000. "I am a true master . . . come to me," he wrote in a small header to his page. He described himself to potential partners as a "48-year-old straight top male from Grosse Pointe, United States. I am a most complete Master who will open to you all this lovely life has to offer . . . I will bring you to my dungeon and train and open to you all you seek to understand, learn and know. I am here . . . kneel."

On another site, he described himself as "male dominant" from "East Side, Michigan," six feet three inches, 250 pounds, fifty years old.

"Welcome to my world, I am Master Bob, a complete trainer. I will open train and guide you in this lifestyle, if what you seek is learning through doing then I am here and look for you to come to me, kneel and have all your desires and cravings opened to you. Are you ready for Master Bob. I will make you love and enjoy the lovely mix of moderate pain and pleasure. Know I am true and skilled in this lovely life so I await you. Come to me, MB. Oh, and I train several so being tied to another is a wonderful thing."

On another site, he listed the activities that he was into under links for sex, S&M, and role play. He reported that he had engaged in all the S&M categories listed except biting, but including nipple torture, vaginal fisting, beating (hard and soft), choking, and hair pulling.

Lifestyle members have a saying, "Your kink is your kink and my kink is my kink and it's all good." Bashara embraced that one with gusto.

"My goal was to help these women in the lifestyle," Bob says. "These women were being abused. You have guys who want rough sex in the name of the lifestyle and they don't know the code, they aren't true to the lifestyle. They don't know how to handle the equipment. A submissive woman is a strong woman; she has to have some strength to her. Most of them have been in bad relationships."

It is, undoubtedly, a lifestyle that is considered shameful by some, passively alternative by others.

Jane "didn't have a take . . . she didn't want to know about it," Bob says. "I did my thing, she did hers, and she gave me the freedom to do what I wanted."

Jane, though, told her friends that Bob was addicted to pornography and was plagued by erectile dysfunction.

"She always said that Bob always lies, Bob always lies," said Patricia Matthews, Jane's friend since her teen years in Macomb County. Jane told her that Bob was a "big flirt, but it's all show because he can't get it up."

Master Bob, for those cruising the BDSM sites, was a widower whose wife died three years before. He was raising his daughter and had a son in college. He used widower because he felt no one would want to date him if he said he was separated, much less married.

In August 2008, Master Bob received an email from a woman who called herself Just Me As I Am. The two were relatively new to the lifestyle—him a couple months and her a couple of weeks—and she was looking for someone to dominate her. She lived in Dearborn Heights, twenty miles away. They flirted on email and talked on the phone a few times. He name was Rachel Gillett. She wanted to meet.

The widowed status evaporated quickly under Gillett's questioning.

"I suspected he was married, and I confronted him," Gillett says. "He told me that he wasn't really a widower but that he was married to Jane but separated."

Still not convinced he was being truthful, she pushed.

Okay, Bob said, he was living a loveless life with his wife, a mutually unhappy existence in which they lived "separate" lives and he slept in a guest room. It was, as Rachel put it, an "emasculating" situation for Bob.

She pushed it harder, Googling Jane and finding that the couple hosted community functions in their home, even finding pictures of them, smiling, in the community newspaper.

"Once I thought they were a real married couple, I ended it," Rachel says. But Bashara wouldn't have it. He texted, emailed, called her. He even called her daughter, asking her to talk some sense into her mother and get her to start seeing him again.

They were bound by their fealty to the lifestyle. They went to the parties together, sometimes, it seemed, on a weekly basis. And he was so into the lifestyle.

Shortly after they met, Bob asked her to come over to a property he owned on Mack Avenue.

The 14,000-square-foot building on Mack was a cash cow for Bob, when he managed it right. It was purchased by his father, George, in 1998 and deeded to Bob shortly before his dad's death in 2002.

On that first visit to the property on Mack, after ushering her down a set of stairs at the back of the Hard Luck Lounge, Bob unlocked one metal door, then a wooden door that opened onto a small square space. It was, Bob said, a dungeon.

It was a windowless, narrow room with a bed in the far left corner and an older television set on a stand to the right. A single row of five track lights ran for four feet above the bed, and he kept a series of lamps, some with a medieval design, on the floor. He kept axes and swords around the room, and hooks on the wall above the bed were used for binding. A small wooden cabinet with two butterfly doors held a variety of ropes and chains, some candles, and sex toys. A round mirror with a metal frame hung on the wall, tilted toward the bed.

It was the first time they had been intimate, she being bound, him playing with her, without him showing a hint of arousal.

"He used a strap-on," she says. "He thought his impotence was from his diabetes or his weight. He said he had tried Viagra and it didn't work."

Despite his inability to perform, Rachel was smitten. But there were also other women.

"Bob had different hooker-looking girls with him all the time," says Mike Mouyianis, who ran the Hard Luck Lounge with Bob as his landlord. "On Saturday nights, he would come in with them and they'd sit on the couches we had at the back of the bar. They were his dates, and some were with him a while and others not so much."

He was always looking at girls, "and he's not a chick magnet," says Jim McCuish, a former business partner. "But he had big balls. He would approach good-looking women, and I'd think, 'You've got no chance.' And he didn't, but he didn't care."

Bob was a serial philanderer, playing in the BDSM community with an aggressive zeal. To the people at the Mack property, where he gravitated for his extramarital get-togethers, it was just annoying.

For Bob, it was pure excitement to be part of the lifestyle with like-minded women, many of whom didn't care that he was married.

He met Venita Porter in 2007 at a BDSM site. Porter was a pretty single mom in her forties, and in some financial trouble, between jobs and in need of some help. Bob liked nothing more than to feel the benevolent knight.

"He was looking for a submissive, and I was needing food and shoes for my children," Porter said.

She became a friend and confidante for Bob, who managed to integrate her into his life, and the lives of his children, without raising too much suspicion. She attended church with them on occasion, and even bought Bob gifts at Christmas, which he would open along with the other gifts from Jane and the kids, as if she were just another member of the family.

"When I met [Porter], she had no food in her cupboard," Bob says. "Her husband had lost his job. I got her hooked up with a guy who gave her a job."

He veiled his romantic interests by telling everyone that he was helping her out, providing groceries and money when Porter needed it.

Porter was aware of his situation, but as with most of his women, he portrayed his marriage as frayed, although he didn't keep his married status a secret from Porter, as she already knew from being a workmate. She went to the movies with Bob and his mother, worked on plans for a birthday party for Jane, and hit Dylan's Raw Bar & Grill with Bob and his son. She met his Rotary friends.

"I was involved with quite a bit of his life," Porter said,

noting that they had also attended church together. At Bob's behest, she had also joined the local Rotary Club.

They had sex, too; a friends-with-benefits relationship that both of them felt was part of the deal.

"I've been a good man and a good father," he told Porter one night during a visit to her apartment. "But Jane and I, we don't get along, and we don't share the same plans for the future."

Divorce, he said, was the only thing he could think of.

With Porter, though, he shared a love of the lifestyle. She, in turn, was crazy about the dungeon, which she helped paint and outfit. She moved the bed on the top of her car and helped design the concealment of the dungeon.

The Hard Luck space was just being readied for opening when the two met.

Their sex was good, she felt, despite Bob's impotence.

"He was very into dominance," Porter said. Breath play, in which he choked her to the point of unconsciousness, was also part of their sexual repertoire, as well as spanking.

Bob would get angry sometimes over his inability to get an erection, and it came out in his aggressiveness.

Once in a while it tipped over into the sex play, as in the time he choked her small neck too hard. They stopped that particular act for a while, "then we came back to it," she said.

Porter was under the impression that the relationship was solid, despite the fact that Bob was married. They spent time together, shared some family experiences. But the one thing Porter didn't like was that they didn't do "normal" couples things. While she was a submissive, she was also not a fool. She didn't want to be treated as just a sex slave; she wanted that to just be part of the deal.

She began to press him for a more conventional date on occasion.

Then it got weird.

She had agreed to meet Bob at Dylan's for a date. It would be dinner, dancing, "relaxed," Porter said.

She got to Dylan's, and Bob called her on her cell and told her he was showing the dungeon to someone and would be out soon. Then he called back in ten minutes and asked her to come on down to the dungeon.

While it wasn't exactly what she had planned—often the dungeon simply meant sex and the end of the night, but it sometimes also meant they would talk—she walked down the stairs, and Bob let her into the first room, which obscured the dungeon. He then opened the dungeon door and introduced her to Rachel, who was naked. As Porter later put it, "there was going to be sex" between Bob and Rachel imminently. Bob closed the door to the dungeon, and Porter burst into a jealous rage that made her feel like her heart was exploding. She stayed in the storage room, then went upstairs for a drink, maybe two, then went back down again, repeating this for two hours "until they were done," Porter said.

When he came out, Bob stood in front of her and turned to ice, the man she had trusted with her own life, who had once told her it was "you and me against the world."

She begged him, she pleaded with him to make Rachel go away, and Bob towered over her with no feeling in his face at all.

Amidst the clamor, Rachel says she dressed and left.

"He's a good man. He'll be really good to you," Porter told her as she left.

Rachel, puzzled, turned to Bob. "Don't be so mean to her," she said on her way out the door.

Porter was crushed. Bob had used her as a crutch and a sex partner and had now cast her aside.

Rachel Rene Gillett, maiden name Mowery, actually was partially a widow. Her husband, David, whom she had divorced in 1997 after eight years of marriage, died in 2002. He was her fourth husband. She had married all four before she reached the age of thirty. She found herself at fifty-one, still looking for the right one.

The marriages had resulted in four children, three boys and one girl, all of them deeply patriotic and imbued with a sense of responsibility.

One of the sons was a police officer, and the two others had served in the army, one spending time in Iraq. They were both out of the service; one worked as a security executive, and the other worked in security with the United States Department of Agriculture in Washington, D.C.

Rachel's daughter was also army—still in the service after doing a hitch in Afghanistan.

Rachel was born and raised in Michigan as the youngest of ten children. Her father was a General Motors lifer, and her mother died when Rachel was a preteen.

"I had kind of a bad childhood," she says. "I think I was trying to make up for that, creating a perfect family."

Perfect is not easy, she discovered through trial and error. A marriage had taken her to California, then Texas. When she ended up divorced in the Dallas area, she stayed. Like too many Rust Belters hailing from an economy depressed by poor government and unions that pushed companies southward, she knew it was a place to find work.

She had no special training, but she was organized and tidy and found work as an office manager at a religious bookstore. She was deeply religious, raised in faith. She didn't drink and rarely cussed.

In 2006, Rachel went back to Michigan to be nearer her family. She was close to some of her siblings and also to one of her sisters-in-law, Linda.

Rachel got a job as a secretary at Wayne State University.

But Rachel was alone. Bob had always fancied himself a knight of sorts, and despite his other dalliances, he felt a special tenderness for Rachel. She had self-esteem issues and was a lost and hurt soul who would someday wax poetic on her life with Bob, after it was over. But for now, this was the real thing.

A year after meeting, he convinced—actually, in the arena of their dom/sub relationship, he ordered—Rachel to move from her place in Dearborn Heights to an apartment over the storefront on Mack Avenue, where they would pursue what he called "their future," Rachel said. She insisted on paying the $650 rent, plus utilities, just as the other tenants paid.

As for Bob and Jane, "I never thought they had some

kind of marriage, a solid relationship," Gillett says. "I was in love with Bob."

Several times he told her that the divorce was pending. Rachel clung to hope after hope. Shortly after she moved into the apartment on Mack, their relationship became more obvious, at least to those who hung around his properties.

"You'd see her around all the time," says John Montgomery, who managed Dylan's. "Rachel and Bob would ride around together in her yellow Saab convertible, with the top down. They didn't even try to cover up the fact that they were hanging out together. They never seemed to think Jane would see them."

Bob agrees that they were hiding nothing: "I never did anything behind anyone's back. There was no secret deal, although there was some privacy in some of my dealings. I didn't keep anyone under a stone; there was none of that."

Bob and Rachel were exploring that world on a different level, as a couple not quite coupled, and of course, the rest of the world wouldn't understand.

He gave her a family heirloom ring sometime in 2010, calling it a promise ring. The diamond came from deep in the family history; Aunt Jenny, to be precise. It was meant to eventually go to Jessica, his daughter.

Rachel put it first on her left hand, and Bob chastised her.

"No, you can't wear it there until I am free," he said.

For Christmas 2010, Bob gave her a necklace that he said was made of cuff links from his father's tuxedo.

MURDER IN GROSSE POINTE PARK 79

"I didn't know what to do with his tuxedo after he died," Bob explained to her. "So I did this. I want you to have it."

They were having sex in the dungeon regularly; it was a "safe" place for them. They were into breath play. They had other partners. While Bob could not achieve an erection—he blamed it on his weight—he wore a strap-on device to penetrate Rachel.

"He thought that was just normal," Rachel says.

Once, they had a three-way in Bob and Jane's bed at the house on Middlesex, after which, as a proper submissive, she slept on the floor. Another time, Bob needed someone to drive Jane's Mercedes SUV home from the repair shop and asked Rachel. She couldn't say no.

Rachel now took on a new identity at alt.com, becoming "MB's Bella," or Master Bob's slave, Bella—Bella being Italian for "beautiful."

Bob kept his benevolent activities in the community alive, although he was beginning to crack a little. His sexual endeavors were taking away from his ability to earn a living. He fell behind on his country club dues—a membership that gave him access and status, as well as considerable pride. In 2010, he withdrew $10,000 from one of Jane's retirement accounts without asking her. She had to change the online password to the account they shared.

He watched pornography, focused on the videos at alt.com and other BDSM sites.

He even told friends.

"I like spanking girls," Bob said, almost offhand, to Jim Wilson one day as the two were golfing at Lochmoor Club.

He repeated it a few times in similar conversations, just buddy-to-buddy, with Wilson. As if to clear up an unanswered question, Bob added, "Jane doesn't like that stuff."

At home, the kids would catch him watching Internet pornography, and it would set off a series of arguments.

"I have ED," he told Jessica, ED meaning erectile dysfunction, a term that has hit the mainstream for all ages since the commercialization of drugs like Viagra. "I want to make sure it's not your mother's fault."

It wasn't; Bashara could not perform with anyone.

One night, Jessica, sensing something was wrong, decided to do a quick check of his cell phone texts.

"Get down on your knees and give me head, bitch," read a text her father sent to one woman, whose identity came up blank.

"What is this message?" Jessica said, pointing to the phone. Bob was in the family room, alone, when she approached him.

He took the phone gently from her hand and deleted the message.

"What message?" he asked.

The message was not to Rachel. It was sent to another girl Bob was courting, as he was compulsive in his pursuits.

A couple of months later, Jessica found a card her father was sending to Rachel, on which he said, among other things, that "the sex was great."

Again, she asked her father about what was going on.

He was brutally honest. He was not physically capable of having sex, he told her, "but there are other ways," he said.

He was oblivious how these things upset Jane. At one point, he told her, "just wait until Jessica graduates from high school, and if you want out of this marriage, fine."

The couple, despite their outward appearing happiness, was in counseling, mostly due to Bob's sexual proclivities but also for his poor money managing.

He owed $18,000 in back taxes on properties. He was continually in court over his failure to maintain his properties to code, with ten misdemeanors over such things as rodent infestation and lack of proper inspections. He was in and out of court chasing money from tenants and seeking evictions for nonpayment.

"It was always about money with Bob," says Jim McCuish, a fellow Grosse Pointer who met Bashara in the late eighties. For a few years, he and Bashara partnered on a couple of properties.

McCuish generally liked Bashara because of his weird quirks. Stealing money from the coin laundry machines at the properties, for example.

"You'd look at him and say, 'Bob, why are you stealing money out of the machines?' and he'd deny it. We had him on security video doing it," McCuish says.

Rent would disappear; even cash from friendly sports betting pools would turn up a little short if Bob was handling it. "He gambled, he was terrible with money, and he was always into shady dealings."

McCuish played golf at Lochmoor, and Bashara was

always looking for an angle to make money from his wealthy colleagues.

"One guy owned a car dealership, and Bob got into a bunch of lightbulbs, which he sold to the guy. Half of them didn't work, but when he asked Bob about it, Bob just said, 'Of course they work. They're fine bulbs.'"

What was most amazing was Bob's ability to be oblivious to protests and accusations, "like nothing had ever happened."

He also had to defend himself in a couple of cases in which tenants sued him for allegedly keeping their security deposit without cause.

"We were on the way to a court hearing and Bob said, 'Now just lie when you get in there,'" McCuish says. "I said, 'I can't do that.' This was over a $500 security deposit."

Another time he connected the entire electric bill to one of his tenants at the property on Mack Avenue, a battle she had to fight with the utility company.

By the end of 2011, two of his rentals in Grosse Pointe Park were in foreclosure.

Jane had thought she could retire in 2001, but no; there she was, back at work.

"She retired because we had good income," Bashara says. There was an attractive buyout program at Edison when it merged with another company, and "she was off for three, three-and-a-half years. That was when Jessie and Rob were in high school. Then she decided to go back to work."

Was it so simple? Records show Bob's income was never better than half of Jane's from 2009 forward: In 2009, she made $77,356 to his $28,534. In 2010, it was Jane, $96,442, to Bob's $21,829, and in 2011, Jane made $92,984 to Bob's $18,201.

Doing a quick inventory, Bob realized there was no more hiding. His personal life at home was a wreck, and his financial endeavors were failing. Jessica's departure for college at the University of Michigan in Ann Arbor had left the tidy home a mess, at least emotionally.

And when Jessica was there, ever protective of her mother, she was looking for more signs of his troubled behavior, and she was pretty good at spotting it.

His son, Robert, was launching his career as an engineer for General Electric in Iowa.

Bob and Jane were alone, except when Jessica came back for holidays.

More and more Bob was spending time outside the home, working on his properties, he said. It didn't seem to matter how much he worked on them; Jane always thought they looked run-down. No wonder Bob was running back and forth from the county courts building, filing actions against tenants who didn't pay their rent.

On January 5, 2011, Jane wrote a note in her journal, kept in a loose-leaf notebook: "Why we fight," she wrote and underlined at the top of the page.

She started, "We make plans," but crossed it out.

Then, "Bob makes plans—doesn't tell me," was her first reason.

"Bob says he says things he doesn't," was another.

"Can't trust what he says. Bob says things w/o talking to me—selling house. Going out w/guys."

While they seem small and typical, these were the concerns of a woman worried about her marriage.

The pressure of his growing sexual obsessions being discovered, the unraveling of his marriage and being involved in multiple dalliances, as well as balancing that with the demands of Rachel that he get divorced was becoming messy.

In early 2010, Rachel was starting to think Bob wasn't going to go through with his divorce. One evening, distraught, she composed an email: "Master Bob—you are you with your boisterous laugh, romantic, playful, wearing your heart on your sleeve. I can't protect you from this, it must be done. We both made choices that now demand payment. I tried, I just can't do it anymore but I put on a brave face for a while. But here it all is and I am not the other woman type. I am too soft, too emotional to picture the other lives involved . . . remember me and know what we had was real it was not long enough for either of us and it has to end here, Rachel."

She tried to break up with him eight times between their meeting and January 2012.

At each attempt she made, he begged and pleaded for time in personal visits and emails. He went to her work and her home and called her incessantly. He cried openly. One day, as she tried to extricate herself from him, Rachel came home to find Bob sitting in a lawn chair in her driveway, crying and begging her not to end it.

At other times, he was oblivious to her demands to break things off.

"Hello and good morning my slave," one email from

Bob began after yet another email from Rachel trying to end their relationship. "I do not understand about how you can love someone, stay with me and now as we are about to be out, you wish to leave. It is true I have rescued us. You say you love me and I love you like no other. I can not imagine and will not do so, live a life without you, plain and simple. No one has ever given the kind of love you have and now you wish to pull it all away. What we have and what we will be is so special. It's almost been two years and I'm sorry if you have been tortured. I'd like to think of us as evolving and growing. I am ready to make a life-changing event for you and us and now that it is happening, you choose to leave. It is in the Bible, it says 'love conquers all' and it will bring us to where we want to be: In a home where you want to be with a man you say you love. I am here and will not release you. I am your man and you are my woman. I remain Master Bob."

What he didn't tell her was that he and Jane had begun to hang out a little more.

Jane had lunch in mid-January with Lois Valente, a longtime friend from the Pointes and the ex-wife of Dean, who handled some of Bob's legal affairs.

"What's it like to be single and dating again?" Jane asked Lois, who was freshly divorced. It wasn't a hint of trouble, but simply a curious inquiry.

Jane told her that she had prayed about her own marriage and all that had gone wrong with Bob's finances and his dalliances. He had mismanaged his properties, she said, but things could get better.

"I'm going to try and build this back with Bob," Jane said. "We did it before, and we can do it again."

And life at home on Middlesex was moving along quite nicely. His sister, Laura, had visited for a few days beginning January 15. Jane was scheduled to visit Rob in Iowa on Friday, January 20, but weather cancelled her flight. Instead, Jessica came home for the weekend from Ann Arbor.

On January 22, as Bob recovered from a BDSM party the previous night with Rachel, Jane told Jessica that she was starting to go on actual dates with Bashara, "like in the old days."

Jane was optimistic about her marriage. Maybe they could salvage things.

"For the last eight months of our relationship, I thought he was finally divorced," Gillett says. "We looked for a house. We went many places in Grosse Pointe and in the area. I never tried to hide my relationship. My friends, my family, my co-workers all knew of Bob as my boyfriend. This was a relationship that I thought was mutual. He led me to believe he wanted a future with me as much as I wanted it."

Bob was courting her as if Jane didn't exist. Lunches at least twice a week at Mario's. Mama Rosa's for pizza.

They would hit the Blue Goose Inn in St. Clair Shores, which was run from 1979 to 1985 by John Engelbrecht, Jane's father. Small world, as they say, and for those who knew Bob, it was even smaller.

He and Rachel went to the Village Grille, two miles

from Bob's house, and held hands. They shopped together at Kroger, a half block away, sharing a cart.

"Everywhere we went, people would see Bob, and he'd greet them, they'd greet him, 'Hey, Bobby,' and all that," Rachel says. No one ever batted an eye or wondered where Jane was or asked why Bob was introducing Rachel.

Jim and Joy Wilson were among those many friends. In the summer, Jim and Bob would sneak off and play golf, sometimes smoking weed and doing some lines of coke in the golf cart. As couples, the Wilsons would come over to the house on Middlesex for Bob's beloved euchre tournaments in the winter, and sometimes they hosted the Basharas at their vacation home in Northern Michigan.

In other words, they were solid couples friends before Joy and Jim split in 2009.

While they hadn't been close since then, Joy was surprised in August 2011 when she was showing the house of her recently deceased mother and in walked Bob and Rachel, with a local Realtor.

"What are you doing here?" Bashara managed, a bit surprised. He hadn't done his homework. He managed an "I'm sorry" regarding her mother's passing and explained quickly why he was there.

"This is a friend, Rachel. I'm helping her find a place to live," Bashara told her. They made small talk while Rachel gave the house a walk-around.

Joy, though, was suspicious. She called Bob at home later, leaving a message on the family phone, asking about his friend Rachel where Jane could hear if chance permitted.

Within two hours, Bashara was back on her doorstep.

"Rachel is a friend who needs a little help," he repeated. He wasn't upset or angry, just being Bob. He spotted some boxes in the living room.

"Do you need some help moving or anything?" he asked.

No, she said. And they left it at that.

Bob and Rachel settled on a house on Kensington Avenue in Grosse Pointe Park, a twenty-minute walk from Bob's current home. Bob placed a small deposit on the place. The five-bedroom, two-and-a-half-bath house was a large fixer-upper, a brown brick job of 3,300 square feet, worth about $300,000 in a neighborhood of $500,000 homes.

Bob contends that the home was not for him and Rachel.

"All these houses that we looked at were for Jane and me," Bob says.

Bob also put Rachel on the deed for the home on Cadieux Road, the first property he had ever bought, so that she could help him manage it. They could be partners in his real estate holdings, he told her.

In December 2011, Bob and Rachel went into the Hard Luck with her daughter, Sonia, and Sonia's fiancé, Richard. They were getting married on New Year's Eve in Aiken, South Carolina.

"I'd like to get some vodka to take with me on a trip to South Carolina," Bob told Mouyianis. "I want to take care of everyone at the wedding with it."

The group of four was acting like a family, Mouyianis noticed. Bob was hugging Rachel, and Sonia was using her iPhone to snap photos of everyone at the table, all of them giddy with revelry. Even the other patrons were noticing. Yet Mouyianis knew—Jane, not Rachel, was Bob's wife.

A week later, Bob went into the Hard Luck with his daughter, Jessica, and two of her friends. They sat at the same table that he had shared with Rachel and her family, and Bob bought them all drinks, laughing and talking with them all.

Before the top-down drives with Rachel in her convertible, Bob had been more discreet with earlier girlfriends and keeping his two worlds separate. Why was Bob suddenly being so brazen?

At the wedding in South Carolina, Rachel and Bob, with him clad in formal black and a blue and silver tie, laughed and danced. And danced and danced . . .

He mugged for photos and seemed to get into every single one. He was loud and sometimes obnoxious and always flirtatious.

"He was creeping the girls out," says Andrea Annis, who was photographing the wedding. "But he was really, really happy."

On New Year's Day, Rachel and Bob walked on the South Carolina beach before driving home.

Rachel was buoyed by the notion that she and Bob were finally really together, free to come and go and do whatever. She had just added Bob to her personnel form as her emergency contact as she amended some paperwork. She was looking forward to moving from her upper-level two-bedroom apartment on St. Clair Street into the new house on Kensington. He was her emergency man; they were a couple now, after all. Bob had finally divorced Jane, as Rachel was led to believe. What she didn't know was that Bob was using a friend as an excuse for being gone from Jane for the week. He had called his pal Jim Wilson, who was now living in Florida, and asked that if Jane queried him, Bob was there with him. A divorced man, of course, would need no such alibi.

Rachel was completely fooled.

The month before, November, she moved to a slot as a secretary in the Division of Development and Alumni Affairs at Wayne State. She was moving from the Department of Computer Science offices, where she worked under department chair Farshad Fotouhi.

As her relationship with Bob moved forward, she began to take more time off for sick days. Her new supervisor wrote that Rachel "seems to be somewhat distracted, which may be affecting the quality of her work."

Rachel agreed and wrote that she was "somewhat distracted" due to family problems, but things had been sorted out, and she promised her performance would improve.

Bob would stop by the office grandly, bearing flowers and announcing his presence, as well as his name.

He called Gillett at work, which was okay in the less formal, friendlier office she had been in before, but her new colleagues and supervisor were not happy.

Rachel acknowledged that she left the office for personal calls and asked that the phone time count as her required fifteen-minute break.

In a quickly filed evaluation in the new office, Rachel was accused of not completing her work, and her behavior was described as "aggressive and disrespectful."

She took time off when she wasn't allowed to, the report said, and Rachel was having trouble getting along with her colleagues. She even refused to speak or acknowledge her boss on some days, according to the personnel reports.

Rachel was also having trouble doing the work of a $29,000 a year administrative worker. She "struggled considerably" to produce efficient work and reportedly failed to correctly process checks and paperwork crossing her desk, her evaluation said.

Additional training, forced on her by Wayne State, didn't help.

"Attitude while being trained is non-cooperative and negative," the review stated, adding, "Rachel has an 'I already know this approach' attitude to the extra training."

Rachel asked to be transferred to another department on January 18.

Rachel, though, thinks something else was behind the bad reviews.

She said her first few days were fine, until Bob showed up. Someone knew him and knew Jane. Rachel thought Bob was divorced. She talked of him as her boyfriend and praised him, proud of her man.

Others in the office knew the truth, she believes, and in their eyes, Rachel was the other woman who didn't even have the dignity to keep things on the down-low.

"I'd always gotten good reviews at work, and things were

fine," Rachel says. "And then all of a sudden, this. Someone in there knew that Bob was a bad guy, but no one told me. In fact, a lot of people knew that Bob was not divorced but just went along with things and didn't say a word. And there I was, looking completely like a home-wrecker."

6

Bob and Rachel Seek a "Very Special Girl"

The dating site where Rachel had met Bob involved more than just dating. It was alt.com, a gathering place for people with "advanced" sexual and romantic tastes.

In August 2011, Rachel posted on alt.com, "We are looking for a special girl, a third to round out our relationship . . . someone who would live with us on a full-time permanent basis who is free to commit to being a part of a loving, nurturing male dominated home. Master Bob is the head of our relationship."

In September, she again posted, "We are looking for one unique individual who can fit with us and our personalities . . . an attractive female, age from late 30's to early 50's, must be able to relocate to us . . . willing to obey his directions concerning finances, health issues, and self growth . . . gainfully employed."

They were seeking what is known as a "triad," a third

partner to live in a BDSM household that would have Bob as the head. The arrangement, while popular in the lifestyle, is also difficult to pull off for understandable reasons.

The third woman in such arrangements is often referred to as a "unicorn" because of how difficult it is to find her.

A posting from Rachel in November announced they may have found what they were seeking. This time posting as MBs_triad, she wrote, "We are a true D/s triad . . . a group of three. Master Bob is the head of our home, respected and cared for by His two lovely slaves, bella and J."

Rachel was especially happy with the direction her life was taking. In May, Bob had told her that he and Jane were officially divorced. All the breakup threats had ended then and there. Bob was living in the house on Middlesex with Jane only as a convenience, although no one really knew of the divorce outside of his immediate family, Bob told her.

On January 12, 2012, a Thursday, twelve days before Jane was murdered, Rachel wrote, "Oregon also has one very special girl that I am just dying to meet! And now for this weekend only . . . Oregon also has my Master!"

That woman was Janet Leehmann, a fifty-something dental office worker.

Leehmann was an Oregon native who was adopted at four months into a ranching family with four children, three boys and a girl. Her adoptive mother was a World War II nurse who went to Europe on the *Queen Mary*, and her father was a paratrooper who was in the Normandy invasion. The couple met in France and returned to the U.S. to become cattle ranchers. Leehmann was riding horses by the time she was three.

By the time she was seventeen, she was married with two sons, and Leehmann found herself divorced in her early twenties, raising her children alone.

She was raised to be resourceful and driven—dashed with a generous dollop of assertiveness that she says comes from her mother—and wound up working in dental administration. By 1996, the kids were out of the house and she married again, this time a hairdresser and platform artist. The couple moved to New York City where he taught at L'Oreal Professionnel SOHO Academy. By 2006, he had run off with another woman, and by 2007, Leehmann was back home in Oregon, settling in Bend, population 80,000, about three hours southeast of Portland.

"I was looking for a nice man to spend my life with," Leehmann says.

Bend is a hidden part of the nation's recession recovery. The town's population increased 47 percent between 2000 and 2010, and 6 percent between 2010 and 2013. Ski resorts, a booming brewpub culture, a younger population, and relief from the increasing traffic of Portland and Eugene pulls people in, and a favorable cost of living keeps them.

She dated occasionally, and Leehmann was introduced to rougher sex and a touch of role-playing through a boyfriend. She liked it. She headed to alt.com, which is a connection site for people interested in various sexual/relationship endeavors.

Leehmann began communicating with Bob the week of Thanksgiving 2011, thanks to the alt.com post from Rachel.

First there were messages, "well thought out and well written," Leehmann says. Later, after talking to Bob a couple of times, she wondered if someone else had written the messages, as Bob, while intelligent enough, did not present himself as a man of letters.

Soon there were phone calls and text messages.

Still, among the things he asked her about was relocation.

"I think that's premature," she said.

"At some point in the future?" he pressed.

"Years from now I might consider something like that," Leehmann told him.

Rachel says that Bob almost immediately began calling Leehmann "all the time."

"She had moved across the country for a man before, so it wasn't new for her, she told us," Rachel says.

Leehmann was puzzled about how any of this would work; she wasn't looking for a full-time relationship. And as far as being a third wheel, that was fine.

"I was just looking for someone to go on a couple trips with," Leehmann says. "I just took it that she didn't care and they were playing. He was talking about this triage, and I thought it was ludicrous. But I was like, 'Whatever you're into.' Rachel had this idea, and she was writing about it on her blog all the time. I've had lots of people in my life with open relationships, but here I was running this dental practice, and he was just a diversion."

Rachel insists the hope was real.

"My idea was that she gave me a night off," Rachel says. "And also someone to shop with. If she plays euchre and cooks, even better, because I don't do either, and Bob liked to eat and play euchre."

Bob backed off his pursuit of Leehmann after her rather cold response to relocating, but after Thanksgiving, he called her.

They began with simple dominance commands—she would refer to him as Master Bob. That sure is a diversion, of course, but it was also part of the role Bob insisted on playing.

"Master Bob here," would begin the text Leehmann received every morning and evening. And she was into it.

"Sleep well with thoughts of your master."

Leehmann: "Thank you, sir."

On December 12, after a few weeks of frequent phone calls and messaging, Bob sent her a text: "Between you and Bella I know I will be taking care of both of you . . . I'm glad you are mine."

Leehmann: "Thank you sir."

Bob: "I am a good judge of character . . . Your slave-hood to me is very real and valued."

More often, the conversations were rote, but sometimes they dealt with serious things, like money.

Over the weeks as they had talked, it had dawned on her that Bob was in some serious financial trouble despite the fact that he and Rachel were planning to move into a house worth over $300,000.

"He was always working an angle," Leehmann says.

"He said he spent his days driving around picking up rent, and he did this every day. Don't people give their rent to you? Why did he need to be picking this up? And he would never answer me. He laughed it off."

Rachel told her that Bob received some money when his father died but had long blown through that. His mom, who would help him out financially, had stopped.

"From what I could tell, Bob wasn't wealthy, and it's really telling, because I kept interviewing him," Leehmann says. "Not that I was looking for wealth, but he was representing himself as wealthy while he was desperately trying to put his house deal together, the house for him and Rachel. He couldn't get a loan. He asked me if I knew anyone who had $60,000, and he said he couldn't come up with $60,000 if his life depended on it."

He later called her and said his mother had loaned him the money.

At one point, he texted her, "My father was a big-time judge," lest she think he was not a man of resources.

Another warning sign was Bob's enthusiastic response to her father's cattle ranch.

"He was beside himself," she says. "He wanted me to drive down and talk with my dad and change his will and make sure I am in it, as Bob was interested in my earning power. He brought it up a couple of times in phone conversations. When he heard my dad had this ranch, he thought it was like the Barkley Ranch in the TV show," meaning the show *The Big Valley*, a sixties' western that featured a 30,000-acre ranch.

He also sent her a package that contained a used dirty

T-shirt and two Olive Garden gift certificates. With it was a letter written by Bob that read, "My slave—This is my shirt that I have worn next to my body for three days—it is sent to you to sleep in and keep near you!! When I come to see you I will replace it with another . . . I remain Master Bob, your Master and Man."

A week later he sent her a studded black leather collar and another letter that called the collar "a symbol of my ownership of you." He instructed her to wear it on her left wrist and said, "You are not to wear it around your neck until I am there to place it there . . ."

The instant messages came in as well, promising big things. Of the play between him and Rachel, Bob said, "I can choke her just enough to make her woozy. Having my large hand on her neck excites her."

"I'm almost a breath play virgin," Leehmann responded.

Bob: "You will be like a kid in a candy shop."

In early January 2012, Leehmann visited her brother and his family in Portland. They knew she had been talking with a man from the Midwest on the phone, and they had an idea that it had romantic overtones.

"I'm a little scared of this guy," she confessed to her daughter-in-law, Jude.*

A day after she returned, on January 9, 2012, Bob dropped a bomb on her: he was coming to visit that weekend. By then, Leehmann was feeling put out by the drama and the persistence of what was really a stranger from the Midwest.

---

* Denotes pseudonym.

She had tried to back off and had told him only the week before that he needed to stand back and not be so persistent.

He called the next week on a Monday and told her he was coming on Thursday. Bob told Jane he needed to train for a new chemical that he would be selling. They were scheduled to go to a play with another couple, a friend of Jane's from work and her husband.

Now Leehmann was trying to put him off. Bob was adamant, since he had already made the excuse. She stood down.

"No, I can't have company this week. I'm just too busy," Leehmann said. It was true in a way; she worked full-time and had no interest in hosting someone she was already a bit tired of, and let's be honest—she was also a little afraid.

"You want to see me, don't you?" he asked. "I can't come on the twenty-first because my sister is coming out from LA and I have family obligations. You need to make this happen."

"Yes," she said, almost automatically.

She now says, "It was like pulling the Band-Aid off."

The sister visit was an excuse, but it worked. For Leehmann, regret was just a few short days away.

He came in on a Delta flight that arrived in the early afternoon, switching planes in Salt Lake City. On the twenty-five-minute drive to Redmond Municipal Airport, Leehmann emotionally steadied herself, putting aside her reservations. This could be okay, she thought.

First impressions are not everything in some worlds. While the rangy, pudgy Bob Bashara was not a guy who turned heads, she found him well-mannered and polite at first. He walked to her with an assurance that bordered on swagger, a gait of confidence.

To ensure he had control, Bob insisted on driving her Honda Accord.

"I'm not going to be a passenger," he informed her.

Leehmann relented, and he drove them to Portello, her favorite wine bar in a city awash in them.

Immediately, there were more power moves.

"I'd like you to unfold my napkin and put it on my lap," Bob said.

Okay, she thought, this is not good. But remembering the role-playing—this is Master Bob, after all—she acquiesced.

As they got up to leave, he reminded her that she needed to help him with his coat.

Now, there were warning bells going off in Leehmann's head. Again, she relented. A couple weeks later, a waitress at Portello, where Leehmann was a regular, pulled her aside. She had been introduced to Bob during his visit.

"Are you still seeing him?" she asked.

"No, I'm not," she said.

"I don't think that man who was with you last week was right for you," she said, whispering. "He was very pushy. He gave me the creeps."

But at the time, it was a beautiful, sunny day in the Pacific Northwest, and there was little to keep Leehmann down. The peaks of the mountain ranges that surround

Bend, which sits in a valley, were snowcapped: Mount Bachelor, the Three Sisters, Broken Top, all as pretty as a picture.

Bob drove and talked as she pointed out the landscape. But he seemed distracted, acting as if he grasped the beauty.

They returned to Leehmann's house. As the couple walked into the entryway to the house from the garage, Leehmann's year-old dog, Virgie, ran up to greet her, looked at Bob, and peed in fright on the spot.

It was the first time Leehmann had ever seen a dog scared like that, let alone her own Australian cattle dog. Was it animal intuition or simply a confused moment?

If the visit was intended to be part of the courting of Leehmann for this three-way funfest life in Grosse Pointe, it wasn't working out.

Bob spent an inordinate amount of time on his laptop and cell phone, claiming to be running his rental operation long-distance.

He mentioned he was trying to move money around, from one account to another. Leehmann was aware of the new house and all the financial movements that go on before a purchase. With the closing to take place the last week of the month, he no doubt had some work to do. Leehmann, like Gillett, was operating on the belief that Bashara was a divorced man.

At one point, as she moved about the kitchen, Bob yelled at someone in the background, and the responses to his barked orders were muffled.

"I want this taken care of, and I want it done right," she could hear Bob yelling through the hand he held over the mouthpiece of his cell phone. "I don't want to deal with this when I get back."

He hung up and went from angry to easy in ten seconds.

"What was that?" she asked.

"I'm having to deal with this handyman," Bob said. It was nothing, he assured her. But he sure was worked up, she thought.

The first night, as if things couldn't get any less romantic, brought an unsexy surprise in the bedroom. Bob took a shoebox-sized plastic device out of his suitcase and plugged it into the wall next to the bed.

It was a continuous positive airway pressure machine, and it included a mask that Bob had to wear when he slept to treat his sleep apnea.

"I have to use it in order to breathe when I sleep," Bob explained stridently, attaching the mask to the machine. It wrapped around his head and had a long tube protruding from the mouth.

If it put a damper on sex with a new partner, it didn't matter, as he had no intention of having sex. It was like a slumber party, Leehmann later thought.

On Friday, Leehmann took the afternoon off and invited Bob on her usual walk around the area, a hilly expanse, at a hefty pace. In any companion, Leehmann sought fitness, or at least someone who could keep up with her.

"I nearly killed him on a ten-block walk," she thought. This would not do.

Saturday they headed to the Sunriver Resort for lunch. The luxury spot was another enchanting drive away, and once again, Bob seemed preoccupied and didn't appear to notice.

They got there and ordered some food, and Bob almost immediately disappeared to the restroom for twenty minutes.

"It doesn't take rocket science to know he ditched me to make phone calls," Leehmann says. She was trying, though.

From there they headed to the lodge at Mount Bachelor, a ski resort at the end of a beautifully scenic drive through the Cascade Range that runs twenty miles west of Bend. They landed in the bar and talked about politics and current events, and he had a beer while checking out whatever football game was on. It was cold, the tourist season was in full swing, and the early evening crowd was coming in.

At one point, Bob advised her that he would be sending for her soon, "after I get moved. I'll show you around Grosse Pointe and take you to some parties," meaning lifestyle parties. He and Rachel had been to a couple when they first met. It had been a while.

"No, I don't want to go to any parties," Leehmann told him.

But she had a question for him.

"How would you explain having two women living with you?" she wondered.

"I'm not so worried anymore what people think," he said. "I would introduce you as Rachel's friend who is down on her luck."

That would not work at all, Leehmann thought. But it hardly mattered; by now, the third day of his visit, she knew that the notion of being part of anything that included a move across the country to be with Bob was a pipe dream on his end.

It didn't stop the conversation. They were not hitting it off, but she didn't hate him, either. He was evasive, she thought, not based in reality. It was as if he was living in a make-believe world that combined lifestyle, riches, and women.

They talked about Rachel, and how she was okay with Bob's visit, even encouraging.

"For you being the dominant, it looks like she kind of controls things," Leehmann said.

"I only let her think she does," said Bob, a typical suburban husband.

He paid for the drinks—he paid for everything, often loudly and with some ceremony—and they moved on. Through the night, he was boorish, becoming short with bartenders and waiters in places that were Leehmann's regular haunts.

It was Saturday, the last night of his visit. The hours were dwindling. She was already relieved to have him leave. But they had already agreed, in a dom/sub unspoken contract, that they would be having an encounter that night. They stopped at a farm implement store on the way home. Bob bought a twelve-foot bullwhip and some heavy rope. Leehmann said nothing. They went back to her house, and he took the role of director.

And they were going to do whatever he wanted in her garage, not her bedroom. Still, she was not afraid; light bondage and a spanking, she thought. One of her ex-boyfriends had used a small crop on her, and she found it exciting.

He told her to undress, and once she was naked, he tied her up, binding her hands and feet on an overstuffed chair. She knew the game, and she enjoyed the light swat, a slight pain rooted in pleasure. She realized, though, that Bob was unaroused. How could that be for someone who is basing an entire episode—this visit, the idea of a triad, and an embrace of the lifestyle—on sex? But then she saw the arousal, not in his crotch but burning from his eyes. Deep brown, they went wild, a story told by so many victims, where the aggressor, however mild mannered, is taken over by a force and an urge.

"Predator!" flashed in her mind. She was aware that she was in trouble.

She said nothing, closed her eyes, and waited for it to be over. And he beat her with a piece of coarse, thick rope until she thought she was going to pass out.

It was the worst thing that had ever happened to her, the most traumatic confrontation. Bob's size alone made it impossible for her to fight back, even if she could get free. She was five feet, one hundred pounds.

After a few minutes that seemed like hours, he untied her and began to talk kindly to her.

She was shaken but managed a smile, as if her life depended on it. Welts were raising on her body, and her leg was already bruising—a bruise that would take three months to heal.

As she composed herself, without warning or saying a word, he wrapped his hands around her neck and choked her. This was not agreed upon, as is protocol, if such a thing can be applied in such an intimate setting, where things often move fast and a plan can be a real buzzkill.

She passed out. She thought she was going to die. She woke up after a few seconds.

"I didn't know you were getting woozy," Bob said to her. "I could have really hurt you."

Leehmann was terrified, even after he untied her and talked her down, with some tenderness.

She put on her best face and acted as if she were fine with him. She gathered herself, and they moved inside, to her bedroom. They never had actual sex, to her relief. His flight was leaving in a few hours. She could make it. At 6 A.M., they left her place for the airport. She dropped him off, and she wouldn't see him for twenty-one months, when he would be the one bound. Just in case, though, he left a trinket for her back at her house: a pair of his blue Jockey underwear.

"The visit went fine," Bob told Rachel when he returned. "She's not as submissive as you are. But she'll be fine."

Rachel says Leehmann told her she liked him. Leehmann says it was part of the act. As long as she never had to see him again, it would just be a lesson she would never forget.

On January 21, 2012, Bob and Rachel were invited to an event in the suburb of Lincoln Park for members of the lifestyle community.

"There were a number of my friends going, female

friends," Rachel says. "I hadn't been to a party for a long time, and they were feeling like they hadn't seen me for a while. So we went."

There were usually three such parties a week in and around metro Detroit, set up by various organizers with different names. Detroit Space was one, Dark Nirvana another. Many are held in one of the numerous civic halls in the region, some in hotel conference rooms, and still others in private homes, the latter of which tend to be the most risqué, as nudity is not an issue.

Bob and Rachel had been to dozens of such parties over the past two-plus years, where Bob could be seen leading Rachel around by a leash connected to a dog collar on her neck.

Patrick Webb—Sir Patrick in the parlance of the lifestyle—held some of the best at his place in Milan, a community south of Ann Arbor and about an hour from Grosse Pointe Park.

Webb had started with a two-bedroom home where he held parties for swingers. People would come from all over Detroit for the parties, where sex, conversation, food, and drink all flowed together, and $50 was the price of admission for a couple. They would stay for the weekend, and the money was a donation, of course, because to charge an entry fee would put them into club territory. Getting a permit is nothing anyone cared to do, for the most part. And sex, both public and private, was legal because it was a private residence.

After a while, Webb queried some of his patrons who

were both swingers and part of the BDSM community if they would help him expand to a larger space.

On a property he owned about three miles from the two-bedroom house, Webb had ten acres, enough room for a larger building. But his clientele was unschooled in BDSM practices. So before he embarked on an effort to construct the bigger building, some of the people from the BDSM scene came in and acted as dungeon masters as he began to hold parties aimed at that lifestyle, teaching some of the newcomers from the swinging scene about protocol and practice.

One night, the two-bedroom house burned to the ground. Webb blamed the local establishment that wanted to rid the community of his parties. Still, the loss created the opportunity for the new space, which was called the A2 Reformatory.

Many of the people from the BDSM community helped raise money to build the Reformatory, and when it was opened, it became a 10,000-square-foot mecca for people of all varieties of sexual lifestyle, from swinging to BDSM.

"He had a play floor. Showers. They built bedrooms in there so you could stay the whole weekend," said one patron who knew Webb, Bob, and Rachel.

"I'll tell you, I like the parties, but my wife would really be unhappy if she knew," Bob once told Webb. "She wouldn't understand it, and she wouldn't condone it." It was somewhat common among attendees; they had an itch to scratch, but their life partner didn't dig it. So they went on the sly, and the feeling was that little harm could come of it. Some did it for years and maintained a healthy, loving relationship with their spouse.

Some of the parties were real blowouts, running from early Saturday night into the next day. Others were simple house parties like anyone else in the region would have on a weekend.

"The music was playing; people come to let their hair down. They live their life Monday through Friday, and they want to let their hair down," is how Webb described his parties.

Bob and Rachel stayed all night a few times; his excuse to Jane was a golf outing with his buddies, a standby when the weather was right.

"He and Rachel came the first time, and he said, 'We're not swingers. We're not into that,'" Webb says. "But later in the night, he came up to me and asked if he and Rachel could get together with my wife and I."

There was also buddy talk among the men in the group, and there was one thing that Webb would recall much later.

He and Bob were at Bob's place, the dungeon, which doubled sometimes as a social club among his male BDSM pals.

Bob had been talking about Jane, and the fact that their relationship was soured, he was unhappy, and she seemed about as discontented. He said he felt trapped, though.

Divorce crept its way into the talk, and Bob noted that it would be cheaper to "kill the bitch."

It was an odd thing to say, unpleasantly dark and aggressive.

MURDER IN GROSSE POINTE PARK 111

But then, Bob could be exactly that at times.

He was often compared to the proverbial bull in a china shop and would sometimes violate social protocol— talking to someone who didn't wish to be talked to or approached, once in a while some touching.

"We were invited to some places and told not to come back," Rachel says. "Bob pissed the hostess off or something."

Whatever, Webb liked Bob and kept inviting him and Rachel.

Webb said one of the more difficult times he had with Bob was at one of the swinger parties, in which he had Rachel tied up and was hitting her with a belt. The others were aghast. Webb stopped it as soon as he could.

That same night, he found Bob and Rachel cavorting in public, with Bob rubbing a two-foot dagger against her. This time, he told them to find a bedroom.

Later, in December 2011, Bob told Webb that he was going to begin a new life with Rachel. He didn't reference a divorce but instead let it be known that he would be coming into some money. Soon. Very soon.

The January party was held at a VFW hall and was initially titled Detroit Wicked and then changed to Deviation.

Bob and Rachel were invited by Carl Epstein,* a friend who knew Bob through online interactions. The couple had clearly made a mistake from the outset. Dressed in

---

* Denotes pseudonym.

semiformal attire, Bob in a thinly striped button-up shirt and Rachel in a green and yellow blouse, the two looked like they were going to dinner rather than an alternative lifestyles event.

For Amy Weber, it was one more event in a lifestyle that she had come to embrace for fifteen years. The parties were her social connection, one that she and her boyfriend, Paul, looked forward to. Amy was recently retired after seventeen years as a Wayne County sheriff's deputy, and the couple lived in Grosse Pointe.

"Amy, there's someone here I'd like you to meet," Epstein said as she and Paul shed their coats at the door and looked around. "He's from Grosse Pointe. You're also from Grosse Pointe, too, right?"

"Yes," Amy said, as he guided her through the crowd. They approached Bob and Rachel, who were standing, looking, and saying nothing.

"Bob, Rachel, this is Amy and Paul," Epstein said, motioning around the circle. "They're from Grosse Pointe."

Bob looked blankly at the couple and began talking, not really saying much, about the lifestyle and how great it was to see all these people that shared their tastes.

It was dislike at first sight for Amy. The words "arrogant" and "cocky" came to mind. She wanted to get away, but she asked him about himself.

"What do you do?" Amy asked.

"I'm in real estate, buying, selling," Bob said, looking away.

It was a mercifully brief two minutes of her life that

Amy immediately wished she could get back, as Bob and Rachel indelicately walked away.

Bob immediately tried to engage another couple. Good riddance, Amy thought.

"But it was strange the way he walked around, trying to be seen and make people know he was there," Amy says later. "I don't know if he was trying to cement his image as being in the lifestyle, but it felt like that."

While the couple had been to dozens of lifestyle parties, she didn't feel it showed. In fact, both of them came off as rubes, or as Amy says in the ultimate insult, "They were tourists."

1

"Without a Doubt in My Mind
I Know That He Did Not Do It"

On the night of January 24, 2012, after he'd cleaned up the alley adequately, Bob headed back to his house on Middlesex a few blocks away. It was around 8 P.M. on a routinely chilly January night in Michigan.

His cleaning, he says, was typical. The cigarette butts gathered; it was a de facto smoking area for the Hard Luck Lounge, he thought, and the tenants of the four apartments upstairs never cleaned. It was always left to him or a helper.

He climbed into his gray Lincoln Navigator, the one with the vanity plates that shouted "BigBobb" was driving. The plate was a gift from his mom and a lighthearted poke at the nickname he had among friends.

He drove the few blocks to his house on Middlesex.

It was emptier these days, with his daughter, Jessica, away at college and his son, Rob, working for GE Energy in Iowa.

Jane would be home by now. Her twenty-five-minute commute to downtown—eleven miles, counting for traffic—was an easy one, the winter weather being soft at a time when many days make even the smallest drive an adventure.

Jane was in a good spot. She was drawing a pension from Detroit Edison, the city's public utility company where she had worked for twenty-five years with an ending salary of $110,000. Her salary at KEMA was a solid $90,000.

"But I am doing fine financially as well," Bob would tell anyone who inquired. He had complained before that he didn't feel in charge in his family life. It was a driving reason for why he would occasionally stray.

He drove straight down Balfour Street and made a right-hand dogleg on Windmill Pointe Drive and another right on Middlesex, his street.

The lights were on in the house, which had a couple inches of snow on the wide lawn but a clean driveway. The dog was there, wagging hello. Jane had obviously been there while he was out cleaning. But there were no signs of her now.

Bashara did all the things a concerned husband would and could do. He reached out to all of Jane's friends to see if they had any ideas as to where she might be. He called her cell phone several times.

He also called his son, Rob, in Iowa, around 9 P.M.

Rob didn't think anything was amiss; his mom ran errands all the time and sometimes would get caught up if she ran into someone she knew.

Bashara also called Rachel. He was frustrated, he said,

because Jane had asked that they set aside the evening to go over their taxes. It was to be at 8 P.M., when he had returned to the house.

At 11:30 P.M., he called the local cops at the behest of a cadre of people who were now gathering at the house.

"I don't want to overreact; maybe this is too soon to call, but my wife is not around, and she's not answering her cell phone," he told the 911 operator. "I don't want to panic anyone, but at this point, it's been three hours."

He was effusive and, as usual, gave out more information than anyone needed. Bashara mentioned he'd been at his property on Mack. He said he went to the garage "and I didn't see anything scattered about."

The 911 operator suggested she send a squad car over to take a report, but Bashara was hesitant: "Why don't we just hold off; that's not gonna help us in any way."

Bashara then called Jessica again at her dorm at the University of Michigan. She was going to be picked up the next day so she could help in the search.

"Maybe she checked into a hotel, maybe she needed some space," Bashara said to her.

Doubtful, Jessica said. She had just talked to her earlier, and her mother was on the way home. And Jane would not deceive Jessica.

Now she was worried, as was her father, or at least it appeared.

A few hours earlier, on January 24, as he cleaned behind the Mack Avenue property, Bashara had called Rachel around 5 P.M. and they talked for a while. Nothing seemed amiss.

He called her later that evening when Jane hadn't come home. Bob was really worried; she could hear it in his voice.

"He really sounded upset," she thought after one of several calls he placed to her that evening.

"Why worry? You're divorced. Maybe she's eating, maybe she's having dinner with someone," Rachel told him. He was inconsolable.

She went to bed, and he called again at 1 A.M.

"She's still missing. I just don't know what to do," he told her. "Jane's friends have been here. They had me call the police."

She pondered what could have happened. Rachel thought of a gas station not far down Mack that would have been on the way home to Middlesex from downtown. She had been approached there by a shady character while pumping gas, a favorite thug tactic. She'd never met Jane, but it was the ex-wife of her boyfriend, so she wanted to help in any way she could.

But there was nothing she could do.

On the evening of the twenty-fourth, Janet Leehmann texted Bob: "I'm home." It was around 9 P.M. in Detroit. No response. She had already decided she would cut off communications with him.

"That was easier than I thought it would be," she said to herself, hopefully.

Leehmann felt safe being halfway across the country from him, but she was sleeping poorly since she was almost strangled to death. She knew she would have to tell Bashara to count her out on the triad thing, and anything else that involved him, for that matter.

Early on the morning of the twenty-fifth, she texted him a greeting once more, and he came back immediately.

"MB here. Family emergency. Stop all communication immediately." It was about 8 A.M. Detroit time. Oddly the message came from a different phone; it was a phone belonging to Bob's mother, Nancy.

Shortly after that, Rachel called Leehmann.

"I don't know if Bob told you, but his ex-wife is missing, and we're worried something has happened to her," Rachel said.

"Oh, I don't know, she may have just had a date and stayed out late," Leehmann said. "She's probably mad that Bob is moving out."

Like Rachel, she also believed that Bashara was divorced.

Rachel went to work on the twenty-fifth. Bob usually called her every morning to tell her good day. This time, it was a terse and frightened Bob on the other end.

"We still haven't found her," he said. "Should I call the kids?"

"You don't know anything, so no, don't call them and worry them," Rachel said.

In any city, a missing person, especially one so solid and reliable as Jane, would cause concern. In a place like Detroit, where predatory murder—the killing of an innocent person—is higher than in most cities, being missing often means presumed dead. The city had 386 murders in 2012. And Jane worked in Detroit, not Grosse Pointe Park.

By the morning of the twenty-fifth, the worst nightmare of friends and family was confirmed. Jane's body was found in a shady area of the city eight miles north of Grosse Pointe Park.

But what was Bob doing at Middlesex around 6:30 P.M. the previous night? He insisted that he was at the Mack Avenue property all evening, until 8. Was it true?

It was one of the stranger death notifications Detroit Police homicide detective Donald Olsen had ever made. He's done so many murder investigations that "they're a blur," he said. But this one was almost weird.

On the morning of January 25, around 10:45, Olsen, joined by Captain David Loch from the Grosse Pointe Park Police Department, arrived at Middlesex. Bashara was looking for them, and he walked out the front door. The looks on the faces of the officers told him all he needed to know.

It became formal when they sat at the table in the dining area.

"We've found the missing vehicle," Olsen told Bashara, looking him straight in the face. "Your wife was found dead inside."

The impact and reaction to such news varies greatly among individuals. Some people simply don't believe it. Others fall apart, screaming. Still others simply stare and try to absorb the news.

Bashara reacted by telling Olsen of his own whereabouts the day before. True, Olsen had asked, part of the normal process, a kind of "by the way" thing.

Often, the bereaved doesn't even hear such a request, being caught up in their own thoughts.

Instead, Bashara quickly recounted the cleaning behind the building on Mack, the phone calls to his wife, and a meeting with his Rotarian buddy, Mike Carmody, for a drink at the Hard Luck around 7 P.M.

He talked of the wave of other women found dead in car trunks in Detroit. He talked about putting $80,000 into the addition to the house. His rental units around the city were losing money, he said.

Finally, he asked how Jane died.

Man, that was some kind of unusual grief, Olsen thought as he left Middlesex forty-five minutes later.

Bashara began another round of calls. They were straightforward and to the point.

"Robert, they found your mother. I'm so sorry. I'm not sure what happened," he told Rob who was working in Burlington, Iowa. "She was murdered. She's dead."

He told Jessica the same thing; her mother was murdered.

Roxanne Flaska, a friend of Jane's who volunteered to fetch Jessica, pulled up to Jessica's apartment located just off the campus at the University of Michigan.

"Mrs. Flaska, someone murdered my mother," Jessica said.

"We don't know, honey," Flaska replied.

"My dad said that," Jessica said.

How could he know already? Flaska thought.

Bashara made more calls, dialing up Rachel and some friends and family who were not at the house.

Leehmann learned of the death the morning of January 25 after she tuned in to the news in Detroit online for an update. She saw that Jane's body had been found. And Bob was bemoaning the loss of his wife to the media.

"And I realized that he was married this whole time."

Rachel, too, was in for a terrible surprise.

Around 11:30 A.M., he called back. Jane's body had been found. He wept uncontrollably. There was nothing she could do. She couldn't go over to the house; no one knew her, and there would be too much explaining to do. Besides, they were scheduled to close on the Kensington house on Friday. What would this mean for that? She felt helpless.

But after they hung up, the broadcast appearances hit the airwaves, and Rachel Gillett's phone was buzzing off the hook with calls from friends. Wasn't this the same guy who had been her boyfriend for the last two years? They thought, or presumed, he was single, or at least divorced. Didn't they see her at work-related parties, a bar mitzvah, a restaurant with him being introduced as "my boyfriend, Bob Bashara"?

Rachel walked out her office door and drove home to her rented upper two-bedroom flat on St. Clair Street. The two and a half miles between her home and Middlesex homes might as well have been a million.

She got on her home computer and began surfing, reading every little news bit she could find on the discovery of the body. This was the ex-wife of the man she loved; she wanted to know anything she could.

She was confused, in shock herself, not over the murder

but the deception. During that day, he called over and over, crying. She tried to be supportive.

"Take care of your family. Don't worry about me," she told him at one point. She offered to pick up Jessica in Ann Arbor, but he told her Roxanne Flaska was going to do that.

"Can you come over?" he asked.

How awkward would that be? she thought.

The two had planned on coming out as a couple after a few months in the house on Kensington, Rachel says. It was supposed to be a soft introduction, integrating her as part of his family. She imagined it would be a romantic, easy change as Jane faded into the sunset and Rachel came into her own new life. Maybe they could all be friends, Rachel had thought.

Instead, Jane was dead and Bob was asking her to come to his side, in front of all of his family, as a friend.

"I can't do that," Rachel said. She was in shock already from the revelation that there was no divorce. To ask such a favor was almost unthinkable. But then, this situation was becoming surreal anyway.

"Why not think that was an appropriate thing to ask?" Gillett says.

Finally, after a few more calls from Bob, who continued to wail and ask her to come over, Rachel broke down and cried, long and hard. She wasn't quite sure why, but she felt like she and Jane had something more than Bob in common.

Then it dawned on her that they did; both had embraced the love of a man who was playing them. His declarations of love flew away when he did a TV interview after giving a statement to the Grosse Pointe Park police.

He repeatedly referred to his "wife" in the interviews. She counted three times. Her next call was to her landlord.

"I need you to come by and change the locks on my doors," Rachel said, her voice wavering, registering an octave higher as she was about to cry again. In the coming weeks, Rachel would go into a full state of shock, shaking uncontrollably, scratching obsessively, and not eating. She never returned to work at Wayne State University.

But she knew she had some things to do and some questions to answer, and it was just going to make things worse for her, although it would be nothing compared to how bad things could get for Bob, her once beloved.

On the evening of January 25, Bob made time to call Leehmann.

"How are you doing?" she asked him.

"I'm fine," he said, a little too chipper.

How can you be fine? she thought.

"We're going to find the person who did this, but the police are looking at me," Bashara said.

"You need to get a lawyer," she said.

"I don't need to, because I've done nothing wrong," he said.

She asked how the children were doing. Losing a parent at such a young age opens the door to some massive emotional trauma, Leehmann thought.

"They're fine," Bashara said. "Rob is getting a flight back from Iowa tomorrow night, and Roxanne is going to get Jessica, and we're going to get through this."

Leehmann knew he wasn't crazy about his wife, but, she thought, to think your kids are going to be fine is not clear thinking.

His online fib of being a single parent to those frequenting the lifestyle websites had come true. Bashara had lots to tell the cops.

He walked into the Grosse Pointe Park police department at 1 P.M. on January 26 to talk with investigators. Olsen was there to lead the conversation. Loch served as his sidekick.

They sat in a white cinder block room with one half-moon table, Bashara on one side, Olsen on the other, with Loch near the door.

Again, it was a strange encounter for Olsen. They talked about cars, wives, and bowling scores almost like a couple of beer buddies bellied up to a bar. Bashara asked about getting the garage door opener out of Jane's car and the keys to the house. Again, Bashara recounted the evening of January 24. He talked about his work as a sales rep for United Laboratories.

He sold cleaning products, he said. In fact, he sold products to municipalities, and the products were great for cleaning vomit out of cars or whatever. That's a product that Olsen might find usable for the squad cars. Then he stopped.

"Ah, look at me," Bashara said. "Here I am trying to make a sale."

As they continued to talk—it was actually a friendly

conversation—the detective began to become suspicious of Bashara. It was his almost flippant attitude combined with the reserved and almost uninterested response the day before upon receiving the news of Jane's death that had him wondering.

Olsen asked if maybe Jane was up to something she wanted to keep hidden. Bashara nixed the idea.

"I can't imagine, because she's such a straight shooter," he said.

"I'm sure there's something out there she's done, probably a lot of things that, you know, you may not know about and vice versa," Olsen said.

"There's not a lot of secrets and a lot of things we hide," Bashara said.

He added that Jane smoked a little pot, to deal with symptoms of menopause, hardly worth mentioning.

He had another idea as well: "I don't want to narc on my wife, but she smoked marijuana, and maybe she went out to get some marijuana and the rest was history."

He added, with a chuckle, "I'm kinda slammin' my poor wife."

Olsen didn't raise an eyebrow, but on reviewing the tape, Bashara comes off way too flippant.

"Let me tell you, gentlemen," Bashara said at one point, "I have racked my brain. I assume she wasn't going to be gone long, because she didn't leave a note."

Olsen asked if he had any ideas what Jane would have been doing in that area.

"I believe she was out running an errand and doing something and someone either carjacked her, kidnapped her, did something like that. I have no reason to believe she would be at Seven Mile and Hoover for any reason," Bashara said.

He said that perhaps she went to fuel up her car for the next day and something happened there.

He ticked off a list of Jane's friends: Debbie Breen, Roxanne Flaska, and her closest from Mount Clemens, Patti Matthews.

"Patti introduced Jane and I," he piped up.

And they talked about social media, sites like Facebook and Twitter.

"I don't do any of that, Twitter, Skype," Bashara said disdainfully, as if it were beneath him.

Bashara left the interview and walked into a group of TV cameras outside the station. And he kept on talking to any media that would have him.

"When I walked in the house, I thought she was in the house somewhere. It wasn't until I went up and changed and then searched through the house and went out to the garage to see that her car was gone that I knew she was out," he said. "I, frankly, thought she was running an errand. It's just unthinkable that this happened to her, that she had to suffer. I've lost my girlfriend, my partner, and it's absolutely, absolutely unthinkable. I am just so upset by it."

He told a national reporter from ABC News that he and Jane had "a good and open relationship."

Still, the idea that he was at the station talking to police conjured speculation of his involvement in the murder. But his family kept a strong and united front of support for him.

His sister, Laura Maurer, said, "Everybody knows my brother and knows that he is incapable of this act, and we are totally supporting him, family, community friends . . ."

Jessica, who had confronted Bob numerous times for his infidelities, also gave the occasional interview and defended her dad.

"Without a doubt in my mind I know that he did not do it," she told one crew. "There's no way. I just know how my mom felt about him, and there was never even any hint toward violence."

At around 7:30 P.M. on January 24, Joe Gentz walked quickly down a beaten-up stretch of Gunston Street in one of Detroit's many lousy areas. He walked past the PPH Lounge, N & N Tire and Auto, and a couple shuttered grocery stores and hit Gratiot Avenue just south of the Detroit Police Department's Eastern District headquarters. There he kept walking past a couple of party stores that offered check cashing, lottery tickets, and liquor. He needed all three, but he also needed to get the hell out of that neighborhood.

Gentz had a friend who lived in that neighborhood and knew all the shortcuts, but Gentz, not being the brightest guy in the world, took the obvious route, down a main artery on a dismal Tuesday in January, his breath showing in great white plumes as he hustled away from the SUV and the body of Jane Bashara.

He had driven the Mercedes from Middlesex to an alley at Annott Avenue and Pinewood Street, tossed the keys on the driver's side floorboard, and walked away.

There were no streetlights, of course. Forty percent of the city's 88,000 streetlights didn't work, and you could be sure that the ones in this area would be among the last to be fixed.

He was breathing heavy and was terrified. The left side of his face stung, although the blood on the one-inch gash had dried. It throbbed. That was going to bruise, as he had taken a punch there from the woman.

She was dead. He had to get away from the entire episode. He needed the money that Bashara had promised him for this sordid chore worse than anything else in the world. It would allow him, hopefully, to keep his young daughter, Brittany, out of foster care and with him, the father she loved.

Now, he walked into a McDonald's at the corner of Gratiot and Seven Mile and headed to the bathroom to check himself over.

While his Supplemental Security Income from Social Security was cut off over a failure to pay child support, he had some money coming to him and felt safe to shell out for a couple of cheeseburgers.

He walked out just in time to catch the 34 bus to the main Rosa Parks Transit Center on Cass Avenue downtown, at 9:15. From there he got the 25 bus that took him up Jefferson toward his place on Wayburn.

Gentz got off near the police station and walked to Art's Party Store on Kercheval, which was his regular place for things like booze and smokes. He got a pack of cigarettes and left.

Two days later, on January 26, Gentz went back under

unique circumstances; he had a check to cash. It was for $452, from BNB Investments, a company Bashara had formed in 2009 to handle rental property income. Gentz had missed his rent payment for January but promised his landlord he'd be getting some money soon. This would at least help. The check was dated January 29, but the clerk cashed it anyway.

It bounced.

8

"I Made a Mistake"

By 9 P.M. on Friday, January 27, two days after Jane's body was found and a day after his interview with Olsen, Bob Bashara was a suspect, a status cloaked in the shaded parlance of the cop world as a "person of interest."

A person becomes even more interesting when they fail a basic polygraph test, as Bashara did that evening. Jane's murder had been officially ruled a homicide that day.

Bashara had no lawyer; as he told anyone who would ask, "Why would I need one? I didn't do anything."

Regardless, late that Friday, Grosse Pointe Park director of public safety David Hiller put Bashara on the map with his "person of interest" declaration. Hiller also pissed off the other agencies that were part of the investigation.

Rarely is a suspect named so quickly, and experienced detectives often work themselves into positions of trust with a person who committed a crime. Hiller effectively removed that tool from the arsenal.

The partner of a murdered spouse always gets scrutiny and is often the unspoken suspect. Relationships, be they wedded or not, are often hotbeds of unspoken frustration and hidden anger.

But Bashara was sure he was beyond that. And he was indignant that anyone could even think he would kill his wife.

"How could I have killed my wife if I was president of the Rotary Club?" Bashara told Mark O'Riordan, an agent with the U.S. Secret Service, pointing to the Rotary pin on his suit coat.

The feds were involved as part of a task force, which allows departments with leaner staffs and less experience—Grosse Pointe Park police hadn't had a murder case in ten years, and few officers in the department had much homicide experience—to benefit from the knowledge and numbers of more advanced agencies, who also have access to the better warrants and better technology.

O'Riordan asked Bashara if he was having any extramarital affairs, a usual question.

"I had some issues with that eight years ago," Bashara told him. "We worked it out. We got counseling. Things were going fine."

It was the first of a trail of lies spun by Bashara, little fibs that were leading him from person of interest into suspectville. There were already whispers of a girlfriend; people were calling in anonymous tips that reported Bob and Rachel, described as "a stocky redhead," together in public and Bob visiting a secretary at Wayne State University, presenting himself as her boyfriend. His grinning mug was all over the television and newspapers. It was hard to get away from him.

"That's all people [are] talking about," Betty Howell, a cook at Janet's Lunch in Grosse Pointe Park, told one reporter. She and others vowed they wouldn't be cowed by the murder and said they had no fear of a crime wave in the Pointes. Grosse Pointe Park had registered ten violent crimes between 2006 and 2010.

"This doesn't happen here," Gwenn Samuel, Bob's aunt, told another reporter.

Indeed, who was this monster among them? If it wasn't a Detroiter, it had to be someone local. Samuel's claim was just not true. Things, very evil things, happen everywhere.

"Dear Maria—I have lost my wedding ring. Keep your eyes open for it. Thanks, Jane."

It was a note to the family maid found by Jane's friends who were searching through things at the house on Middlesex, hoping to find clues, doing their own sleuthing. They turned the note over to the cops.

The note joined the growing mountain of evidence that put Jane's death into a time and place. She was killed in the home, investigators believed. Bashara had a girlfriend, according to some of the notes and other communications found on his computer. In fact, Bob had a few girlfriends. The lost wedding ring was symbolic, if not important.

The memorial service was held Monday evening, January 30, at the A. H. Peters Funeral Home in Grosse Pointe Woods. Several hundred people passed through, some complete strangers, drawn by both a lurid fascination with murder and pure sympathy for the sad demise of a well-regarded wife and mother. For six hours, Bashara, Jessica, and Rob greeted the well-wishers, mustering any reserve of emotional strength they could, held up only by the surreal facts that just didn't seem believable.

They returned with other family members to Middlesex at 10 P.M., Bob and Rob carrying vases of flowers that had been given as gifts of solace. People were torn apart both by the loss of Jane and by the impossible suffering these three, Jane's family, were going through.

There were news teams gathered outside the home, but Bashara declined, politely, to talk. His sister, Laura, handed out a statement to the reporters asking for some privacy. It was on the stationery of John Brusstar, a local criminal defense lawyer.

Bashara had finally lawyered up, on the advice of Dean Valente, a family friend and lawyer who handled some of his legal real estate squabbles and contracts.

Jane's brother, John Engelbrecht, had earlier defended Bashara after the memorial service, saying, "I don't see him doing this to my sister." But when a reporter pressed him about the state of the marriage, Engelbrecht stopped talking. There was already heat about the marriage and Bob's affair, and the cops couldn't keep a very good secret. Besides, they used every opportunity to make themselves look good even though they were simply fielding calls.

Cops told reporters that they had found Rachel Gillett, but actually she had voluntarily, but reluctantly, come to them. She'd handed them a present, essentially, by coming in on Saturday, January 28, and spilling it all.

"I had thought about it over a few days," Rachel says. "I still didn't think it could be murder."

Which is what she told Grosse Pointe Park police detectives during a three-hour interview. She went to them simply hoping to clear Bashara.

"He was divorced, he wasn't really married to her, we were together and were buying a house," Rachel told the two detectives in a small conference room.

They looked at her sadly.

She told them about their relationship, how they met online and about the romance, the trips to Chicago, to Michigan's west coast beaches, the South Carolina visits to see her children, and the recent trip for the wedding.

They took notes and looked at each other, exchanging glances that said, "This woman is so naïve; she has been so played."

"I realize now that I looked like a complete fool," Rachel says, two-plus years later.

She left out everything about the lifestyle, the BDSM parties, the dungeon under the Mack Avenue property, the other girlfriends, and the actual site at which they met, alt.com.

They didn't need to know that, she thought. It had nothing to do with the case.

That same Saturday, Brusstar, the defense lawyer, drove over to Middlesex to meet with Bashara.

"The police really think that I have something to do with Jane's death," Bashara told him.

Brusstar had handled some heavy crimes: bank robbery, cocaine transport, firearms, often in federal courts as appointed counsel.

This time, he was connecting with a potentially huge case representing the son of an esteemed state judge and respected member of a wealthy community.

The two were alone in the house, the first time the place had been empty since Tuesday night when Jane's friends began to discuss her disappearance.

"Is there anyone who might have something against you, against Jane?" Brusstar asked.

Bob had a ready answer, although he didn't have his name quite right. Some fellow, he said, named Joseph Goetz, who had called him the day before.

To make sure he had the time right, Bashara showed Brusstar his phone, with the number he claimed was that of this "Goetz" fellow. The call was from 9:46 A.M. Friday. But why would Bashara refer to him as Goetz, when he had the day before mentioned Joe Gentz, the guy who did occasional odd jobs for him, to investigators as a possible suspect?

At any rate, with Bashara dictating, Brusstar put together a one-page letter outlining a suspicious character.

"A part-time worker, Joseph Goetz, whom Mr. Bashara has hired and assisted in getting his own apartment, has become disgruntled and aggravated with his relationship with Mr. Bashara," read the letter to Grosse Pointe Park police chief David Hiller dated January 29. "They had one disagreement in particular involving a roofing project at one of Mr. Bashara's properties. Another disagreement arose when Mr. Bashara had Mr. Goetz's electricity cut off . . . for non-payment. Veiled threats were made by Mr. Goetz, but Mr. Bashara thought nothing of them until yesterday." The letter referred to the call from the day before from Gentz.

"Yesterday, at 9:46 A.M., Mr. Bashara received a disturbing phone call from Mr. Goetz demanding $1,500 because 'I helped you out . . .' Mr. Goetz also started into a rant about the death of Jane Bashara in this same phone call." Bashara told Brusstar that the caller was talking "gibberish," although that didn't make it into the letter.

Brusstar dropped the letter with an officer at the front desk of the Grosse Pointe Park police department on Sunday, January 29. Bashara was pleased, but he was busy. He had a funeral to attend.

On a crisp, clear January 31, a Tuesday, hundreds of bereaved people drove to the Grosse Pointe Memorial Church in Grosse Pointe Farms, a week after Jane's murder.

At the same time those attendees drove to the church, radio stations began to report that Bashara had failed a lie detector test. The polygraph is inadmissible in a legal sense but very damning in the proverbial court of public opinion. That bit of news was unconfirmed, a leak, but many had that on their minds as they entered the Grosse Pointe Memorial Church for services.

Bob was surrounded again that morning by family: his

mother and children, Jane's family, and her tightly knit circle of friends. But some had heard the news and had a doubt planted. He had always been a decent guy, but there were the girlfriend rumors.

"We hear he was having an affair," a newscaster told viewers as he stood with the brick church in the background that morning. It was solid reporting in an awkward venue. The funeral was a tribute, but the possible murder was the real news.

Police also told reporters, in one of many well-planned and calculated leaks to the media, that the murder happened at the Middlesex home and that there was more than one party involved in the killing.

Bashara was doing some maneuvering of his own. He reached out to people outside of the mourners and sympathizers. As the girlfriend situation began to provoke questions about his motives and his morals—men have killed for love, of course—he sought to control the flow of information.

"I had nothing to do with this, even though I'm probably going to have to defend myself," he told his golfing and drug buddy, Jim Wilson.

To his son, Rob, he said before one press conference to be sure he expressed support for his father.

He called tenant and sometime handyman Robert Fick and told him, "Do not speak of anything to the police about Rachel Gillett." Bashara also asked him to let him know of any fellow tenants who were cooperating with the police.

Bashara began placing calls from phones other than his;

he used his mother's phone to call Janet Leehmann. He used Fick's to make a call, then when Fick got the phone back, the number called had been deleted.

Bashara began following Kristy, who was bartending at the Hard Luck the night Jane was murdered. He drove by her apartment and went to a park in the neighborhood, hoping to catch her for a second to chat.

"He started bugging her, trying to get her alone to talk," says Mike Mouyianis. "He was driving by her place. He would go to different bars after she left working at the Hard Luck, hoping to find out where she went. He spent some time on it."

That afternoon of January 31, a week after Jane's murder, Bashara came home to meet with another lawyer, the replacement for Brusstar, a showy, dramatic defense attorney named David Griem, a former prosecutor whose shock of white hair, nonstop chatter, and sometimes outlandish statements made him a pariah on some circuits and a sought-after savior on others.

In 2007 he had briefly represented the accused in the last big murder case in the Detroit area, that of Stephen Grant, who strangled his wife, cut her body into fourteen pieces at his father's machine shop, and hid the parts in plastic storage containers in the garage of the family home, which was located in the northern reaches of Macomb County, north of Detroit. Griem quit that case after finding that Grant had lied to him about a number of things, just before Grant was arrested. Sans Griem's representation, Grant was convicted of second-degree murder.

Like the Bashara case, Grant's was a "this-doesn't-happen-here" circumstance with the husband being the suspect.

Now Griem was back representing a suburban father and husband accused of upsetting things in happyville.

Griem had more in common with Bashara, though; Griem lived in Grosse Pointe for a while. And he was used to high-profile cases, representing everyone from cops to mob bosses to terrorists, often getting them diminished sentences and charges.

Griem's first chore was to keep the heat off Bashara. His second was to find out who really killed Jane.

He didn't know that his new client was furiously trying to reach the former handyman he had named in the complaint to the police, this man, "Goetz," who had issued "veiled threats." Records show Bashara made a number of calls to Gentz—"Goetz"—on January 24 and 25—the day of and the day after Jane's murder.

At 4:30 A.M. that morning of January 31, before one bell had tolled for Jane's funeral, Joe Gentz—not Goetz—walked into the Grosse Pointe Park police department in his finest suit and told them some amazing things.

"I'm here to confess to the murder of Jane Bashara," the man told the officer at the front of the police department. "It was a conspiracy."

Gentz was distraught about what had gone down in the garage of the Bashara home on the evening of Tuesday, January 24. It was true that he was on the borderline of mental impairment, but he did know right from wrong. He had impulse control problems, judgment issues, and an advanced fondness for alcohol that bordered on addiction. He'd been in various programs as he got in trouble from alcohol, but they didn't take.

He watched the TV news the night before, in which the funeral notice was passed along to viewers, and understood what he had to do.

He grappled with his crime all day on January 30, a Monday.

He called his friend Frances Natale for a ride to Mount Clemens earlier that day. He had another custody hearing in his bid to take care of his daughter, an effort that was costing him money for both a lawyer and transportation.

"She's going to stay in foster care. I just know it," Gentz said to Natale after the hearing as the two sat in a diner in north Detroit. His voice dipped even lower than its usual thunder. She wouldn't have been surprised to see the coffee in her porcelain cup move as he spoke.

Natale tried to console him. She had met him a few months earlier on singles.com, a matchmaking website. It was no love connection, but she was sympathetic toward Gentz, a gentle giant, she thought. She herself was hardly killing it in life, but she'd just bought a used car at one of those places that don't check credit. It was the only way she could have done it, and the 21 percent interest was just part of the cost of living on the margins, she figured.

And what about that money Gentz had said he was going to make? she thought. He'd told her a month ago that he was going to come into $6,000 AND a car. That was tantamount to winning the lottery among Natale and her friends.

"It's a secret," Gentz had told her. "No name, and he's out of town a lot. But it's $6,000 and a Cadillac."

She asked him again in the diner. What ever happened?

"I don't know, I don't know," Gentz said, brushing it off. She guessed it was still a secret.

They parted ways after eating, as she headed to her boyfriend's place, which was nearby. Gentz took off walking.

They connected later on, when Gentz called again. He needed a ride and was at a McDonald's almost next to the diner they had been at earlier.

It was evening, and this time, he needed to go home to retrieve something and then on to a friend's place in Mount Clemens. Again, Natale was a good friend with a car.

They stopped by Gentz's place on Wayburn, and she waited for him. He came back with a suit on a hanger. She didn't ask about anything, but he told her a story that was scary as hell. And then she dropped him off at the home of a friend of his named Steve Virgona.

"I made a mistake."

Gentz had picked up the phone a few days earlier and called Virgona, a longtime and trusted ally who lived in Warren, a solid twenty-minute drive from the flat on Wayburn.

He told Virgona an amazing, tragic, and almost unbelievable story—he was the killer of Jane Bashara.

Virgona had a headache from listening to Gentz, whom

he had known for twenty years. Gentz collected benefactors who often felt sorry for him, and Virgona was among them. Many people thought Gentz had a good heart but was so mentally disabled that he had a hard time discerning who might be trying to take advantage of him.

The two periodically talked on the phone, and Virgona had generously helped Gentz in his ongoing child custody dispute.

There was one other thing sticking in his craw about Gentz, though, that made him believe exactly what he was being told. Months earlier, Gentz had asked Virgona if he was interested in being part of a "hit" on someone.

Virgona declined and wrote it off to Gentz being goofy, which he was most of the time.

But a few days ago, Virgona had been following the coverage of Jane's murder and was watching television footage of the vigil on January 25.

"That guy looks familiar," he thought, when the camera panned to Bashara, holding a candle, surrounded by others doing the same.

Virgona thought about it, pored over his memory banks. He kept watching, and it hit him: Bob Bashara was the guy who got the apartment for Joe on Wayburn. He had seen him when he helped Joe move.

And now, Joe was telling him that he was part of the murder of this guy's wife. While Gentz could find trouble, this was way out of character.

It was around 3:30 A.M., and Virgona was in his kitchen washing down a couple of aspirins when Gentz knocked on his door. He knew why he was there—Gentz wanted

Bob Bashara dancing at the wedding of Rachel Gillett's daughter on New Year's Eve 2011, twenty-four days before Jane was murdered.

Photo by Andrea Annis/Charisma Photography

Jane Bashara's work badge.

Photo by Mandi Wright @Detroit Free Press/ZUMA Wire

Where Jane Bashara was murdered, 552 Middlesex in Grosse Pointe Park. "A real estate buddy of mine sold it to me, a real good deal," Bob Bashara said. "A great street."   *Photo by author*

Alley and garage next to the spot where Jane's body was found in her SUV on January 25, 2012. "I seen a Mercedes amongst a bunch of abandoned houses," said the tow truck driver who discovered the vehicle.

Photo by author

The entrance to the dungeon, looking down from above. "He was very into dominance," said one of his numerous lovers.

Photo by author

Online profile that Bob Bashara created for himself on an alternative lifestyles website to advertise for potential partners. "I will open, train, and guide you in this lifestyle," he promised.

Photo by author

Joe Gentz in the courtroom. He confessed to the murder of Jane Bashara and claimed he was paid to do it by Bob Bashara, but refused to testify in Bashara's murder trial.

Photo by Patricia Beck @Detroit Free Press/ZUMA Wire

Joe Gentz said that Bob Bashara offered him $2,000 and this old Cadillac to murder Jane Bashara.

Photo by Mandi Wright @Detroit Free Press/ZUMA Wire

From left to right: David Griem, Bob's second lawyer; Christine Utley, co-counsel; and Bob Bashara.

Photo by Susan Tusa @Detroit Free Press/ZUMA Wire

From left to right: Laura Maurer, Bob's sister; Nancy Bashara, Bob's mother; and Bob Bashara.

Photo by Eric Seals @Detroit Free Press/ZUMA Wire

Rachel Gillett, whom prosecutors claimed Bob Bashara wanted to start a life with after the murder of his wife, Jane.

Photo by R. Gillett

Janet Leehmann was courted by Bob and Rachel to be the third party in their domestic ménage à trois.

Photo by Mandi Wright @Detroit Free Press/ZUMA Wire

Therese Giffin, a former Chicago police officer, was one of Bob Bashara's lifestyle partners and lied to investigators to throw them off his trail. *Photo by Mandi Wright @Detroit Free Press/ZUMA Wire*

Bob Bashara, sitting in jailhouse scrubs, watches as his lawyer, David Griem, and assistant prosecutor Lisa Lindsey argue a point in a hearing. *Photo by Deb Jacques, courtesy of C & G Newspapers*

some support when he went to turn himself in. He was carrying his only suit.

Gentz was wearing the leather jacket he wore the night of the murder, a black leather Triumph motorcycle jacket with "World's Greatest Motorcycles" emblazoned in white on the back, zippers up both arms and across the collarbones on each side, and white stripes on each arm. He showed Virgona the unmistakable scratches on it that looked like they could have come from exactly where Gentz said they did—a woman's fingernails. Gentz gave his friend the coat, his wallet, and his watch and handed over two cell phones, an iPhone and a BlackBerry, that he said were used in coordinating the murder.

Gentz showered and dressed up in the beige suit, lacing on a gray tie over a white shirt. He cleaned up well, actually, burly and barrel-chested, his stiff gray hair standing at attention in a neat row. Gentz had a mustache and beard worn in a neat Fu Manchu.

Together, they headed to the Grosse Pointe Park police department. They expected some interest when Gentz, after taking a deep breath, walked up to the desk and told them of his part in the town's biggest murder case in history.

Instead, the bored officer tried to get rid of him.

"There's no detective on duty," the desk jockey told them. "Come back later, after eight."

Virgona insisted that Gentz needed to talk with someone. This was real. But when a night-duty cop came back to headquarters to hear them out, he, too, was unprepared to take a statement.

"Nobody confesses like that," he told them.

"This is no joke," Virgona pressed.

It had been a half hour since they had walked in. Virgona showed the officer the jacket, with the scratches on it. He showed them the phones, from which they could take numbers and match them with those of the other parties, including Bashara.

And finally, Gentz was shown a cell while police took a statement from Virgona. As the talks went on with Gentz, the cops became convinced that there was another person involved in the killing. "Conspiracy" was being bantered about, meaning a possible murder for hire.

Competency became an issue as they talked as well; Gentz was clearly not the brightest or most credible guy. But he told his story, and it was a confession.

He told police that he was a handyman who worked occasionally for Bob Bashara. A few weeks after starting, Bashara began complaining about his home life with Jane. Then it got worse.

"He goes, 'I want you to knock my wife out,'" Gentz said. "'Kill her. Make it look like an accident.'"

Gentz played it down. But he said Bashara came by his apartment a few days later.

"Why haven't you taken care of it?" Bashara demanded.

"Bob, you know, it might not be for me," Gentz said.

"Bullshit. I need you to take care of it."

There was money and a Cadillac in it for him.

Gentz told police investigators the story with a steady voice. He sometimes contradicted himself in places, but there was some continuity that showed knowledge of certain details of the case that hadn't yet been publicly divulged.

For weeks, Gentz said he pondered committing the murder, with Bashara bugging him constantly. Phone records show over four hundred calls between the two starting in the fall and ending on January 25.

On January 24, 2012, Bashara told Gentz he needed some help moving boxes at the house on Middlesex. It was around 6:30 P.M. when he arrived, Jane was home. Bob told him the boxes were in the garage.

Do this now, Bashara told him. Use whatever. He pointed to an extension cord.

As they talked, Jane came into the garage.

"I want this shit out of here," she told Bob, pointing to boxes of junk that had stacked up so high that it cramped the space. It was a typical hoarder's garage, with stuff everywhere.

She was angry and gesticulating. She began to explain what she wanted to Gentz, both of their backs turned to Bob, looking at the boxes and some golf clubs she wanted moved.

She saw the gun first.

"What are you doing, Bob?" she asked.

Bob looked at Gentz.

"Shut the woman up now," he commanded. He pointed the small handgun at Gentz.

"Bob, what are you doing?" she asked again.

Gentz reached out and punched her squarely on the jaw, a full-force shot. She fell to the floor.

"Please don't do that."

Those were Jane Bashara's last words.

"Do it now," Bob ordered. "You better do the job or

you're going to die right here with her. Choke her. I want you to take her out."

With that, Gentz crushed her throat with his Red Wing boot. He pushed down as she fought. Then she stopped.

He said he put the body with the help of Bashara into the SUV and drove to the alley near Seven Mile and Hoover, where the SUV was dropped.

Gentz suggested the area. Bashara followed him in his own vehicle, and once the SUV was dropped, he left Gentz to fend for himself.

Gentz was to be paid somewhere near $2,000 and given a used Cadillac. The stories were sometimes rambling, sometimes inconsistent, enough that they made the detectives wary. But some of his information checked out or coincided with things they already knew.

It's said that the real achievers get things done, but additionally, they react well and have the ability to see opportunity and make the most of it. Open doors are often walked through by the victors.

In the Bashara case, the Grosse Pointe Park police became the losers when they let Joe Gentz walk out the door on February 3 after holding him for seventy-two hours, the maximum a person can be held without being charged.

The details of Gentz's confession implicating Bashara were leaked almost immediately, a tactical move by loose-lipped cops to foster a negative image of Bashara, whom they were still convinced was guilty of murder. They just had to get the pieces to fit, forcing them if necessary. It was good PR—taking down the wealthy, or at least the better-to-do, was a sure route to positive headlines. A poor black man doing the killing was just another day at the office—even the last Grosse Pointe Park murder was committed by exactly that. But a white scion of the community arrested for murder? That got the attention of the nation.

Griem, though, was outraged by the leaks as he watched comment boards and blogs light up with hatred for his client.

"It's like Swiss cheese," Griem told one reporter. "It's like being on the *Titanic*. And the leaks are meant to sound incriminating. They are calculated. They are an effort to smear Bob, to establish negative public opinion and contaminate the potential jury pool out there."

"Anything where Joe Gentz implicated him was untrue," Griem told another news outfit. "Completely untrue and a fabrication to get back at Bob."

There were other miscues in the investigation.

The local police went by the Hard Luck after Bashara had provided them the name of Gentz as a possible suspect. An officer showed Kristy, the bartender on duty the night Jane disappeared, a picture of a guy with black hair, someone they thought might be involved. No, she said, the guy who was with Bashara had gray or silver hair.

She told the cops that there was one of their own in the bar that night, at the time Gentz and Bashara were in there. Shouldn't they ask him? The investigators showed no interest.

And the security camera video that swept the back alley behind the Hard Luck? It was a loop that was taped over after seven days, erasing Bashara's sweeping project. No one thought to preserve it in the aftermath of the discovery of Jane's body.

It was one more miscue in an investigation that was hindered by rookie ineptitude. Much of the legwork fell to the Grosse Pointe Park police, who had zero experience in solving a murder.

"We can't pick our investigative team," Lisa Lindsey, a Wayne County assistant prosecutor who was part of the team handling the case, told a witness who complained about the poorly conducted interviews being done by the Grosse Pointe Park cops.

As for the security video of the night of January 24, Bashara says, "We had asked for it," referring to himself and his then-lawyer, David Griem. "But they told us it was gone. That was proof of where I was."

Other witnesses experienced the same response that Gentz initially received when he tried to turn himself in: disinterest.

The same day Gentz walked out of the Grosse Pointe Park holding cell, February 3, Janet Leehmann, the Oregon woman that Bashara and Rachel were courting as part of their live-in threesome, tried to call Captain David Loch at the Grosse Pointe Park cop shop.

Leehmann was "consumed with this poor woman," she says, referring to Jane. "And I knew they were going to find out about me anyway, and I wanted to help."

She left a message for Captain Loch with the officer on duty that Friday. Loch called her on February 6, unaware that she had ever called.

"And how many others were trying to give tips and help

that never got through to these investigators?" Leehmann asks.

Now, feeling that Gentz had not given them a strong enough case to charge him, they let a confessed murderer walk free, if only for a little while.

"I don't own a firearm, I absolutely had nothing to do with this, that is a sick assessment," Bashara told an ABC reporter six days after Gentz was released. Sitting next to him for the interview was Jessica, his daughter. The family was holding together, despite the statements of Rachel Gillett and Joe Gentz.

He had succeeded in casting the blame on Gentz, who was still being watched by investigators. Agents from the state police and the Federal Bureau of Investigation as well as Wayne County Sheriff's investigators and detectives from the Detroit Police Department were now part of the team trying to solve Jane's murder. They were looking hard at Gentz, even after his release.

Finally, they had what they needed to connect Gentz to the crime scene: a drop of blood found in the garage with the DNA of both Jane and Gentz. There was more blood on the garage door. It was Jane's.

While Gentz was ready to give up, though, the contingent of law enforcement needed some public relations juice on the case.

Gentz was embroiled in a child custody battle for his daughter in Macomb County, attending regular hearings at the courthouse in downtown Mount Clemens.

On March 2, just over a month after telling police that he killed Jane, Gentz was in Mount Clemens for such a hearing in the afternoon when he got a phone call from Virgona. A detective he had talked with sent word to him. A warrant had been issued for Gentz. He was wanted.

There was no use running. Gentz had already tried to give himself up, so he did it again. He walked into the courthouse, past the security metal detectors, and into an elevator to the second floor. He was already in his suit for the hearing, the same gray one he had donned for his confession at the end of January. He was met at the elevator by a Macomb County sheriff's deputy and led into a conference room, where detectives from Wayne County awaited.

"Sit down," one said. "Here, have a seat. You're under arrest for the murder of Jane Bashara."

9

Epicenter of Detroit Wealth Tarnished

Rachel Gillett watched the five unmarked police cars descend on her apartment on the television set of her dentist's office.

It was a Monday, March 5, and she hadn't returned to her job as an administrative assistant at Wayne State University since she walked out a day after Jane Bashara was found dead.

Investigators from the Michigan State Police and other agencies hauled seven boxes out of her upstairs apartment, including personal pictures not just of her and Bob but of her family, including her police officer son.

She left her appointment in mid-cleaning and got home to find that the officers executing the search were dumping plants upside down and throwing books and clothes on the floor. The place was ransacked as savagely as if she were a criminal. The cops took four hours to plunder her place as she sat in the flat of her downstairs neighbor.

Much of the material taken she would never get back.

Rachel was thoroughly dispirited.

She loved Bob Bashara. No doubt about it. Enough so that she believed him when he said he was divorced but living in the house on Middlesex for the convenience. And after all, he had managed to secure a down payment for a house for the two of them, also in one of the ritzy neighborhoods of Grosse Pointe Park.

Then, after the murder of Jane, she watched the news.

"Were you having an affair?" he was asked by a local newscaster.

"No, I was not. I loved my wife," Bashara had said. "She meant everything to me."

What about this woman, Rachel, whose name had come up?

"She was a good friend, that's it," Bashara said.

Devastating.

Rachel lived her life on an elevated emotional level. She spent her life searching for love, and like so many who obsess over finding that perfect mate, she had kissed a lot of frogs.

Weave into her quest a predilection for a lifestyle that much of society rejected, and you get some interesting head space.

She had been writing in hopes of ridding herself of the overwhelming grief she was feeling, but even those words just made things worse.

What do you do when a police officer looks at you and says you are the motive for someone else's death?

Who do you turn to when the person you are closest to, who you lean on to be your solid rock, is not there?

How do you cope with the realization that everything you knew and were so sure about was nothing but a lie?

She was even emailing friends about it, similar words on a theme: "The anti-Bob bandwagon is huge here with all my family and friends who thought he was divorced!!" she messaged one pal from out of town.

And the cops and the prosecutor's office continued to pester her, treating her like she was a criminal, threatening her with jail whenever she didn't provide an answer that fit their story line.

And that wasn't the worst of it.

Bashara would not leave her alone. It was just like the previous breakups. He went to her house, he called, he texted, he hit the BDSM websites in search of her. He beseeched his friends to reach out to her. One night, as he drove by her house, he stopped and searched her garbage out by the curb, later explaining to his cousin, Stephanie Samuel that he had spotted some exercise equipment and wanted to check it out.

One night he went to her house around 9:30, and she was not home. Bashara rang the doorbell, knocked on the door, and rattled the doorknob, scaring the downstairs tenant. She looked to see Bashara standing at Gillett's door.

On April 2, she found a palm frond cross in her mailbox.

It was the same thing he had given her on each Palm Sunday since they met.

It was bad enough that Rachel had her lawyer send him a letter demanding he stop pestering her. He also threatened that if he didn't stop, she would file a personal protection order (PPO).

Bob was upset, as he knew such an order would go public quickly, given the local media interest in the case. He didn't need to give the cops any more ammo in their crusade against him.

Rachel kept herself physically isolated, but online she kept up a social scene that would be the envy of any high school girl.

Then there was Therese Giffin.

A rail-thin, five-foot-ten-inch ex–Chicago cop, the fifty-something Giffin met Bashara in 2010 at alt.com. He said he was divorced, but that lie came undone quickly. Giffin's law enforcement background ensured she could suss out that kind of factual bullshit.

She wore her short bleached blond hair in a wave across her forehead, giving her a look that would be at home at any alt music venue in Chicago. A native of the Chicago area, Giffin spent ten years as a street cop and since then had spent time as an office worker and a seasonal tennis instructor for the Chicago Park District.

Giffin was immersed in the lifestyle as a submissive, and Bashara was a smooth-talking dom who scratched her itch. They became fast friends and sexual partners. Giffin went to Detroit routinely, and the two cavorted in the dungeon. His impotence was no problem for her; she was into

Bashara, and the vibrators, nipple clamps, and anything else he could work in was just fine with her. He would tie her to the makeshift cross he had in the dungeon and whip her with a cat o' nine tails, a leather whip with multiple "tails" or tassels.

Now, with Bashara as a murder suspect, she became his closest ally and, for him, a hopeful connection to Rachel.

Giffin and Rachel had become tenuous friends after Giffin "applied" in November 2011 to be the third person in their dream lifestyle in the new house on Kensington. She failed to be that person, as she still had a young son living with her, which kept her out of the running.

In turning her down, Bashara sent her a message: "You know what I seek. I seek 2gether serving me in concert serving me as one."

After the murder, as Rachel retreated from Bashara, Giffin stuck by Bashara while still staying close with Rachel.

"He always wanted you and I to become best friends, and I really couldn't understand why we didn't connect," Giffin wrote Rachel.

"Things happen for a reason, and maybe this is the start of that friendship."

By mid-March, Bashara was hoping to get Giffin to help create a bridge to Rachel, maybe even convince her to talk with him.

"[S]he just replied to Me saying she hoped I am ok, and that she does not want Me to communicate," he told Giffin, whose email handle was "obedient slave," via instant message. "I replied that I will not bother her again, but please do not do this ppo . . . she said she won't if I leave her alone . . . I said great, [good-bye] and good luck."

As a point of style, any word referring to himself, the dom, Bashara wrote in caps, and any word referring to his slaves was in lowercase. Correspondingly, submissives refer to their superior in upper case, such as with the word "You."

"Why is it that cannot get her out of My head? Like you said she is no beauty queen but to Me something special . . . wow."

In another exchange, Giffin asked about her rival in Oregon, Janet Leehmann. "Any word from Oregon? Thank You," Giffin wrote one afternoon.

"No, why should there be, she sent Me a letter thru an attorney here telling me not to contact her so I'm not."

"Good, I didn't trust her, I trust r," Giffin came back, referring to Rachel.

"Why am I like this . . . I feel terrible that this has hurt her so."

"Because You are a caring person."

The exchanges went on and on, Bashara beating himself up over his situation and Giffin supporting him.

Then, Bashara, realizing that Giffin's past as a cop might earn him some credibility in the public eye, had a brainstorm.

"Could you write me a character letter?" he asked her during one of their late-night phone conversations. He insisted that she not mention Rachel.

Of course, she said. What do you want me to say? He gave her a start, and she took it from there.

"I can no long sit back idly, watching the news and

listening to law enforcement portray Robert (Bob) Bashara in such an adverse manner," Giffin wrote in the letter. "One cannot meet a gentler, more caring person, with an enormous, generous heart . . . Bob has always been very involved in the community, always giving . . . Bob, in my opinion, is a dedicated family man. He has always spoken very highly of everyone in his family. Not only would he speak of Jessica and Bob Jr., but also his late wife, Jane . . ."

She emailed the letter to Griem. They never told him of their scheme. Giffin was just another person who thought Bob was terrific and, more important, innocent.

The same day the letter was sent, Bashara drove by an old friend's house to say hello.

Venita Porter, the mistress he had treated so cruelly in front of Rachel that night a couple of years before, was home with her youngest son.

She heard someone open and close her mailbox on the porch—two metallic clicks—and then a knock.

He went in with a smile and the day's mail.

"I know it sounds crazy, but I bend to Bob," Porter said.

She hugged him warmly. She recalled what he used to say to her in warm moments, "You and me against the world," and felt it for a brief second. She had read all the stories, of course, and knew that he was a murder suspect.

"I understand that people have probably threatened you because you know me," Bashara said. She nodded. It had been rough; she was a friend and had been seen with Bashara over the years. Now, with the Rachel affair being aired out, the locals were aware that Porter, too, had probably been one more of Bashara's mistresses, and more than likely was part of the lifestyle, with all of its unseemly connotations.

"You know Rachel isn't standing with me on this," Bashara added. "I think she's working with the police against me."

He was oblivious to the fact that Porter harbored no love for Rachel. She considered her an interloper and was still stung from the episode at the dungeon a couple years before, when Bashara had called her to come over—summoned, actually—for what she thought was a date, only to find a naked Rachel in the dungeon bed.

Quickly, any warmth Porter felt for him melted. She wanted him gone.

"You know, I was at the Mack property the night Jane was murdered, cleaning up in back," Bashara blurted out, a non sequitur that startled Porter. "I was having drinks with a friend at the Hard Luck."

He mentioned a wine tasting that was coming up. Would she be his date?

"No, I'm busy that night," Porter said. It was getting uncomfortable. Why would he talk about what he was doing the night of the murder?

He left after she declined his invitation.

As soon as his car pulled away, she called the prosecutor's office.

On April 26, Gillett filed for a personal protection order in Wayne County court.

"I am very concerned about my safety in and around my home due to the harassment of Bob Bashara," Gillett wrote in a statement to the court.

She said she had told him repeatedly that she wanted to discontinue their relationship and asked him to stop contacting her, yet he had persisted via email, phone, and through friends and personal visits.

"He is deliberate enough to drive different vehicles when he comes to my house and will park on nearby streets rather than in front of my house . . . Bob Bashara repeatedly contacts me although I have consistently told him that I do not want to have any contact with him at all."

She told the court that his behavior was intimidating, and she added that "the fact that his wife was found strangled terrifies me because I think that it could happen to me. He knows that I am a potential witness for the prosecution for the case regarding Jane Bashara's murder and I am afraid of what might happen to me if he is charged. Also, he has consistently stated that if I were to move, he will find me."

The order was granted the same day.

The order was served to Bashara at Middlesex. He called Griem—another fire to put out—and asked that he talk to the media.

"My client has not been in contact with her. We have not seen the proposed personal protection order," Griem told a local radio station. He was relying on Bashara's word. "Anybody can walk in, make allegations, and attempt to get a personal protection order."

Griem also included Rachel among those who might

have killed Jane. Maybe she was filing the order to deflect Bashara's people.

"Our investigators have developed several persons of interest in our search for the truth," Griem said. "I would indicate to you that Rachel Gillett is one of those persons of interest that we have developed."

"You're killing me, Bob."

It became David Griem's epigram, a phrase he uttered every time word came out of another public fuckup, another secret exposed, of his client.

He said it when the news of Bashara's affair with Rachel came out in the days after Jane's murder. He said it again when he heard Bashara had been pestering Rachel despite her attorney's letter demanding he stay away and again when the PPO was granted. Another time when the dungeon hit the news.

There were leaks from the Detroit Police Department and the Wayne County Prosecutor's Office daily at the start of the investigation. Anyone who talked to the cops would find their statement, or at least the meaty part of it, blared in the news the next day. Griem was defenseless to halt the public persecution of his client.

Griem was holding regular news conferences to appease Bashara's wish that he address every blip that hit the news. When he didn't do so, Bashara would get angry.

"Even if we respond, the media is going to give us a half inch of print to respond to twelve inches of the other side," Griem told Bashara.

"I don't care. We can't have people just saying things," he responded.

Griem tried a different tact.

"Look, these reporters only get a story from me every year or two," Griem explained to his client. "They have to deal with these cops every day, and there are a number of stories they can get from them over the course of a year. So they are going to use whatever they can from the cops."

It didn't sway Bashara; answer these charges, he insisted.

So press conferences took place everywhere, from outside a police department to the sidewalk in front of Griem's office building in downtown Detroit, where reporters caught every third word between the city noise sound track.

Griem also sicced his investigator, a former FBI agent named JD Gifford, on anyone close to the case, including Joe Gentz, Rachel, and anyone else making noise. Gifford, a former street cop in Indianapolis who spent ten years as an agent in the Detroit office of the FBI, was a smooth piece of work. He was a fearless and skilled surveyor and knew every crevice of the city.

Gifford was first assigned to follow Gentz. He came back with valuable intel almost immediately; the day Gentz was released by the Grosse Pointe Park Police, he headed to the Travis Coffee Shop, a nearby diner, where he was joined by a cadre of pals, who glad-handed him and pounded him on the back in congratulations.

Griem wasn't sure what to make of that, but he took it as a sign that Gentz was beating the system and his shady associates were treating him like a hero for doing so.

It also gave Griem the confidence that his client was, indeed, not guilty.

That helped, because he was starting to get some heat close to home.

"No one spit on me," he says. "But I could see it in the faces of people when I went to the grocery store that they were thinking about it."

No matter how much he believed in Bashara's innocence, Griem knew he was aligned with a local scourge.

Bashara told him of being asked to leave a local church festival when he showed up unannounced and volunteered to work in the Vegas tent and the food area. Parishioners at St. Michael's were no longer welcoming to Bashara and his mother, who continued to attend services.

He was heckled at kids' sporting events and was asked to stop coming into Dylan's Raw Bar & Grill, despite the fact that he was the landlord.

The Sunrise Sunset Saloon, where he used to like to go to play his beloved card game of euchre, was less than friendly to him, so he stopped going there as well.

He was also being beseeched by his lifestyle pals to keep their names out of the news. Bashara had them call Griem.

They might have been into the lifestyle, but there were various shades of sensitivities. Some were in the form of public persona—how would it look if the boss of a corporation were revealed to spend weekends at mysterious sex parties? Others were of a more personal nature, as in someone's wife surely didn't need to know that her loving husband got his swerve on in a BDSM parlor in rural Michigan.

"We were finding all of these people, everywhere, involved with Gentz or Bob, these characters out of an Elmore Leonard book," Griem says.

The locals were getting spooked, as the unsavory episode threatened to taint the community's glowing reputation as a step away from that mess just down Jefferson, Detroit.

The local newspaper, the *Grosse Pointe News*, handled calls from locals asking them to cool it on the coverage of the Bashara case. Who wanted to read about trouble in the ranks?

"They wanted us to scale back the references to BDSM," says Joe Warner, the paper's editor, who took most of what he estimated to be three hundred calls from readers giving their opinion on how to handle the story.

The Lochmoor Club, Warner says, asked him to keep its name out of it, as if laundering the truth out of a story were a routine among the locals. Never mind the coke snorting taking place on its links; it had a reputation to uphold.

The paper moved much of its coverage inside the front section, obedient to the residents to a fault. But no doubt the readers checked out the local news for the latest sordid twist.

When Joe Gentz was charged with Jane's murder, it was clear from his arrest in that conference room that law enforcement didn't want just him. On that day, he was also charged with conspiracy to commit murder. His co-conspirator was Bob Bashara, although no one said as much. And it was also made clear that Gentz could help himself by helping the cops nail Bashara.

That would do wonders politically: the takedown of a son of power and influence, of a state appellate judge and corporate lawyer who represented the epicenter of wealth, the Pointes, which existed amidst the squalor of Detroit.

Plus, Bashara was an easy target. The more the cops talked to people, the more they found that Bashara wasn't well liked. While it was indisputable that he was a pillar of the Pointes in some circles, namely the Rotary crew, he was also considered a philandering, coke-snorting loud-mouth who rubbed elbows with some shady characters.

The cops dispersed to talk with these sketchy folks, people with names like Ponytail Bob and folks with criminal records that involved armed robberies. A couple of these sources were homeless, and some were incarcerated.

At the same time, investigators visited the moneyed elites of the Pointes, friends of Bob and Jane, who were treated like the upper class they were, unless they showed the smallest inkling of support for Bob Bashara. Even the blue bloods wouldn't be afforded any quarter if *that* was the way they were gonna be.

The investigators fired off subpoenas, jumped on flights, and flew potential witnesses into Detroit.

They eventually compiled what would amount to a tera-byte of documentation in the form of witness statements, photos, recorded material, and other materials. In other words, more information than your average home computer could hold.

"They had a lot of time on their hands," said Lillian Diallo, a Detroit defense attorney who would eventually represent Bashara.

In many cases, the authorities promised anonymity to witnesses, vows that they never kept. Materials that were seized from innocent witnesses, people who were never charged with a crime, were never returned.

Janet Leehmann called the Grosse Pointe Park Police to tell her story. The department was doing its best to be part of the team looking into the murder, but it was part of a joint effort of far more experienced agencies, including the Detroit Police Department and the Wayne County Prosecutor's Office.

When Janet Leehmann first called the Grosse Pointe Park Police, she left a message for someone to call her back, a message that was never relayed. Finally, Captain David Loch called her. Investigators had found her number on Bob's computer. They knew of her communication with him and Rachel.

In fact, she was still talking with Rachel, hoping to help her. They wanted her to keep the communication active.

"No, I can't do this anymore," she told him. Since she had first reached out to the department a few days earlier, the scene had gotten too heavy for her. She was starting to believe that Bashara had something to do with Jane's murder. Rachel was falling apart, and Leehmann, who had gotten involved inadvertently by just looking for a little excitement, was bailing out. This was not her kind of excitement.

"Please, it would really help us if you would keep talking to them and telling us what they are saying," Loch told her. He was setting her up as a witness. He told her he was flying to Bend, Oregon, to interview her, only to change his mind a week later to tell her he wanted her to come to Detroit.

"No, I'm not going to do that," she said. Leehmann worked in a dental office, had limited means, and had no intention of taking her vacation time in Detroit.

"You are coming because we're issuing a subpoena," Loch told her.

Interstate subpoenas can be fought. Testimony can be given via phone, satellite, or other technological means. But when Leehmann, whose grasp of criminal law was nonexistent, called a Detroit lawyer for some help, he told her she had to come. It was simple as that. After all, there are few attorneys who are going to buck the Wayne County Prosecutor's Office. Helping a woman from Oregon fight the system would only cause problems for a local attorney. So Leehmann found herself on a Delta flight into Detroit.

After spending the afternoon at the Grosse Pointe Park police department, she wound her way downtown to her hotel, the Hilton Garden Inn. After checking in she walked the two blocks to Fishbone's, a cavernous restaurant with a huge bar running through the middle. It was a recommendation of the cops; she figured they must know the places, and they handed her a generous $200 per diem.

She was alone at the bar when a young man approached her. He wasn't hitting on her, exactly, although that wouldn't have been out of place; Leehmann was an attractive woman in good shape and with a lively line of patter. She looked approachable and had a ready smile. And on this evening, she was enjoying a glass of wine before dinner.

He wore a soul patch and a cabbie hat and claimed he was a Red Wing. Leehmann had no idea what a Red Wing did. Locals knew he played hockey for the NHL team.

"You don't look like you're from here," the man said.

No, she said, she was in town for a hairdresser's convention.

"My name's Jennifer," Leehmann said. Never give a stranger at a bar your real name. She knew that.

"Wow, that Bashara case is really something," he said.

"I'm not from here. I don't know anything about it," Leehmann said.

The stranger went from light and chatty to demanding and nasty in one second.

"Yes, you do, and your name is not Jennifer, it's Janet, and you're from Oregon," he said. She stared at him for a second.

"Who the fuck are you and what do you want?" she said, her voice raising. She was scared and angry. He turned away and pulled out his phone. While he was calling someone—getting orders for his next move?—she slapped a $20 bill on the bar and walked out, back to her room, checking behind her as she walked to make sure he wasn't following her.

The next morning, she had another interview, this time with the Wayne County Prosecutor's Office. Lisa Lindsey and Robert Moran were heading the prosecutorial team, and they met Leehmann at the courthouse.

They talked for a while, Leehmann giving them some good information. They were aware that Bashara was still in touch with her.

They were talking about the nature of those conversations when Leehmann's phone rang. She looked at the digits.

"It's Bob," she said to Lindsey.

"Take it," Lindsey said.

The conversation was brief and mundane, Bashara complaining about the police and the way they were treating him. Did she know they had parked an unmarked blue sedan outside his house?

She made the perfunctory responses, being sure to inject some sympathy in the right places.

"Listen, I'm at work," Leehmann said. "I gotta go."

"Call me when you get home," Bashara told her. It was clear that whoever was shadowing her at the bar the night before hadn't been in touch with Bashara. Maybe he wasn't even working for him.

Leehmann hung up and turned to Lindsey.

"I am sick of this and am changing my number when I get home," she said. She knew that everything she told investigators was being leaked; the media had never reported that she was in town giving a statement, but somehow this stranger in a bar knew who she was and why she was here. It was a creepy way to treat anyone, but the prosecutors seemed oblivious.

"Please, don't do that. You're getting good information; we need this," Lindsey said. It was similar to Loch's pleading, and hadn't he thrown a subpoena at her after she said she wouldn't come to Detroit?

Leehmann returned to Oregon. She kept her number. She was a good citizen. But now she was in the middle of a murder case.

"Who wants to be 'outed' for being a bit kinky by a homicide trial?" she thought, hoping it would never come to that.

She did feel bad for Jane. She'd read Gentz's statement about the murder and how cruelly and violently Jane was snuffed out. Leehmann had a small patch of land she gardened, where, in Jane's honor, she planted some forget-me-nots.

Jane's clothes went missing almost immediately after her body was taken to the morgue. They were the first line in the investigation, containing DNA that could identify the killer. Blood from a wound she inflicted on her assailant, strands of hair, a bit of fiber—all could be pulled from the last clothing worn by a homicide victim.

The autopsy was conducted at the Wayne County Medical Examiner's Office, one of three thousand bodies the office would see in the year.

Jane's clothes, along with her body, were released to the

A. H. Peters Funeral Home in Grosse Pointe Woods on January 27. Records show the clothing included black pants, a dark purple blouse, and underwear. Her socks and jacket, which she was wearing when she was found, were never sent to the funeral home and went instead to the Michigan State Police crime laboratory. An agent from the funeral home signed for the remaining clothes. When the Grosse Pointe Park Police went to the lab asking for the clothes the first week in February, a week after the autopsy, they were told the funeral home had them.

For a law enforcement agency looking into a murder, obtaining the clothes to send on to a crime lab is among the first steps in an investigation. Among the first things to do with a body is to check for foreign DNA, including anything on the clothing. In this case, the fact that Jane had several broken fingernails would indicate a fight, which would almost certainly mean DNA other than hers would be present.

A funeral home in Grosse Pointe Woods rarely, if ever, deals with burying a homicide victim. Clothes of the deceased are routinely tossed out rather than given back to the bereaved family.

In this case, no one claimed them in the first couple of days, and out they went, potentially crucial pieces of evidence. The Detroit Police Department at first refused to believe it and claimed they were in the possession of the department. Then, in a blame game pattern that would continue throughout the investigation, the department tried to blame the Grosse Pointe Park cops, who were leading the investigation.

But the clothes were in Wayne County, at an office that Detroit PD investigators visited routinely.

The clothes never got to the investigators. Some speculate that Bashara himself may have taken custody of them. Others think they were just thrown out. Whatever happened, defense attorneys down the line had some ammo.

10

"I Gotta Get to Joe"

In the parking lot at the Valero gas station at the corner of Six Mile and Woodward, Bob Bashara watched the afternoon street show that was Highland Park, one of the Detroit area's worst municipalities in terms of crime and poverty.

It was the middle of the week in June 2012, and less than a year earlier, the city was forced to take down over half of its streetlights because it couldn't afford to pay the power bill. The town had lost half of its population since 1990, and the folks left were mostly welfare cases.

Bashara went to buy some cocaine from Paul Monroe, an ex-con with a deep rap sheet that included armed robbery and felonious assault. It was a while ago, when he was in his twenties and thirties, and he'd done some serious, double-digit hard time.

When he was looking for a place to live, he came across the apartment building on Jefferson that Bashara owned.

He told him about the criminal past.

"Doesn't matter to me," Bashara had told him. "Everyone deserves another chance."

He lived in the Jefferson apartment with his girlfriend, April, until she shoved off with another man. He also sold cocaine to make ends meet, and Bashara was a customer. Monroe moved out shortly after April's departure, but he and Bashara kept in touch.

Now, Bashara needed some blow to self-medicate. Bashara wasn't a heavy drinker, but he enjoyed some weed and some lines once in a while.

After sitting in the small lot at the Valero gas station, Bashara spotted Monroe on the corner. It wasn't hard to spot the large black man, who, at fifty-three, was a couple years younger than Bashara and lived in a different universe. Monroe jumped in the front seat. He hadn't seen Bashara for a while but was well aware that he was a suspect in the death of Jane.

Bashara, he noticed, looked stressed. His eyes were rimmed with red, and he had lost weight in the wrong way. It made him look physically weak, and his pale complexion showed up his acne scars more than usual.

"Are you wearing a wire?" Bashara asked Monroe as he drove down Six Mile a couple blocks, pulling off on a side street. In his world, as it had evolved, everyone was wearing a wire.

It was a stupid question to ask a man who was about

to hand over two ounces of cocaine. But then, Bashara wasn't exactly a man of the streets.

He patted him down a little bit, which irritated Monroe.

"What are you patting me down for? I ain't wearing no wire," Monroe muttered.

Monroe placed the baggie of coke in the center console, and Bashara grabbed it. He dipped a finger in, and the powder stuck to the end of his index finger. He inhaled and repeated a few times. It was a wasteful way to do drugs, but with such a quantity, he didn't need to consider it.

Then he began to drive. Bashara had an immediate, uncommon reaction to the blow. His face creased, and he looked like he was going to cry. Then he had a very common reaction: he began to talk.

"I had my wife killed," Bashara said, and he began to cry, softly.

"Why did you do that?" Monroe asked. He'd seen a lot of things—way too many for most people—but he'd never had anyone tell him about having a spouse murdered. Especially a white person who hailed from the best neighborhood in the city.

"I think we were about to start a divorce," Bashara told him. "And a divorce is like losing money."

Was Joe Gentz there? Monroe asked. He'd avidly read the news about Gentz and the confession.

Yes, Bashara nodded. "Joe committed the murder."

"You know they going to hunt you down and convict you," Monroe told him. "You're going to get convicted."

It was hardly what Bashara needed to hear. He really had to do something.

*   *   *

Investigators in the case were tireless. They were every-where all at the same time. Any property Bashara had was like a magnet for them. The investigators heard all of the stories, about Rachel Gillett, about the rumors of the land-lord's financial woes and how he paid tenants to work on the continually run-down properties.

Bashara decided to do a little of his own public rela-tions work, so he began to visit the properties and talk to his tenants. They weren't fond of him; he would harass them unmercifully when they were the slightest bit late with the rent, sometimes to the verge of squaring off with them. He could be aggressive and angry.

So when he went over to the Jefferson Avenue apart-ment complex, Robert Fick—who also went by Ponytail Bob—tensed up. He'd worked on a number of Bashara's properties. He'd heard about the murder and seen that Gentz was referred to as one of Bashara's handymen, but Fick had never met or even seen the guy. Fick had met Jane a couple of times when he did some work at Middle-sex, and he always liked her. She was solicitous and kind, maybe a little too good for Bashara.

"Listen, when any of these investigators come by to talk with you or anyone else here, I need to know about it," Bashara told him. It wasn't a request; it was an order.

"Also, if anyone asks about Rachel, just tell them you know nothing," Bashara added.

Of course Fick, like many of the tenants, knew Rachel, although most didn't know or care that she was their landlord's mistress. But some people have a habit of running off at the mouth when a cop talks to them. They all saw her at a little cookout Bashara threw for them the summer before. He introduced her as his girlfriend. Maybe his wife was cool with it. These rich people have weird arrangements sometimes.

Other than keeping Rachel quiet, Bashara asked that he only tell the truth. He asked the same of Ralph Lee, another tenant/handyman. Lee was a convicted sex offender in his sixties. His beef dated back to 2004, and he had done his time on the list without incident. Still, he wasn't crazy about all the law enforcement attention the apartments were getting.

Will Schatz, another tenant, was courting trouble with Bashara. When he saw news reports of Gentz getting paid off for the hit on Jane with a Cadillac, he looked out his window at the sickly yellow Caddy behind his building. It was a 1982 model, a pretty bad year for the once-regal make, and on a couple of occasions Bashara had him and a couple other guys move it. But it never started, and they had to push it around with a riding lawn mower.

Schatz called the cops. It was too much, the murder, his landlord, the Cadillac. He thought there might be something to it.

Not long after his call, the Cadillac was hauled away. He knew Bashara didn't call anyone, so he assumed it was the cops.

Bashara blew up when he found out about it.

"If you don't shut up, you will be evicted," Bashara

promised. "You know nothing about me or my personal life. And I certainly didn't kill my wife."

As if to cement his fealty, Bashara sent his cousin, Stephanie, over to Schatz's apartment one day in June. He wanted a letter to give to David Griem, asserting that investigators had inappropriately confronted him and demanded to know about speculative things, including the dungeon, which Schatz had no knowledge of.

The letter was composed in accordance with Bashara's wishes.

Schatz had no choice; with only a slight pension, one doesn't have a variety of living options. He signed the letter, fearful of Bashara's wrath. He felt his landlord could be violent if he wanted to be.

Poison in the food, glass in a saltshaker, or a grenade launcher.

This is the fantasy world presentation to Bob Bashara of how he could have Joe Gentz murdered in jail.

And Bashara was into it.

"I gotta get to Joe," he told Steve Tibaudo, who sold used appliances out of his place on a particularly seedy stretch of Warren Avenue in Detroit.

Steve's Furniture & Appliance was a centrally located beater, old-school, with an eccentric and dusty feel.

So was Tibaudo.

In his mid-fifties, the portly merchant carried himself with the air of an Italian don, sans the style. He spoke in halting, sometimes dramatic bursts, affecting a Jersey accent. He'd lean in close when talking about something that others shouldn't hear, which would come in handy in his last dealings with Bashara. Tibaudo wore his thick head of graying hair brushed back from the top of his high forehead. His salt-and-pepper goatee made him look more menacing than he was, or could ever hope to be.

"He was really just a wannabe gangster, too soft to execute anything, and actually a nice guy," one acquaintance said. Indeed, while he claimed to be always armed with three Berettas and a pocketknife, Tibaudo's love for his rat terrier, Mr. Doodles, whom he fed filtered water, betrayed a softy.

In June 2012, though, he transformed himself from small-time purveyor of appliances and wagers to what he said was "a little (Robert) De Niro, a little Jack Nicholson, and a little Leonardo DiCaprio."

Bashara was asking about putting out a hit on Joe Gentz, who was going to turn evidence on Bashara in Jane's murder. He was now sitting in William Dickerson Detention Facility in Hamtramck awaiting a competency hearing.

A couple years earlier, Tibaudo had hired Joe Gentz to work around his shop. An imposing tough who could take orders was just what he needed, and having some extra muscle in the seedy neighborhood never hurt.

But Gentz proved to be more of a liability. He'd call the local street people who were friendly with Tibaudo "niggers" and get frustrated and kick things with his large feet, sometimes damaging the goods.

Tibaudo, though, had a soft heart for Gentz, whose

obvious mental disability made it hard for him to make a living. Tibaudo referred him to one of his many cousins—for Italian families in Detroit are spread wide—who owned a pizza place, where Gentz worked for a while before again wearing out his welcome.

When he introduced Gentz to Bashara in late summer of 2011, the hope was that Bashara could give Gentz some work.

Bashara did him one better; in addition to the work, he also found Gentz a new apartment after Gentz was bounced from his old one.

Now it was June, and Gentz was the enemy Bashara had to face down.

"You're dealing with a guy who is not mentally stable," Bob says now. "He totally used me for his own game. Whatever happened or transpired between he and my wife was a matter of him overreacting, and he killed her. I was not there."

The cops wanted Gentz to turn state's evidence so they could put Bashara away. Since his arrest in March, Gentz was appointed an attorney, whose investigators began to work with the Wayne County Prosecutor's Office to ensnare Bashara. They were convinced that he caused Jane's death even though Gentz committed the murder.

While Gentz was charged with first-degree murder and conspiracy to commit murder, charges that both carry a mandatory sentence of life in prison without parole, the authorities were sure he would play ball with them to link Bashara to the crime.

The only obstacle was the ability of Gentz to grasp both

the consequences of his actions and the impact of his statements.

It was well documented that he had a hard time understanding the world. Could he perceive a deal in which he could receive a lesser charge in exchange for testifying against Bashara?

The authorities quickly began to arrange a competency hearing for Gentz, fast-tracking a process that ordinarily takes weeks or even months, given the languid pace that almost everyone operates on in Wayne County.

But even a murder case couldn't beat the system's inertia. The competency hearing was scheduled for July. Now it was June, and Bashara couldn't wait. Gentz had to be killed.

"If I don't, it's my life," he told several people. The one person he should have avoided in the matter was Tibaudo. Instead of helping him find a guy to do a jailhouse hit on Gentz, the used furniture salesman went to the cops.

They'd already visited him a couple of times, asking about Gentz and Bashara, and he had the cell phone number of Tim Matouk, the very able investigator for the Wayne County Prosecutor's Office.

Shortly after Bashara and he talked about hiring out a hit on Gentz in early June 2012, Tibaudo went to the cops. For all of his tough talk and his gunslinging, murder for hire was a serious crime he wanted no part of.

Plus, he wasn't crazy about Bashara. For twelve years he had dealt with him and witnessed numerous times that Bashara had kept the deposits of tenants for no apparent reason. And he thought he was a bully, blowing up on him more than once, using his size and bluster to intimidate him. While he may have been armed, Tibaudo surely didn't want to shoot a man with the community connections of Bashara.

"Your friend Joe Gentz has got me fucked up big-time," Bashara told Tibaudo on June 18. The two were sitting in Bashara's SUV. "I didn't realize he's a loose cannon."

They chatted on about $50 Bashara owed Tibaudo, who was trying to make the conversation more civil. He wanted to change the tone, actually, although he knew it would keep coming back to Gentz. Bashara was now obsessed with getting rid of Gentz.

"Joe Gentz is a terrible, terrible man who killed my wife," Bashara told him. "Because I wouldn't loan him money. Because I wouldn't help him get more work. I'm an innocent man, and they may charge me."

"Listen, the Wayne County prosecutor's people are coming by my store," Tibaudo complained. And that wasn't all. Steve Virgona, Gentz's friend, was coming by as well, in addition to a couple more people from the Gentz support group.

"You got all these people coming down here fucking up my business."

Bashara was hardly listening. He had nothing to do with the Gentz people, anyway.

"I'm as big a victim here as you are," he said. "Bigger, because I lost my wife. I didn't know how goofy this guy was."

After Tibaudo promised Bashara he would look into putting out a hit on Gentz, they talked again the next day.

They chatted about Tibaudo's health, a constant in any conversation with the merchant. It was the case of two guys with parallel interests by now; Bashara trying to contract a hit, and Tibaudo trying to get something on tape that would serve as evidence to get Bashara put in jail.

"Lookit, Steve, here's the deal: I didn't kill my wife," Bashara said. "I didn't pay Joe to do it. I didn't hire Joe to do it. He's an idiot. You think I'm going to hire him to kill my wife in my garage when I'm in town? You think I would actually do something like that, the mother of my children? You have a fucking thought coming if you think I'm capable."

"Well, anybody that would hire Joe Gentz for anything but cleaning his toilet out gotta be nuts," Tibaudo replied. And he meant it. But still . . .

Over the next week, they would meet at the Mack Avenue property, at Tibaudo's store, in Bashara's SUV. They settled on a price: $20,000 with Bashara giving him a few thousand as down payment. If the job didn't get done, Bashara would get his money back.

Tibaudo said he had a number of people who could do it, ranging from a cousin to a guy who ran a check-cashing place in the neighborhood.

"Okay, let's do this, the sooner the better," Bashara said. He was getting worried about the seeming onslaught of detectives and private investigators. They were talking with his tenants, and he thought that two guys, one black and one white, were from the Iverson Agency, a local detective firm. He was convinced that the two were hired by Susan Reed, the court-appointed lawyer for Gentz.

There was a little bit of paranoia creeping into Bashara's thought process, and it was impeding any clear thinking. He was making mistakes. The biggest one was to trust Tibaudo.

Every time they met in June, Tibaudo was wearing a wire, a car key fob in his shirt pocket that was outfitted with a recorder.

But they talked and talked, two guys who seemed to have watched too many seventies-era gangster movies, with Pacino and Brando and Pesci.

Bashara and Tibaudo were funny, though, as in Three Stooges–style nyuk-nyuk humor. Throughout the week, they talked of ailments—"You gotta have your gallbladder removed. It does nothing," Bashara advised him. They talked of dogs, Madonna videos, refrigerators, and, finally, murder.

"When you gonna come up with the money?" Tibaudo asked.

"Monday, I'll be here," Bashara said.

Bashara walked out. Tibaudo quickly dialed the FBI agent who was working with him on the recording. The agent demanded that Tibaudo keep him continually updated.

Tibaudo was also cooperating with Matouk, the investigator from the Wayne County Prosecutor's Office. They had talked so frequently in the past week that Tibaudo had put his name in his phone for quick reference.

Tibaudo had his back to the front door and didn't hear Bashara come back in.

"Who the fuck are you on the phone with?" Bashara bellowed. "Let me see that phone."

"I'm trying to get a girl for the night," Tibaudo said, caught red-handed.

Bashara, who towered over Tibaudo by six inches, grabbed the phone and began to page through the numbers.

"Tim Matouk," one entry read. Bashara exploded.

"You're talking to the cops," he yelled. "This guy is making my life hell."

"No, that's my buddy Timmy Mac," Tibaudo said.

"You took two calls from Tim Matouk," Bashara said. It was not a question. "I want to know what's going on."

"Bob, really, I ain't, fuck you, you're fucking yourself," Tibaudo yelled back. He was in a panic, caught because of the stupid mistake of adding the detective to his phone contact list.

"You got two calls yesterday from Tim Matouk," Bashara insisted.

"You're unraveling," Tibaudo said. He was still yelling. He stood facing Bashara.

"You said you wouldn't call anybody," Bashara said, softening his tone. "I think you know my concern about being setup. They could be offering you twice what I'm offering."

It was the emotional space Tibaudo needed to come up with an excuse that Bashara would be inclined to believe. Matouk, he said, had called him while he was in a doctor's appointment, and he couldn't answer the phone. He had no idea who it was.

"So I returned the guy's call," he said.

It worked. Bashara lowered his voice and started to talk

Tibaudo down. Once explained, Tibaudo handed Bashara his phone, allowing him to screen through the past calls.

Bashara said he would be back Monday, June 25, with some cash. He needed Gentz dead.

"Hey, work it," Bashara told Tibaudo as he walked out.

That Monday, Bashara went by the appliance store. This was the day, and he had an envelope. He went in and took off his sunglasses, put them on the table along with the envelope, and ran his fingers over Tibaudo's shoulders, brushing along the blades and up the collarbone. He was searching for a wire, the kind people used to wear in old detective TV shows, where the bulky wires would lead to a recording device, or, in the early 2000s, a wireless microphone that was broadcasting to a remote recording device.

"Bob, what are you doing?" Tibaudo asked.

"If you're wearing a wire, kill me now," Bashara said.

"I'm Sicilian. We don't go around wearing wires."

"All right. Now just yes or no. Do you think you can do this?" Bashara asked.

"Listen to me. I told you. I can only try. I got a cousin," Tibaudo said.

Bashara picked up the envelope and pulled out twenty $100 bills, plunking them down on the counter, counting as he plunked. $2,000 in all.

"Hey, Bob. You know, you said three. You only gave me two," Tibaudo said.

"Okay. Two. I'm doing the best I can do."

"Okay. Okay."

"I never cheated you ever."

It was a fair point. While he had never actually cheated him, Bashara was a slow payer. Tibaudo reminded him of the time he saw him at the gas station and grabbed his thumb, twisting it painfully in hopes of putting some payment pressure on Bashara.

Then the two chuckled.

"Get out of here," Bashara said. They were friends, he thought.

He asked for an invoice for $20,000 worth of appliances, applying the $2,000 to the balance.

"Put cash special," Bashara said.

"This is ridiculous, Bob," Tibaudo said.

"Make it to BJR Management."

Bashara was still uneasy. He wanted to take the conversation outside. They stood in front of the store, looking as if they were just shooting the breeze on a beautiful early summer day.

Bashara was looking better than he had the Friday before. Not as wound up. He looked then like he needed some sleep. In fact, he looked as if he'd been up for days, with huge bags under his eyes and forehead creases that were far more prominent than normal. His pasty complexion was a shade of gray.

Today, Bashara was looking rested and seemed more at ease. The deal was finally getting done.

With a sigh, Bashara tilted the conversation back to Gentz, the man who, if all went right, would be dead soon.

"If I knew he was as bad as he was, I never would have involved myself with him," Bashara said.

Finally, they were done. Bashara should have been happy. But while he looked better, he was feeling down.

"What's the matter, Bob?" Tibaudo asked Bashara as the two parted. It was still a fine day outside, around noon. Plenty of time to work.

"Nothing. Just fucking lost, like a lost puppy," Bashara said. He got into his SUV and drove off.

From the appliance store, Bashara drove west to Dearborn Heights. He wanted to see Venita Porter, the woman who had painted his now-defunct dungeon. Bashara had always liked her, and he was sure she liked him despite their rough times. Sure, she had been devastated when she found him with a naked Rachel that evening in the dungeon. But that was years ago, and he had visited her after Jane's death. It wasn't a great visit—Venita seemed a little nervous—but she didn't exactly kick him out.

They were going to meet for lunch, but he called her and asked if she would meet him at an area in Hines Park, a large link of wooded trails and pathways that runs through southeast Michigan.

"I'm in trouble," Bashara told her. "The police still think I killed Jane."

He was down, almost inconsolable. Venita was scared of him. Before leaving her place, she had put the only weapon she could find, a box cutter, in her purse.

They began to walk down a narrow paved path, obscured by shrubbery and other flora that was in full green bloom.

"Why did you turn me into a whore?" he asked her. It was out of the blue, and Bashara suddenly seemed threatening to her.

As they walked, he nudged her, not violently, but assertively, toward an area behind a large bush and put his hands around her neck. To him, it was a gesture of intimacy, no different than they had engaged in before.

To Venita, it was closing in on death. He lifted her up, his large hands and upper body squeezing her. She furtively moved her hands toward her purse, searching for the box cutter, at the same time resisting.

"No," she said, trying not to panic.

"No" worked. Bashara stopped. He didn't have the confidence to push any further. Maybe she wasn't into him.

"Come back to my house and stay with me," he asked. "I don't have much time. No one will know."

As they walked out from behind the bush and back onto the trail, Venita spotted two men together, pretending to not look but looking at them anyway.

Detectives, she thought for no apparent reason.

She declined his invitation, and he took it with a sigh.

Late that afternoon, he was moving things around the property on Mack. It was his favorite of all of them.

He knew he now needed to sell it and had put it on the market. He wanted $550,000. Dylan's Raw Bar paid $4,000 a month in rent, and the six apartments fetched $600 each per month. He now had two empty storefronts. The Hard Luck Lounge had closed the day after Jane's body was found. The bar's owner, Mike Mouyianis, had locked the door, dropped the keys, and, during the frenzied days of the funeral, the cop interrogations, the vigils, and the visitors, moved out.

"He left with a year on the lease," Bashara says. "Never even told me he was moving out." Mouyianis had held a final closing party on January 26. Bashara wasn't invited. Some of his friends were.

Dylan's Raw Bar was still operating, and Bashara went in for a beer. Then he headed downstairs, toward what was once the dungeon. He had carried the whole thing out of there—the cross, the bed, the sex toys—and put it all in a storage bin attached to the back of the building.

As he was walking down the alley behind Mack, an unmarked cop car pulled up at the end of the alley. He looked behind him to find another unmarked pull up, blocking the other way. A Grosse Pointe Park police car came up behind that one. Agents emerged from both unmarked cars.

"Bob Bashara, you're under arrest for solicitation of murder," one of the plainclothes officers told him.

David Griem was on his way to a Detroit Tigers game, wearing his Dave Dombrowski jersey, with the Detroit Tigers general manager's name and the number 00 across the back. His cell phone went off, and it was Bashara. He was at the Grosse Pointe Park cop shop. He had been arrested. Griem had predicted this for some time, knowing that the authorities were working on a deal with Gentz to testify against his client. He assumed they finally got enough to haul Bashara in. But that could be taken care of; a murder charge with nothing but the statement of the confessed killer wasn't much.

This was worse. Solicitation to commit murder. Bashara, Griem says, was distraught.

"Bob, you're killing me," Griem told him when he arrived at the jail. There would be no bond at least until charges were finalized and Bashara was arraigned.

In his baseball jersey, Griem addressed reporters outside the police station.

"I don't have a crystal ball. I find that far-fetched for this reason: We all know that Joe Gentz was released by the prosecution and was out on the streets . . . before he was arrested again. If that were the theory then Joe Gentz wouldn't be around today," Griem said.

"I don't know what to say at this point in time, but right now I'm speechless."

Griem still seethes.

"Tibaudo went to the cops almost immediately after Bob approached him," he says. "He didn't pick someone out of a phone book to call. He wanted to build up a snitch bank account with a law enforcement agent. He could have just walked away and told Bob he was crazy. But he didn't."

11

"It Is What It Is"

The Andrew C. Baird Detention Facility sits to the east of downtown in one more torn-up block of institutional buildings. It is one of three jails operated by the Wayne County Sheriff's Office, which holds 2,600 prisoners on any given day.

Across the street are the ruins of what was supposed to be a new jail, before it all fell apart in mid-construction amidst cost overruns and a federal investigation into those overruns.

A couple years before Bob Bashara was checked into the jail, Detroit mayor Kwame Kilpatrick served four months on an obstruction of justice charge, then again spent time there when he was being convicted on federal charges of racketeering, bribery, and extortion.

Bashara was taken from Mack Avenue to the jail's sally port, where he was processed—fingerprints, mug shots, the usual TV drama stuff—then issued some green scrubs and plastic slippers.

He was taken to an upper-floor cell, fifteen feet by ten feet, where he would bunk alone. The cell was typically spare, with a thin mattress pad on a single bed running along the wall, a toilet, a sink, and a shower. He had a phone inside his cell that could only place calls; no incoming.

Freedom was history for Bashara. Whatever he knew to be the truth was irrelevant. If he had approached and paid Joe Gentz to kill his wife, it was erased from his mind by now, as he truly believed he was the victim of a wrongful targeting, "a witch hunt," as he told me.

The prosecutor's office, on the other hand, was confident in pursuing Bashara to the end of the earth and was sparing no expense. Lisa Lindsey met numerous times with the Engelbrecht family and soon became their hero. She gave family members copies of the book *The Sociopath Next Door* to read in hopes of getting them to grasp what Bashara was, in the opinion of the prosecutor's office. The book includes interviews with several individuals who simply lack what can be called the "caring gene." That deficit allows them to use people for anything they need and go to any means to carry out that exploitation. Sometimes even murder.

To visit Bashara, Stephanie Samuel drove to the jailhouse from Middlesex, where she had been staying off and on since Jane was murdered. While she grew up in Grosse

Pointe, Stephanie had moved to Windsor, Ontario, across the bridge two years earlier with her wife, Kathy.

Stephanie was Bashara's cousin on his father's side, and she had looked up to him since she was a child. He was always so fun loving, so easygoing, and he could make her feel better when things were tough.

It was his gift of soothing and talking that made Stephanie feel better. When she was diagnosed with cancer in 2002 at age thirty-one, he was part of the strong family unit that supported her and gave her strength. When she was diagnosed again, once more her older cousin was a source of strength.

Now, she was going to reciprocate.

"I trust him with everything that I am," she told a television reporter a month after the murder. She carried an actor's demeanor of drama, and indeed, her passion was acting. She had been part of the local theater community since she was a child, and her words often came with hand gestures.

"He's the best big brother I ever could have wanted," she told a reporter in February 2012. "And I just know without a doubt that he had absolutely nothing, nothing, to do with Jane's murder."

Now, she was checking in at the desk of the jail to visit her de facto big brother. The building had a wide lobby with polished linoleum floors and an airy, high ceiling.

She was directed to a bank of elevators.

The ride up to the seventh floor is like the ride in the movie *Angel Heart*, a 1987 flick in which Mickey Rourke plays Harry Angel, a private detective who sold his soul to the devil for fame as a World War II crooner. The elevator in that movie symbolizes the ride down to hell, where his alter ego, singer Johnny Favorite, will reside for eternity.

There are clicks and clacks in the creaking ride, and it stops and opens onto a dark hallway.

Just beyond a double-paned room is a dim light, and a man beckons Stephanie, pointing her left, down the dark hallway. He holds his hand up with three fingers. Door number three. All the doors are coated in multiple layers of military beige paint. There was no stripping, sanding, and primer used here.

She walked down the hall and heard a creaking on the other side of the steel door to her right. She entered, and there he was, in his prison scrubs, a clear plastic identification bracelet on his wrist. Her big brother, the man who lived a storied life, the son of an esteemed judge and a community leader who just a year earlier had been mentioned with reverence in his hometown only a few miles away.

She picked the greasy plastic phone receiver up with her left hand so she could speak to him, as the glass made it impossible to converse directly.

And all of a sudden, she was angry.

"Bob, what did you do?"

"Steph, I was setup."

"Bob, even if you were setup, if someone asked if you wanted to hit someone, all you had to do is say 'no.'"

He hung his head down.

He nodded then said, "I know, I know."

"What?" she demanded.

"It is what it is," he said with a shrug, raising his head and looking her in the eye.

It was the breaking point for Stephanie. She would remember that one for a while.

He added that he got sucked in.

"I'm sorry if I let everyone down," he offered feebly. "I did the best I could do."

Griem would be coming down, and they were going to figure out a legal strategy.

From that point going forward, Stephanie said, she would be in charge of everything, from the disposition of the house to the legal matters.

"I understand," he said.

"Should you get out on bond, if that happens, we are still making the decisions," Stephanie said, referring to the family and implying that he was out of the picture.

"I understand. It would be nice to come home and get things squared away before trial."

"Who's going to come up with bond?" she asked.

"I was hoping Mom would float it until we sell the house in Middlesex and the money comes back," Bashara said. He'd borrowed tens of thousands from his mother over the years, and this was no time to stop.

Stephanie knew that, and now it rankled her.

"You know my main goal has shifted, do you realize that?" she said. "You know for forty-one years what you've been to me? You know since this happened what my main focus has been?"

"Me?" he asked.

"You know what my main focus is now?"

"No. My mom?"

"Yes."

He paused. Then repeated the magic words.

"It is what it is."

This time, she admonished him. It sounded callous, she said, uncaring.

"I don't mean it to sound that way," he offered.

Stephanie told him that she will always love him, no matter what, and that his mother will, too.

It was all too much to bear. She had to go.

There was little chance that Bashara would bolt if he were given bond. A normal bond in this case would be $1 million, perhaps; a lofty if not political sum that would make the prosecutor's office look like it meant business but an amount affordable to the Bashara family. It was not something they might be able to raise in a hurry, but nothing insurmountable, as bond requires that 10 percent of the total be issued, or $100,000.

The charge of solicitation of murder is a felony, with a maximum sentence of up to life. But that sentence is rarely handed out.

Given the amount of time and money already put into the single charge, there was no way the solicitation rap was going to be the only one. The authorities needed time. They could use that time to drain Bashara's resources so that his ability to pay for a solid defense would diminish. They could also use it, of course, to build additional charges; it's the common strategy used to charge mob bosses—get them for something that you can put them away for and start piling on.

In a press conference—because for Wayne County prosecutor Kym Worthy, there's a lot of stock in political appearances and pomp—the office handed out a press release before the June 27 gathering at the 36th District Court downtown, outlining the charges and also noting that the investigation into the murder of Jane Bashara was continuing.

The presser announcing the arrest was a ceremony of credit, with seventeen people flanking Worthy, agents from the FBI and the ATF, investigators and officers from the Wayne County Sheriff's Office, the Detroit Police Department, and the Grosse Pointe Park cops. Lisa Lindsey, Robert Moran, and some others from the prosecutor's office stood to Worthy's right as she delivered her triumph.

Among those watching was David Griem, accompanied by Bashara's mother, Nancy.

"These are serious charges," Worthy said. "The evidence will show that money was exchanged. We don't think that he should be granted any bond at all."

Such a request cannot be made. Lindsey instead asked for a $25 million bond as the lawyers discussed the issue with the judge.

Street thugs are given lower bonds.

It was an extraordinary amount for a hometown boy who had few connections outside of his little burg.

He had property in the area worth over $7.3 million, Lindsey insisted, and his mother, Nancy, was a wealthy woman.

Bashara appeared via video, looking stunned.

"He's still grieving the loss of his wife," attorney Christina Utley, who was enlisted as co-counsel by Griem, told Magistrate Charles W. Anderson III.

"He's a substantial danger to the community," Lindsey added, citing the restraining order Gillett was forced to resort to and her fears of being harmed by her former lover. She added that there were "rumors" that Bashara was trying to "silence" Gillett.

"We're trying to verify," she said, although in reality, Bashara had no idea where Gillett was.

Gillett was doing a good job of staying hidden. She had obtained a prepaid cell phone with a Pennsylvania area code but moved elsewhere. Her secret hiding place was well kept from both Bashara and the media.

Judge Anderson drew the case by chance, and it was unlikely that he would hear the case from start to finish. But his decision was key here. The political heft of the prosecutor's office could have a bearing on his future, an unspoken fact in the Wayne County justice system. Cross them and you could have real trouble getting reelected.

He settled on a bond of $15 million, cash only, so the full amount would have to be paid. There was little chance of meeting that.

The revelation of Bashara's sexual preferences and conduct was lurid and titillating, there was no doubt. The dungeon, the mistresses, the threesome household with an import from Oregon; it was all enough to cast more than a *Fifty*

Shades of Grey on the whole episode. Sometimes, it threatened to cloud the fact that Jane Bashara was brutally murdered and dumped in an alley.

Still, watchers of the case, of which there were many, were predictably enticed by any little salacious detail or development, be it credible or not.

So when a woman calling herself Lady Geanna called local radio host Charlie Langton on the morning of July 2, she aroused some locals.

Langton was a lawyer and media personality with solid credentials, a smart guy with a bent for entertainment. The Detroit market is blessed with such characters that blend sound news instincts and flair. Both Langton and Drew Lane, a sharp-as-nails shock jock, are radio stalwarts. Charlie LeDuff, a former *New York Times* reporter, is a Pulitzer Prize–winning journalist who moved over to television after conquering the print medium.

Lady Geanna opted for Langton, who took the call earlier in the case from Steve Virgona, who told him extensively about Joe Gentz's involvement in the case.

Val Hall, who ran a housewifey, gossipy crime blog called *The Hinky Meter*, also called Langton in February to air out her not-so-professional opinion of the case, pretending to be an investigative journalist in the know. The audience lapped it up. It was amateur hour, but as entertainment, it pulled in listeners.

Geanna had also called in February to talk about the dungeon. But this July call was a little heavier, if not incredibly difficult to believe.

"I didn't want to say until he was arrested," Geanna

told Langton, her self-importance ballooning with every word. "I was getting some strange phone calls, kind of threatening. But from what I understand they did participate in the slave parties together, and Bob was the master with Joe being his slave. Joe would do whatever Master Bob would tell him to do. They participated in the shows at the S&M parties . . . A slave does what he's told. It can go on to extensive role-playing where literally slave contracts are made, of ownership. I'm sure probably when police dig around a little more they'll find some kind of contract with Joe."

Few believed it. But it showed just how the prurient overtones of the case drew out the characters. Reality became a muddy TV show.

There was little clear thinking going on for Nancy Bashara.

Her only son was now in jail and facing prison, her beloved daughter-in-law was dead, and the relationship with Jane's parents was fractured. The Bashara family was always tight, though, rallying around the women. When George Bashara divorced Nancy, it seemed that more of the family rallied around her. And over the years, she had been more generous than anyone could imagine.

Every spring she handed out $80,000 to her immediate family—$10,000 each to Bob, Jane, their two children, her daughter Laura Maurer, her husband, and their two children.

"It started with my father in my family," Nancy said.

There were also the vacations, for which she footed the bill. Starting in 2000, the families of Bob and Laura would gather in a designated location that everyone agreed upon. One year it would be Cancun, maybe the next would be a ski trip, then the Bahamas. The last year was 2008 with a trip to Jamaica. She loved her family and was pleased to be able to bring everyone together for the gatherings. The kids were getting older and having more adult concerns; as Rob, Bob's son, was starting his career as an engineer and Jessica was getting ready to start college, she realized the trips would have to end.

Still, she was there for anniversaries and birthdays and holidays.

When Bob and Jane would have a fund-raising event, she'd be there. Anything at St. Michael's Church, of course, as it was where Bob was married—twice—and baptized.

Nancy Bashara lived in a modest apartment in Grosse Pointe Woods and ran errands for the family when needed. She was independently wealthy and had plenty of time and a helping spirit. She spoke with Bob at least two or three times a week.

She answered questions with a matronly "oh yes" if you caught her right and stuttered if you didn't. She was portly, with gray hair cut tight to her head, sometimes severely so, in that it looked as if she might be fashioning a prison cut.

And when Jane was murdered, it was Nancy who paid for the funeral, $8,000 for the service and the meals, plus the interment and the high-end casket.

The incarceration of her only son was a blow to her, and, no, she was not thinking clearly.

Her birthday, July 3, would be one of the worst days of her life.

David Griem knew there was a recording, and audio proof was often the death knell to a defense. Worse, it was inevitable that he would have to hear the recording of his client soliciting murder.

At the same time, he also knew that sometimes recordings didn't tell the whole story. Or there was a reason behind what was going on in the recordings that wasn't being told.

So on the afternoon of July 2, Griem listened once, then again. He sat with his co-counsel Christine Utley, assistant prosecutors Lisa Lindsey and Robert Moran, and a couple of clerks in the conference room of his twenty-fourth-floor office in Detroit's Guardian Building.

Griem listened to the recordings of Bashara agreeing to pay $20,000 for someone to kill Gentz in jail. Never mind that it was close to impossible; how stupid could someone be to think a used furniture salesman could make it happen? It was out of a Tom Waits song, or one of those Hollywood comedic crime capers with a so-called dark edge.

Guilty, he thought.

He took his copy of the recording and knew what he had to do.

Nancy Bashara had paid him throughout his work on behalf of Bob, and he truly liked her.

"There are recordings," he told her bluntly in a phone

call later that evening. "And Bob is on them, and he's going to be found guilty."

"I want to hear this for myself," Nancy said.

He tried to talk her out of it.

"No. Come by Middlesex. I have to hear," she said.

He brought the recording, along with a transcript, the next day. He wished her happy birthday.

"It was the right thing to do, for anyone who has a heart," Griem says of allowing her to listen to the recording. "Nancy had been through a lot already, and it took a lot for her to cut the umbilical cord."

Stephanie was at home when Nancy called, sobbing. She had read and heard enough, too much, probably.

Stephanie went over immediately. By the time she got to page four, she knew. Her cousin was guilty.

She stayed up all night, listening, reading, and crying.

"We're done here," she thought. The family could not support Bashara anymore.

In a phone call on July 4, Nancy told Bob, "I'm through," meaning that what was on those tapes was the last straw. She loved him, of course. But this was too much. The money would not dry up—indeed, records show she floated a $25,000 loan to him in August—but her emotional support was waning.

After hearing the recordings of her own son trying to arrange the murder of another man, no matter how awful that man might be, it was clear that Bob had lost his moral compass. The philandering, the lifestyle, those were pretty bad to her. But murder?

The cord, as Griem noted, was cut.

* * *

So some might think it odd that as she sat at Middlesex, after hearing that her son was capable of having someone killed, that she thought back to when that very son had asked her in March for a favor.

"Mom, I have all these things for Robert, and I need them to be safe in the safe-deposit box," Bob had told her. "I lost my key."

He was in the master bedroom upstairs, sorting through things the way people do after someone dies. There are things that get distributed, and he said he wanted Robert to have some keepsakes, as well as a couple of watches, some coins, and some man jewelry, like cuff links and a couple of tie clasps.

The stuff was in two large plastic bags. They weren't too heavy, and she headed over to Comerica, where she and her son had shared a box since 2010. Records show it was March 5 when she placed the bags in the box and left, another errand completed.

Now it was the end of June, and for some reason, she thought again about those watches and some other thing for Robert. There were some clothes she was going to send to him in—well, where was he now?

His job as an engineer at General Electric was taking him to several different places. He had gone from Burlington, Iowa, to Greenville, South Carolina, to Houston, learning the different elements of management.

His timing was perfect, as the nation was enjoying an unprecedented energy boom, and part of what he was learning was the undersea excavation for oil and gas.

As a result, he was scattered, as was Nancy.

So on July 5, she decided to go back to the bank and fetch those bags.

"Bob is in jail. I better handle this," she said to herself.

She opened the box and pulled the bags out. She felt the weight in her hand and decided, right then and there, she'd have a look. She hadn't checked them before. But for some reason, on this day, under the circumstances, she'd look in there.

Everything she'd seen on the bed was in there, and there was another bag, a white and yellow striped pouch with small flower patterns and a snap at the top.

She opened it up, and inside was a silver .32 caliber Smith & Wesson with a black grip and trigger. It was an old-school model, polished and in good shape, with a long barrel.

Hadn't Joe Gentz, in one of his many versions of the evening of January 24, said that Bashara had held a gun on him and commanded him to kill Jane?

Hadn't Bob told reporters that the only gun he owned was a BB gun for keeping backyard squirrels at bay?

"I had never seen the gun before," Nancy said.

She carefully placed the gun back in the bag, took the other bag, and placed them both in the box, locked it, and left. She had to show this to Stephanie, who would know what to do.

Laura was coming into town the next day, a Friday, and on the way in from Detroit Metro Airport, she got a call from Stephanie, who asked her to go directly to the

Comerica Bank branch on Mack Avenue. They might have a problem.

Stephanie and Nancy were already there, Nancy with the key, and they together went into the little room, signed out the box, and sat down at a table.

"Holy fuck," Stephanie said as soon as she looked into the pouch. No one wanted to touch the gun. They peered in as if it were a relic from a bygone era. Then Nancy pulled it from the pouch.

"Nancy, put it down," Stephanie said. "This looks like incriminating evidence."

She didn't say who it could incriminate, but then, she didn't have to.

They all went back to Middlesex. It was no longer a gun, but instead they referred to it as "the pouch." But they also understood that the pouch was loaded in terms of legal impact on Bob.

It was stashed in a drawer in the buffet, where it joined silverware and dishware for the night. They then called Griem, who said he would come by the next day.

"You're killing me, Bob," Griem said to himself after hanging up the phone. A gun. What's next?

"I ridiculed the gun, that Gentz killed Jane because he had a gun on him," Griem says. "I don't know of anyone who committed a murder because they had a gun on them."

Now, there was a gun that had to be dealt with. Griem showed up the next day and joined Stephanie, Laura, and Nancy at the dining room table. They pulled the gun—the pouch—out of the drawer and handed it to Griem. While he had defended some people accused of pretty heinous crimes, some including guns, he was no gun guy.

Nancy was hysterical—"What does this mean?" she asked. Griem simply didn't know. He closed his eyes and held up a hand to say, "Stop."

"I've seen enough. Give me the bag. I'll take care of it," he said.

He left the house and immediately called his own counsel.

"At the time I was given the firearm, I was greatly concerned about the potential conflicts that could arise," he says.

Over the next twenty-four hours, Griem talked with two lawyers, Mark Kriger, who would soon take over as Bashara's attorney, and Kenneth Mogill, a lawyer and adjunct professor at Wayne State University Law School, who taught a class called Professional Responsibility and the Legal Profession.

"I never talked to the authorities," Griem says. "After talking to Kriger on Friday and then Mogill on Saturday, I kept the gun under lock and key."

And that's where the gun inexplicably stayed for over a year. It wasn't smoking, but prosecutors would be when they found out it had been kept from them.

Mogill advised Griem to keep the weapon. He says now, as he did upon getting the call from Griem on that summer day in 2012, that holding on to the weapon was "legally and ethically appropriate."

"In a situation like this, everything is fact specific,"

Mogill says. "There is nothing improper with someone having possession of a gun or a candy bar if there is no reason to believe the police are interested at that point."

A number of other factors entered into his advice to Griem: a gun is legal, while something illegal, like cocaine, is illegal and cannot be held at any time. The gun would not degrade, like a perishable; therefore, if the gun became germane at some point, it would be available.

"I know [Griem's] intention was to make sure he was acting ethically," Mogill says. "He was taking the high road."

Griem was also ready to hit the road, with regard to the case.

But before he did, he would repeat to anyone who would listen that his client had been setup by an overzealous prosecutor's office with the help of a witness who had no credibility.

He also said that Bashara was trying to obtain information for Griem's investigators and "made a terrible mistake."

It was a last hurrah, knowing what he knew, to try and defend what was now the indefensible.

12

"I Apologize to Mr. Gentz"

Running an empire from jail is hard work.

Just ask John Gotti, Pablo Escobar, or Bob Bashara.

Sitting in a jail cell in downtown Detroit, he couldn't figure out how he would maintain the grounds, let alone collect the rent. Given his tenant base and their often dodgy ability to pay, that would be a problem.

He called Stephanie Samuel. His first order of business was to evict Thomas Ramsey from the larger apartment complex. He had started the proceeding in May, but such a thing is sometimes a complex and drawn-out process in accordance with law, especially when a tenant has no place to go.

"He was a menace to the other tenants," Bashara told her. He had no lease; this should be easy. Bashara claimed Ramsey had drug issues and, unknown to him, had a criminal record.

Ramsey had also talked to investigators about Bashara's actions around the time of Jane's murder.

Stephanie didn't know that but declined anyway. She was still angry. So he turned his attention to a more pressing issue, that of revenue.

Bashara wanted to make sure his properties continued to generate income. Facing serious felony charges of solicitation of murder, with first-degree murder charges to follow, he was certain, there was going to be a need for some serious cash.

His mom, who had been there his whole life with an open wallet, had pulled back the checkbook. Hearing those tapes of her son arranging a jailhouse murder of Joe Gentz was too much.

A day after his arrest, United Laboratories terminated Bashara, where he had worked for nearly three decades selling cleaning products to businesses. He had a 401(k) account with United Laboratories worth $21,000. That would go to legal fees.

Bashara called Drew McSkimming, a friend of eleven years, for some help. The two had served on Rotary together, although the club had purged any references to Bashara's contributions over the last few months.

At St. Michael's Church, Bashara and McSkimming chaired fund-raisers. They were solid Grosse Pointe Park buddies. So could he go over to Middlesex? Stephanie was there, and she had the keys to his apartments. Maybe McSkimming could go by one of the apartment complexes and ask some tenants if they could write some character reference letters? And while he's at it, there are some things that need to be done there . . .

"Let her know how much I depend on her right now, and that she's got the keys to my kingdom," Bashara told McSkimming on the phone. Bashara's cell had an old-school phone on the wall, complete with phone cord, and he was wearing it out.

"I had quite a little empire," Bashara told McSkimming. "It wasn't huge, but it was quite a little property."

While he was at it, could he maybe do him another favor?

What is that? McSkimming asked.

Reach out to some politicians and see if they can help me. Bashara mentioned U.S. representatives Hansen Clarke and Gary Peters and Wayne County commissioner Tim Killeen.

Also, when you're over there at the property, check with Robert Fick and make sure he still supports me, Bashara said.

McSkimming followed through on none of his wishes.

With Bashara now behind bars, the prosecution didn't have to think about him meddling in the case, talking to potential witnesses, or amassing money for his defense.

No, now the state would chip away at his backing. The arrest had already alienated some of his family.

"I may be in jail for a while," Bashara told his son, Rob, in one phone call. He beseeched Rob to continue to support him in hopes he could get "some sort of probation thing."

But the family was fading. Rob was moving on and in

fact was becoming close to Jane's family. Daughter Jessica took his calls for a while, until he threatened to cut her out of the will if she didn't support him.

That was that. He didn't see her again for a year under circumstances no child should ever see a parent. She'd moved out in March anyway, even while her father was still free.

Bashara's properties were slowly failing, even as a series of helpers tried to keep them afloat.

Jane had been co-owner of the properties, at one point even taking a hit to her credit when Bashara was late on a series of mortgage payments.

Mother Nancy Bashara had co-signed on some of the loans, and she faced a lien of $9,879 on one property.

On July 18, 2012, Griem filed a motion with the court to be removed from the case.

"There has been a breakdown in that relationship," he wrote the court. "To say anything more would only intensify the media feeding frenzy which has made it difficult, if not impossible, for Mr. Bashara to get a fair trial and therefore would not be in the best interest of justice."

Through the five-page filing, Griem misspells the name of Jane's family—"Ellerbrecht" rather than "Engelbrecht." The motion was refused initially and a hearing called. There were just days until the next hearing in Bashara's murder-for-hire case.

"You just can't come in and say, 'I quit,'" Judge Kenneth King told Griem. "It doesn't work like that."

Bashara, who stood handcuffed next to Griem, said he'd like some time to get a new lawyer up to snuff and that prohibiting that "would not be in my best interest for fairness, for me getting a fair shake and a fair opportunity to defend myself, sir."

A new defense attorney, Mark Kriger, was in the wings. He would take the case and proceed.

And to make things direr for Bashara and his empire, his primary tenant at the Mack Avenue property, Dylan's Raw Bar & Grille, closed its doors.

So Bashara was faced with diminished family support, bailing commercial tenants, and a new lawyer who would have to play catch-up.

While both Bashara and Escobar performed great charitable deeds within their empires while carrying on with dubious and illegal endeavors, Bashara was no Pablo Escobar. He didn't have a cartel to piss in.

In mid-July, Lorraine Engelbrecht, Jane's mother, stopped by Middlesex with Jessica to go through some things of Jane's. As she went through the house, they found a stack of papers sitting on the dining room table and looked through them. The table had turned into the center of activity, a de facto office due to its central location. It was where Nancy Bashara and Stephanie had listened to the recordings of Bashara soliciting murder. Griem had also brought a copy of a transcript of the recordings, which he left there.

Engelbrecht looked through it and pondered the legality of sharing such information.

So she told Lisa Lindsey, the assistant prosecutor who was rabidly pursuing the case. Lindsey promptly told

Judge King, who found it interesting, to say the least. Griem could face a sanction for sharing such material, which was part of an investigation. No one should have that other than the directly affected legal parties, Lindsey complained.

So in late July, Jane's mother went back to the house to find her key was no longer working. The house was battened down, new locks in place and no alternative access. She was locked out. Stephanie Samuel, Bob's cousin, was in the house.

Griem had emphatically advised Bashara to allow Jane's family full access at any time to the house and Jane's belongings.

"Listen," he told Bashara in May, before he was locked up. "This is a horrible time for everyone. Make life easier for Jane's family. By doing that, you make life easier for yourself."

He didn't heed that advice.

So Engelbrecht called the police, then the media.

"She's moving everything out today," Engelbrecht told the camera, standing on the front lawn of Middlesex. "That belongs to the kids; that's Jane's items in there. I don't know what I'm gonna do."

She firmly believed that Bashara was controlling the estate from jail through Stephanie and the power of attorney he assigned her.

"I could not let anyone inside the house outside the immediate family," Samuel says.

The next week, Engelbrecht sought the urn that contained Jane's ashes. This time both Nancy Bashara and

Stephanie turned her away. And once more, she called the media, which dutifully sent a camera crew.

"Bob is controlling every piece of furniture, every dish. Even Jane's ashes," Engelbrecht told the crew. "He doesn't want Jane's ashes. And we can't have them. And that's spite. That's evil. I just can't tolerate much more of this."

The families, Jane's on one side, Bob's on the other, had been divided almost instantly by the murder, Samuel says. The dispute over access was just another symptom of that fracture.

Joe Gentz was competent to testify against whomever he liked in the eyes of the law.

A psychologist with the Michigan Department of Community Health passed Gentz after a June meeting. His lawyer, Susan Reed, told a reporter that she would let an independent shrink examine him as well, saying, "We want to be sure Mr. Gentz is competent before we enter into plea negotiations," nakedly acknowledging that he would be bargaining for a lesser charge to turn evidence on the big prize, Bob Bashara.

A July hearing by an independent shrink also determined he was stable enough to take the stand.

Competency to stand trial is different from being able to testify in court, though, and a judge would have to determine if Gentz was solid enough to do so. Given the power of the Wayne County Prosecutor's Office and the routine subservience from judges, it was unlikely that anyone would deny Gentz testifying against Bashara.

It was all falling into place for the prosecution, which was burning to get Bashara for the murder.

His murder rap stood at first-degree murder, a life sentence with no parole upon conviction. Gentz had already admitted, in front of the cops and God and everyone, that he killed Jane Bashara. He was going to go away forever.

Unless he could help the state get Bashara.

Gentz wasn't making it easy for the prosecutors. Despite having a private cell, he was routinely causing problems, refusing to take his medication—prescribed to keep him calm—and erupting into a loud, frenzied tantrum when a guard tossed his cigarettes.

In one case, after becoming angry with another guard, he formed a pistol with his hand, forefinger extended as the barrel, thumb as trigger, and faked shooting. In another, he stood toe-to-toe with an inmate on the brink of violence after Gentz abruptly changed the channel on the community television.

Jailhouse nurses were so unnerved by his behavior that they asked for extra security when dealing with him. He rolled up a dozen disciplinary write-ups for his actions. He would have more flare-ups over the coming months, including an altercation with a prison guard.

Bashara took a plea in October to the charge of soliciting the murder of Joe Gentz. He had little choice, as the recording didn't lie and he knew it damn well. He wanted to kill Gentz, straight up, and was in a hurry to do it.

"Foolishly and regrettably," Bashara told the court he

solicited the murder of Gentz through Steve Tibaudo. The single count's statutory maximum was life in prison.

While the prosecutor's office pointedly and rightfully contended that the agreement allowed no reduction in charges, it did spare him the maximum. The prosecution noted that state sentencing guidelines called for a sentence of between six and a half and eleven years. The defense believed the range was four to seven years.

The unspoken future was that Bashara was going to be charged with first-degree murder as soon as the state could get Gentz squared away. That is, to get him to understand that the deal it would offer him was a deal he couldn't afford to refuse.

A week after Bashara's plea, Gentz told the court he was not guilty of murder and that he would go to trial. Anyone following the case knew that he would not face those charges and that he was being groomed for a deal. It was a badly kept secret ever since his attorney, Susan Reed, noted in open court that a deal was in the works.

But after Gentz's plea, Reed told a reporter that a plea is "always a possibility. But right now that's not what we're focused on."

Bashara was sentenced for solicitation in December. Gentz addressed the court in a victim's impact statement, read by Reed, saying that Bashara "used and threatened him," claiming he had links to the Mafia and that he could get him anywhere.

"I have been telling the truth from the beginning. Bob has used me and threatened me. He told me he had friends in the Mafia and would have me killed. I was afraid for my life. I was afraid for my life because he said he could get to me anywhere, even in jail.

"I'm still in fear and don't feel safe anywhere," Gentz said.

Bashara stepped up to the lectern facing Judge Kenneth King.

"I certainly do not deny that it was difficult for me to come to the decision to plead guilty and subject myself to certain prison sentence, but I recognize that's what I had to do," Bashara said, reading from a statement. He wore black-framed glasses, a tan suit, and a fresh haircut.

"I can't begin to tell you how ashamed I am for what I did. Throughout my life I have tried to help those less fortunate. A name on a plaque means nothing to me," he continued, his voice cracking. "What does mean something is being able to use those talents and your skills to help those less fortunate. I understand that I must pay for what I've done. I absolutely stand before you and my family and the world to take responsibility for my actions.

"I apologize to this court. I apologize to Mr. Gentz. I apologize to my family and friends."

He was escorted back to his cell with six and a half to twenty years in state prison.

He gathered his things out of the cell—some clothes and papers—and was led to a van that took him eighty miles to the Charles Egeler Reception and Guidance Center in Jackson.

The center was once the state's hardest prison, but as the prison population grew, so did the system, and it was now a place all male prisoners went to for indoctrination.

It's also the place that allows officials to determine where a prisoner will be sent for the first few years of his sentence. Reading tests, physical and mental examinations, and background factors are all considered. Bashara was somewhat famous but hardly the kind of guy who needed to be spending time in isolation. Plus, he was a relative short-timer who would no doubt be angling for release as soon as the calendar switched to 2019; his first release date was projected to be February 24, 2019.

Nonetheless, he was placed in protective custody and a few weeks later shipped out to Oaks Correctional Facility near the state's Lake Michigan shoreline, barely an hour from where the Bashara family spent idyllic summers in long gone days.

"Bob Bashara offered me money to kill his wife," Gentz told Judge Vonda Evans in December 2012.

Wearing the same beige suit he donned when he tried to turn himself in to Grosse Pointe Park Police in January, Joe Gentz nervously scanned the gallery as he was led into the courtroom. He towered over his attorney, Susan Reed, and stood straight as he faced Evans.

"You look nice today," Evans said to him. He was wired, tight.

"Thank you," he murmured.

There was a deal, the lawyers told Evans. She looked

pleased. Then she looked back at Gentz, who took up a sizable part of her line of vision.

"I see you've got your glasses in your pocket. You want to put them on?" she asked.

Gentz smiled: "Yes, ma'am," and he pulled some specs from the breast pocket of his jacket.

Evans read him the dictates of the agreement, under which he would plead guilty to second-degree murder.

"Do you know the court could sentence you up to life imprisonment?" Evans asked Gentz.

"Yes, ma'am."

"But I'm not."

The deal was this: His guilty plea would send him to prison for seventeen to twenty-eight years. In exchange for the leniency, he would have to recite his version of the murder exactly as he had before, at any time he was asked. More specifically, without stating as much, he would agree to testify against Bashara.

Any legal layman could tell that Joe Gentz's admitted actions fit most descriptors for first-degree murder. He had forethought, he acknowledged delivering the fatal blow or blows to Jane Bashara, and, for a finishing touch, he took money for doing so.

"Bob Bashara offered me money to kill his wife," Gentz read from a prepared statement. "He threatened me, if I did not kill her. I killed Jane Bashara because Bob Bashara promised me money and threatened to kill me. This happened in Grosse Pointe Park, Michigan, January 24, 2012."

He stumbled a number of times, tripping on words and initially stating "2012" and "2002."

As the judge prepared to leave the bench, Gentz wished her a Merry Christmas.

He was sentenced in February 2013. The judge wasn't nearly as solicitous this time around. The sentence was already pronounced; this was simply a formality.

"Anything you want to say, Mr. Gentz?" Evans asked in a loud, bold voice.

"Yes, ma'am," he said.

"Well, I'm listening," she said, tersely.

Again, Gentz read a statement, a bit more rehearsed this time.

"I am very, very sorry for what happened. I am asking for the family's forgiveness for what I have done," he said. "My family for forgiveness for what I put them through. My friends and everybody else."

His voice began to falter, suppressing a sob. He stopped, his mouth working and no words coming. He held his head down and meekly cast his eyes up toward the judge.

"Very good," she said. Then, Judge Evans read her own prepared statement, only it was a speech that lasted six minutes.

"Despite your limited mental ability, you knew right from wrong and good from bad," she said. "All your life people have used you and controlled you."

She made it apparent that she was convinced that someone else was behind the killing, while not naming Bashara.

"When you were asked to kill Jane Bashara, it wasn't done instantly. The request was made, and you wanted to obey the request of your master. Despite his request you had time to think about this."

The judge said he took the life "for a man you loved and feared." She was writing her own version of events, implicating Bashara from the bench.

"How many days did you think about the task to take Jane's life, a woman who had welcomed you into her home and her family?"

Bashara told the cops in one interview that Gentz had never met Jane. He told a television crew that she once fetched iced tea for Bashara and Gentz as they worked in the backyard. But neither version had been proved or disproved.

Evans added that he was used by "a person who used you to achieve his goal: freedom from his marriage."

It was a bizarre piece of courtroom theatrics that betrayed the judge's feeling that Bashara was guilty of first-degree murder. Such grandstanding is usually seen on the other side of the bench, from a flamboyant attorney or feisty witness.

Evans closed by making it known she did not think the plea deal was right, and that "in my eyes, does not comport to the damage that you've done."

With that, Gentz was whisked away, a freshly minted key witness.

13

Emails and Conversations with
Bashara: "This Is a Setup, Clearly"

I began my overture to Bob Bashara on January 1, 2013,
with a letter to him in prison. I had no book deal and
actually wasn't even sure I would be writing this book. I
simply wanted to see what could happen.

"I am writing a book proposal about your ordeal and
would like to sit down and talk with you," I wrote. "It
appears that the full story is not being told and, in order
for me to do so, you should be able to speak without worry
of premature judgment. While I can't offer the glamour
that television shows do, I can offer the permanence of a
book and take the time to know your story in a way daily
newspapers or television stations can't. I also understand
that sometimes actions taken are only as good as the circumstances.

"I will speak to everyone affected by this situation, and
with all points of view. No good journalist would fail to

do this. If I did not, any book would not be taken seriously, and with good reason. But your story, including your solid background, has never been examined. It appears that you have plenty of good points and this needs to be part of the record."

I wasn't promising anything except a fair vetting of his situation and story. I had no multi-billion-dollar corporation subtly pressing me for stories that generated web hits that would translate to better ad rates, as many newspapers do. Sadly, reporters are pushed in bad directions when so much money is at stake—directions that often cause great ethical lapses that are not their own fault.

In this case, the best thing that can happen to a media entity is to create a monster. Frankenstein is scary, and if you have a real-life Frankenstein, well, you've got a lively story. I have the luxury of sitting back to write books, and while sales are necessary to any author who wants to keep doing books, they aren't the compelling reason we write. We just want to know what happened without heavy-handed pressure.

Bashara and I began to communicate via email via JPay.

We also talked on the phone in brief intervals, as the system didn't allow prolonged conversations. I was trying to confirm information and understand whatever I could about the family.

I was always careful not to be too critical of him for a number of reasons. First is that I was hoping to get him to open up to me, not to form a friendship or to exonerate him, but to understand what happened. I also knew that he needed a friendly voice, not a judgment.

In one early conversation I inquired about his first marriage at a young age to Priscilla, and also about his former mother-in-law, Beverly.

The emails are exactly as they came in.

From him (no date): *I mentiond that I want to move slwly and must know who to trust prior. As for beverly, she could not be more wrong. I was divorced for two years prior to meeting Jane. Pricilla divorced me and I was totally faithful to her. I would like to say hi to pricilla and know how she is doing, so if you can give her my info, I would like to communicate, as it has been years, and unfortunately she was too young and not ready for marriage, or atleast to me??!!! While I was hurt, I never hated her and moved on, dated a few girls proir to meetig Jane, so I am uncertain as to Beverlys memory. I value opinins as to y life and the goings on, and you are most correct, I have been totally dispariaged and hammered by the law enforcement thru the media . . . who ever heard of a 25 million $ bond . . . lol A stunt to paint me as a dangerous man . . . i am pacificist and a gentle man, sooo here I am, doing ok, coing and surviving. I am helping a nmber of inmates with riting, homework and plans for succes after they release . . . again, my life has always been community service and helping others, and in here i am not changed, but atill pasionte on helping those I know i might . . . I am also seeking out a baptisimal font for the*

Christians grop who worship here, as they want one and the State is of help . . . pps i am out of time, regards.. BB

From him (no date): *S, I was out of time and my last was wrought with misspelled words. Like I said, we proceed and get to know each other.I have not contacted anyone about taking to you and will not for now. I also have no interest in a book for now.*

I also do not know what is goingon, so let us be poaitive. I hope this finds you well, and have added you to my visitors . . . i will look for us to talk later, and until now, know youre correct, I am not a criminal, but a man who has a life of positve good works, even in ALL I was doing . . . more onthat much later, have a great week BB

1/17/2013 1:47:37 PM

SM,I have always know Bev is abit off, but she loved me, until her daughter wanted out, then they both turned on me. Actually I would like to know how Pricila is dong, does she have kids, married, still in GP, etc. I give you permission to give her my contact info should she want them, as it would be good to talk, after all these years. You are correct Margis Smith is a lovey lady, whom I got along with well, as she covered alot of my comunity service PR for the GP News

I also place quite a gew adds for my properties there. I have temporarily lost my phone, as they say i am running a business from prison . . . well if one had a business, why is it so bad to atleast complete your work, or protect your interests . . . On the flip side the want you to come out with emloyment and a future, yet they prevent one from protecting it long enough to keep it . . . lol . . . So, I am looking to start a dictionaty program for atleast my building, and will seek GP ers to donate 20 or so to the place here . . . my cmmunity service work never stops . . . I hope that I a properly represented at gentzs sentencing, as a victm impact statemet should be forth coming, as besides, my Jane, I am his biggest victim. I am here, and while this place is not bad, they were always a level 4, and have not properly adjusted for those of us who are level 2s . . . as they is a clear difference that is not being observed, like other level 2 s.

I bid you a good weekend and hope you discover all you seek . . . have a good day . . . BB

1/23/13

SM, I really would like you to contact my close friend/ atty. Rick*. at ****. Please into yourself and let him know of our talks.. yell him I said hello.. as for any communications from here to GP, it is hard, but once the snow resides, I would welcome the chance to meet.. as for the virgota fellow, do not remember him, but he is not someone i wish to communicate with . . . I know you have a book on your mind, but anthing le that is not on my

---

* Denotes pseudonym.

radar, but I would like to continue to chat . . . you must know that now is a hard time for me . . . please include my Jane in your prayers, as tomorrow is the one year anniv, of her death.

I am really sad, and miss her sooo much, as I do my kids . . . my daughter has been polluted by so may, and I feel for her.. I love her and Robert dearly, more than life itself . . . I do not read much as my eyes tire quickly . . . am due for a procedure sometime soon . . . as for Pricilla, do that as you are able . . . but I never hated her, just very disappointed in the way she ended our time . . . bid you well and may you be well . . . BB

1/31/13

SM, Good morning, and I do have a great relationship with Mark, we were raised like brothers, but I have not had his cell number to call him, but would like to . . . he is on my visit list, as he occasionally comes to Trav. City to vacation. I am curious to know how you know of him?? He is president of Mich. first aid in Roseville . . . if you wish to reach out, have him give his cell to either my cousin Steph. or explain how he might reach me on here.

I am sickened at the way in which the media, thru the prosecution is twisting the story of gentz around to make him sound like a victim . . . I absolutely cannot believe, their nerve and if anyone feels empathy for a cold blooded killer. This friend of his SV, I have never met, is no better, as he seems to love the press and notariarty, again a sad, sorry state for a situation that has terribly transformed soo many . . . enough as this thinking makes me physically sick . . .

I had a very tough time this past week, given the one year, but then i have had little time to actually grieve, but do in my own private way.

As for helping others, I do this in a variety of ways, from spelling and school help, to life planning and advice, soo many come to me, and I do not refuse anyone . . . I did this in ALL aspects of my life, in way you will find amazing. I do not yet have a tv, but then again, i go to bed early, looking for another day, one more closer to my release.. I have learned of another sad stat . . . 95% of those up for parole, do no get released but flopped for another year . . . they say that I can expect this as of my high profile . . . bullshit . . . I will do my time, most respectfully and then best get out. I have lost my phone for 30 days as of jan 15 and yet as of today, they have still blocked all my calls to the several attoneys I have listed, a clear violation of my rights and their rules in their guidebook . . . All here are victims of the whims of those in charge . . . i wonder if they are doing this to isolate me????.. I go merrily along I have much to do, i am writing, and communication with others . . . I love my family and try to reach out as often as I can . . . As for my wonderful son, i am soo very proud of him, his work ethic and just the man he is becoming . . . Jane and I worked very hard with both kids, giving them every advantage possible in their young lives.. my daughter is also a

*wonderful lady, and can debate with the best . . . i see her
as a Senator, someday . . . I was shocked to read an article
wrought with outright lies and misconceptions, as they
need to continue to debase me and drag me thru the
muddy waters of life . . . I must go, but know it is not press
or fame I seek, but only to get back to a life interrupted by
a senseless act, by a man I was trying to help. Had I know
how sick he was, i would have never associated with him.
Finally, if you do happen to reach out to my son, tell him
how much I love him and I hope he is well . . . and did he
get my letter, sent also for jessica . . .*

I bid you well . . . BB

2/5/13

*SM, I am doubtful to trust most anyone . . . I am curious
that you would ask me about her, as you must know she
took out a PPo against me, even though it was not her
idea or wish.. if she wishes to communicate with me you
can give her my info, but she was abused and poisoned
as well, by many and has moved on . . . which leads me
to my friends and family.. they do support me, but soo
many have read lies and mistruths and now here I sit,
they do not know what to think . . . but those who know
me . . . know me and still support me.. As for me I am
ok, I do not have money on my phone, so after the 15th, I
am unable to call, unless money is placed there . . . like I
said, trust is something I must be convinced of . . . I have
directed some to michigan packages. com, to aid in my
comfort . . . I did watch the game, but even thoug this has*

become a level 2, many say it is still run like a 4 . . . I remain, the man i have always been . . . BB

2/15/13

SM, I am busy the whole day helping others needing schooling and tutoring, I play cards, gin mostly . . . as for her, that is on you, I cannot and will not ask you to do that, as there is a ppo in place which I respect, but you should know that, although it was not her idea, but rather the PO, looking to further debase me . . . I most likely will move in a year or so to a level 1, but I might have thought you would know that . . . Tues should be interesting, but if you are who you say, you should also know about his sentencing . . . again . . . curious . . . so have you connected with Rick, or are you not going to do that . . . I am a bit unsure of who you are, so I need you to talk to him and then i will feel better . . . you need to understand there has been alot of deception involving me, so I trust noone, but you atleast reach out, but then there are questions you should know the answer to, so i am leary . . . hope you understand, if not, then sa la gare. (sp) . . . if you do connect with ANYONE, I would most likely like to know . . . so until you talk to Rick, be well . . . as for winters, there is snow . . . talk to you later //or not . . . I remain the man I always have been . . . BB

We stopped emailing when it became easier to talk. I was awaiting the June release of another book I had fin-ished the previous year, *Detroit Rock City: The Uncensored*

History of Rock 'n' Roll in America's Loudest City, and was doing magazine and other stories. I was also traveling a bit, but it was winter and I stayed mostly in Michigan, where I have a house.

The phone conversations read as they were delivered. Here is what Bob Bashara had to say, sometimes prompted, other times apropos of nothing. Some are dated, some are not. Rather than put the dialogue in any order, I take it right from my notes and onto the page, so there is jumping around. It was the nature of our talks.

> **Bob Bashara:** *They said they didn't want me to sell the house. Now I have money to do different things. There was a sheriff's sale and it sold for $64,000 just to satisfy the note I had.*
>
> *Comerica Bank foreclosed on its portion of the loan, and we were going to remedy the foreclosure and pay it off.*
>
> *I don't stick anyone—and whatever's left over I put in a trust for my kids, whom I haven't heard from. I think they're confused. It's a matter of my character being besmirched, but what control do I have?*
>
> *I write my kids on a regular basis, and I sent my daughter a birthday card. I've never been so powerless in my life. Before that I was in control of most everything and had people's best interests at heart. I try to do that—well, it doesn't fare well in prison. If you try to be too nice to someone they wonder what you're up to. So I go along to*

get along. I have few people that I've gotten at least a mild friendship with, and it's who I associate with. I play cards during the day.

I have some tennis shoes coming.

I missed Gentz being off. I was busy with a church fundraiser, and when I hire someone to do odd jobs and get an apartment for them, it wasn't like it was real close bonding or anything. So it's not as if I spent a lot of time with him. Tragically devastating what he did to my life.

I rented to three convicts before, and all three worked out great for me. One of them has money on his phone, and I still am in touch because I gave him a chance to make a life for himself and gave him odd jobs, but I didn't just jump into it. You develop a comfort level with people, and that's what I did with these other guys. I kick myself to this day [over Gentz]. He never told me he was a convict. I asked the fellow that referred him to me, and he lied to me, Steve Tibaudo, the furniture guy. And he's the guy who set me up. That's where Gentz was working before this. I've never been associated with anything like this. It's like a nightmare. I see what's going on around me, and I feel like I'm in a coma.

I had no idea that in my meeting with [Gentz], I got him a place to live and gave him some work. He thought I was a meal ticket, and he used me. He's off my radar screen and has screwed up my life, and I'm going to recover from this and rebuild my life.

Priscilla married me to get out of their house, and I had two people ask me if this is who I wanted to spend my life with. She was sweet; she came from a good family. When she wanted to divorce me, her parents stood by her on that. Beverly [former mother-in-law from first marriage] loved me.

I haven't seen Priscilla for thirty years. Last time I saw her was at the bank in Grosse Pointe at Eight Mile and Mack, about a year after Jane and I were married. I was in line and she said, "Hi." I said, "Hi, Cil, how are you doing?" She said, "Not that great." She had gained some weight. I was in love with her, I don't take marriage lightly, and I didn't want to be divorced. That was the last thing I wanted. We had talked about having kids, but she was just too young; she hadn't sown her oats. She didn't want to be married anymore, and she made excuses about me, I was into this and that. Her parents loved me. Her grandfather was one of the founders of Michigan National Bank.

Any girl I dated, their parents thought I was the greatest thing since sliced bread. I'm the real thing. I've spent forty years doing things for other people, and I learned from my father and my grandfather.

If my father was alive right now, I wouldn't be in this place. This is politics. They had me right where wanted me.

This is a setup, clearly. Did I walk away? No—that's what I was guilty of. I thought the judge would give me more leniency, for all the things I have been into for forty

years, since I was fifteen years old when I started work-
ing. I was my high school class president, and even before
that, in youth group I was active.

(Speaks of Wooden Nickel, a restaurant he owned when
he was young, his first real business venture.)

I had that for three and a half years. My father decided
he wanted me to have it. He always loved business and
was a very accomplished attorney and intelligent jurist.
He had that Lebanese in him, wanted to be a business-
man. He bought this franchise and had me run it. I was
working for my uncle in the first aid business, and my
cousin and I worked together at the Wooden Nickel. It
was his father who was the president of the franchise, and
I realized I was taking the limelight, and within six
months of me leaving, my cousin flourished. I wanted to
step out of the way.

On April 17, 2013, the Wayne County Prosecutor's Office
held another ceremony to announce charges of first-degree
murder against Bashara.

Added to the prosecutorial arsenal were charges of
solicitation, conspiracy, witness intimidation, and obstruction of justice.

"We are alleging he encouraged witnesses to call in
false tips. We are alleging that he tried to get a witness or
witnesses to leave the state so they could not be talked
to . . ." Worthy said once more from a lectern in a room
jammed with law enforcement officials.

Worthy also promised that Gentz would be among the witnesses. She refused to call him a star witness: "He's not the only witness. We have many, many others. I would never call one person a star witness. I never do that."

The investigation, according to Worthy, included three hundred witnesses, five thousand pages of documents, and travel to Iowa, Illinois, Florida, Oregon, and Texas. Ten percent of the witnesses were from law enforcement, the rest civilians.

We talked four days later, on April 21.

Me: *How are you doing?*

Bob Bashara: *I'm okay. They're throwing the book at me. The twenty-sixth is my anniversary. I'm gonna try to hire the best attorney that I've got and defend myself because it's a bunch of lies. There is witness tampering. I never told anyone to do anything, cooperate or not cooperate. I never said anything.*

Me: *Is it political?*

Bob Bashara: *I think so. I think it's driven by her family, and I don't know what's going on with them. The bottom line is I'm not saying a lot. They interviewed the real estate lady who was showing my house, someone I've never met. My power of attorney hired her, and they wanted to know where the money is going. What they are trying to do is squash the sale so I don't have funds to operate. That's how political it is.*

*Mark Kriger is my new lawyer. He was referred to me
by my first attorney. I've been behind bars since I hired
him so I have no idea how good he is. There are opinions
both ways. My mom is pretty upset and it's just terrible
what she has had to endure. She's mad at me as well and
hasn't come to visit.*

Me: *Are we going to have a trial?*

Bob Bashara: *I don't know. It depends on pretrial, and
all they've got is this guy and he's a mess. Anything you
can dig up would be great.*

Me: *If everything is as you say it is, you're going to be
fine.*

Bob Bashara: *I'm innocent as can be.*

It was that last exchange that caused him to disappear.
He was angry that I doubted him. No emails, no phone
calls for a couple of days after two weeks of daily calls.
We talked again on April 24.

Bob Bashara: *They moved me to level 4 yesterday. They
said it was because of my pending charges. My lawyer has
called, and I asked them to get involved. They are putting me at risk. This is way above my security level. I'm
a true level 1 based on my points and time.*

Levels are determined through a system that counts a
number of things, including the crime and the potential
for problems. He was complaining that he was moved to a

higher level in which he would be among the more dangerous offenders.

> **Bob Bashara:** *I had to move to a different block. I'm*
> *with the worst of the worst. I have a cellmate.*

Larry Ellington was among the worst of the worst, a
career criminal serving time for armed robbery. Standing
five feet seven inches, he was a solid mass of muscle, the
kind of guy who could provide protection. Ellington could
navigate his way through prison life, as he knew the peck-
ing order and the various gangs and groups.

He and Bashara lived in the same unit beginning in
April, and in May, they became cellmates.

Ellington claimed to be a Moor, a subset of the Muslim
faith. While the latter was widely practiced in prison, Moors
were essentially black Muslims from Northern Africa, trac-
ing back to the eighth century.

The identity led Bashara to believe that Ellington could
get things done in prison, Ellington said later.

Ellington and Bashara inevitably became acquaintances
at the least. Ellington was certainly no friend, because on
May 21, he sent a letter to Wayne County prosecutor Kym
Worthy.

"I have some very important information I would like
to share with you," Ellington wrote. "I share a two man
room with Robert Bashara, the businessman from [Grosse
Pointe]. I'm sure you would like to know what he has told
me and what he wants me to do for him."

Ellington claimed that Bashara asked if he could help put a hit on Steve Tibaudo, the used appliance salesman who wore the wire to catch Bashara soliciting murder. He said Bashara also wanted him to find a way to have Tom Ramsey hit. Bashara was suspicious that Ramsey was talking to the cops about him, helping them in their push for murder charges.

In exchange, Bashara would arrange to have money put into Ellington's prison account, plus hand over some property to him down the line.

Jailhouse conversations, especially those between cellmates, have sunk many a man or woman. Susan Atkins, part of the Manson Family, took the connection to its height by sending letters detailing her part in the Sharon Tate slaying to her former cellmate, who promptly turned evidence.

Related conversations are dubious as evidence. But that's never stopped an abundance of snitches who are keen on getting their sentences reduced and to be seen as a friend to law enforcement.

Ellington was among them. Like Tibaudo, Ellington was eager to sell Bashara out in exchange for some legal good grace. With his loose tongue and inability to filter himself, Bashara was a blabbing meal ticket.

Bashara continued to talk about his life and his case in our conversations. Outside the mention of having a cellmate, he never mentioned Ellington.

Bob Bashara: [On the house on Middlesex] *We have a purchase agreement and are looking to close for less than I wanted. It's something, and I'm not losing it. Jane's family has no stake in it. They'd like to and have advised my kids to get involved, and that's unfortunate. My kids have been poisoned by Jane's sister Julie, after all I've done to help her. I referred her to a friend of mine when she was looking to get pregnant. He was a neighbor, and I talked her into seeing him after five years of trying, and this is what I get, this type of payback. [Rob and Jessica] have been poisoned.*

I've already lost everything, lost so much. This is about my freedom, and it's also about doing the right thing and knowing you had nothing to do with any of that. Mostly this is for my kids and my mother and her family, but I think her family will always not like me.

I was the leader of that family. [Jane's] father has Alzheimer's, and he was in tough shape. He didn't know who was who, and it's mostly the mom and Julie the youngest daughter taking care of him now.

Me: *Where is Julie living?*

Bob Bashara: *Chattanooga. Julie is a teacher there. She's a pothead. The family is from metro Detroit. All the three girls went to [Central Michigan University], and the boy went to Western [Michigan University]. He knows I had nothing to do with this. He knows me and how much I loved his sister. Julie is the spokesperson for the family.*

I've gotten a little bit of mail from a few friends. I'm thinking they'll move me to Macomb County prison. They may have done this to make me miserable. I've gotta get level 2 back. They said I had controlled movement for my own protection.

Every twist and turn they want to make my life hell, but I'm gonna fight every step of the way. They're in for a battle.

Gentz had them hoodwinked. He was released after seventy-two hours by Grosse Pointe Park Police. His guy picked him up and told him, "You're in a world of trouble. Name Bashara." And the next thing you know that's what he did. It's unbelievable that they believe him.

Me: *Who was the friend?*

Bob Bashara: *Steve Virgona. I am hypothesizing. I've had over a year to think about it. They said to him, "Look, they're the ones who said to turn him in." I was the one who turned him in. That doesn't get mentioned. I was the one who found a letter and sent the letter to the Grosse Pointe Park Police.*

Me: *Did Gentz work for you?*

Bob Bashara: *He did a couple jobs, and I paid him $400. I met him in October. He did a few jobs for me. He was evicted from Macomb, something up there. The bottom line is it's a terrible shame.*

Me: *What does this mean?* (reading:) *"Jane's sister: Our family feels very strongly that this is not over with the sentencing of Mr. Gentz."*

Bob Bashara: *I don't know what this means. This guy [Gentz] had sudden outbursts.*

(talks about the night of the murder)

I was over at my Mack property. I know I wasn't there and I had nothing to do with it. He [Gentz] can rot in prison.

My dad and I never talked much about the courts. He said there are a lot of shady dealings in Wayne County. He would rather see someone sent to rehab or a halfway house than jail. He said prison was his last resort. He said sending people to prison doesn't correct anything. It doesn't help anyone.

Me: *Should Joe Gentz be in prison?*

Bob Bashara: *Absolutely. I'm talking about people who have done far less things.*

Me: *How about drugs?*

Bob Bashara: *Yes, if you're selling that stuff, because you're hurting people. It's a victimless crime, so I would be more lenient. Especially now since they've changed the marijuana laws. I have a young bunky, a nice kid, twenty-one years old, convicted of home invasion. His mother died when he was eight, and he's been in and out*

*of juvy homes. He got into everything, robbing and steal-
ing cars. He's a good kid.*

(On levels, again) *Everyone in here says it's more like a
four than a two. [At level four] the freedom isn't as great
as others.*

In April 2013, the house on Middlesex went up for sale,
asking price $415,000. The deal was handled by Rick
Falcinelli, a friend Bashara met in the lifestyle. The sixty-
three-year-old air force veteran had his own computer
programming company and became a friend to Bashara
after Jane's murder, talking with him frequently and even
drafting a letter testifying to Bashara's character.

The move to sell the house was practical as well as stra-
tegic, staying one step ahead of the cops. The Wayne County
Sheriff's Office tried to unload the home in November 2012
for $64,000 after the bank foreclosed on it, but there were
no takers.

The house sold for $325,000 in May. The proceeds
were divided among the family, including payment to
Nancy Bashara, who had floated nearly $300,000 in loans
to Bob and Jane in the past decade. By now, Bashara was
out of money, his debt leverage sinking him without the
ability to work his properties, which were high maintenance in both the ability of tenants to pay and the constant need of repair.

Being a landlord means a lot of fixing. Sitting in prison,
even with the best of outside help, that just isn't going to
get done.

Bob Bashara: *We bought that big house on Middlesex in 1988. We were married in 1985 and had lived in St. Clair Shores. I got this for a good deal from a real estate buddy of mine. Hell of a deal on a nice street in our price range. We wanted to have two kids. That was always our plan. We had Robert when we moved in there and then had Jessica. I put in work on the kitchen and a screened-in back porch.*

I organized the block parties for ten to fifteen years straight. Jane and I did those. We had winter and summer block parties. There's a median in the street, and people would come out with grills, bring out tables for three blocks, and set out different things on each, like appetizers, entrees, and desserts. A lot of people wouldn't come out; they were older.

I had a judge on one side of me and a doctor on the other.

My father's parents are 100 percent Lebanese. They were born here and went to Lebanon to be educated, then came back to finish college in the States. I think both of them were born here. Arabic was spoken in their home, and I was a fool; I should have learned it. My dad could understand it, and I would have had two people who would have taught me in a heartbeat.

My great-grandparents were entrepreneurs; they had a store. My great-grandfather also had a store in Lebanon, and he came to do business here. My grandfather is partly responsible for the large Arab population in Dearborn.

He was counsel general to Lebanon for the Detroit area, so he helped a lot of people settle in Dearborn.

My grandfather ran twice for state senate. He was hugely political; my father was even more so. He ran three times and won each time.

I never ran for anything. There was a group of people who wanted me to challenge the mayor of Grosse Pointe Park ten years ago or so. It was a bunch of guys, Little League fathers . . . They had a committee and everything, but I backed out. My wife didn't want me to do it.

[Jane] and I were a partnership in 95 percent of everything. She didn't like the real estate; she thought tenants were taking advantage of me.

We were making money, but I was too nice to people as a landlord.

I paid my bills and paid down debt. I had no financial trouble, none at all. I had loans and so on, but I moved money back and forth between properties as I had to. If I was doing some rehab on one, I'd do that or take out a loan.

I started buying properties when I was seventeen. I bought it on my own, but my dad facilitated it. This guy had bought a house for his daughter and her husband, and when the husband left, my dad handled the divorce. It was on Cadieux, and I bought it for $1,000, rented it out. I've been able to buy properties for very *little down. I know how to use the appraisal to work with the bank.*

A few years later I bought some more properties. First I had a restaurant, and I wasn't making any money. I was married to Priscilla for a year, and that sidetracked me for a bit. You have to focus. Once I married Jane, we bought a duplex in St. Clair Shores, three or four years later. I bought that to diversify from a Little League buddy; he gave me a good deal. It needed a lot of work. It was built in 1915. In the summer of 2012 I was going to dedicate it and name it after my father, the George Bashara Building.

We lived on Alger in St. Clair Shores before we moved to Middlesex. We were there three years then had Robert. The people in the house on Middlesex were in a divorce. We had dual incomes, and Jane had a very good job.

I used my tenants to work for me for over twenty years. I gave over a dozen people a chance to work for me and supplement their living or make a living and help me on my houses.

Me: *Did you guys take vacations much?*

Bob Bashara: *I won trips through my company. Our best was having a four-day cruise out of Nice, France, to the Riviera. Her and I and another couple went to Florence and Venice for five days. Then in September, Jane and I and another couple went to Hawaii for ten days. We flew to L.A., then to Honolulu and stayed at* *the house of the couple's brother for three days, then Jane and I took a time-share for the rest of the week. Jane loved to travel; I was never a big vacationer. I wanted to get home; she could have stayed for three weeks. People say, "You were rich," but we worked very hard. We had a great life and a great relationship. My mortgage was $3,200 a month.*

Everything will be made crystal clear, and people will say it all makes sense. My hope is that I can get to boot camp and then serve ninety days and get out on parole. They have this truth in sentencing law that took away good points, which got them out on early release. Now 90 percent of people get flopped and don't get out. It's a business.

The alternative lifestyle had nothing to do with this.

They picked me up in Jackson. Now I'm here.

I had to put my dog to sleep two months after Jane was killed. He had bloating and we had to put him down. It was a terrible day.

(On Joe Gentz) You're dealing with a guy who is not mentally stable. He totally used me for his own game. Whatever happened or transpired between he and my wife, he so overreacted that he killed [her].

I have nothing to hide in my life. I have nothing to be ashamed of in my life. They've made this lifestyle a big deal; they've made it an issue. It's been put on the table. I have to at least explain what was going on. They brought in Rachel, Janet who I knew for two months,

Venita. They even brought Bob (Robert Godard) *in and said I exposed him to the lifestyle. Well, he wanted to learn about it.*

This is my life we're talking about, and 95 percent of everything they have is bullshit. They're using the fact that I had this alternative lifestyle as a motive for me wanting to harm my wife. My wife was not inhibiting me. If I didn't want to have Jane, I would have simply divorced her. But I had plenty of income. Money was never an issue. I was paying for two kids going to college. Both of them had cars, whatever they wanted. If Jessie wanted a $500 pair of boots, Jane got them for her. I was raised that if I wanted something, my parents went and got it for me. Jane never had that. They didn't have the means. My dad had good means.

Belonging to the country club, it was a great club. Jane and I, after a while, decided we needed to tighten belts.

I played golf; both of us did. I had a handicap of 14 or 15. In my heyday I golfed two or three times a week both for pleasure and business. Jane and I played nine holes once a week, and we played in a couples league that I ran. I was also in the nine hole men's league that I ran. I did so much for so many people. You think the media sees that? No, never.

Jane and I raised money over fifteen years when our kids were here. We did wine tastings, fairs, so many things to bring the community together. The principal gave me the honorary title of mayor at Trombly Elementary. Jean

*Rusing. I did a fund-raiser December 16 and 17 (2011)
for the church and brought in $28,000, right before this
all happened.*

*Even in the lifestyle, I was in it to help the women. They
were struggling. Jane didn't have a take on it; she didn't
want to know about it. I did my thing, she did hers, and
she gave me the freedom to do what I want.*

14

"This Is One of the Most
Unusual Cases I've Ever Had"

The second week of September 2013 came in with record high temperatures, hitting 96 degrees on a swampy Tuesday at a time when Michiganders are often embracing the first waves of fall.

The sun baked the sidewalks outside the Frank Murphy Hall of Justice in downtown Detroit, where satellite trucks lined up on nearby Gratiot Avenue to ensure the metro area heard every sordid detail of the state's first-degree murder case against Bob Bashara.

It wasn't even a trial, although Bashara was already serving the first of his six-and-a-half-to-eleven-year sentence for soliciting the murder of Joe Gentz, the man who had confessed to police that he killed Jane Bashara.

"I would hope someone could understand how a man would want to kill the guy who killed his wife," Bashara says.

Rather, the media jam-up was for the preliminary examination, a unique process required in Michigan in which the state has to produce enough evidence to prove it has a case against the defendant.

In Bashara's case, it served as a de facto trial, a trail of people, some cowed and threatened by prosecutors with jail if they refused to cooperate, who went downtown to seal his fate.

It was a five-day parade of Bashara's accusers that for him played out like a nightmare version of *This Is Your Life*, the popular television show from the fifties in which a subject meets by surprise with characters from his or her past. But in the show, these were valuable and trusted friends, mentors, colleagues, and the like.

In this case, the plot of the show had changed.

Loved ones from Bashara's past—including his own mother and daughter, Jessica—were now archenemies bent on seeing him sent to prison for the rest of his life.

"My mother's wedding ring went missing shortly before she was killed," Jessica said under questioning. It was a gold band with a single diamond in the center. "We found it shortly after she died. My dad said it must have been uncovered during the search."

She was implying, knowingly or not, that her own father had stolen a $7,000 ring.

Jessica was a twenty-one-year-old college junior at the University of Michigan in Ann Arbor. She was working an internship at DTE Energy in Ann Arbor, a publicly traded provider of energy for residential and commercial clients.

Jessica was her mother's girl in so many ways, and working for DTE, which had purchased Edison, where Jane spent almost thirty years as a manager, was one more tribute to her mother.

As concerns her father, Jessica was now a damaged, vengeful witness.

She was coached by the prosecution and willing to tell about her occasions of accidentally finding her father watching porn and discovering disturbing text messages on her dad's phone.

"I caught him using a website, alt.com, and viewing pornography multiple times," she said during the hearing. It created problems after Jessica told her mother because "she thought he had quit using it."

She also described how she found an outgoing text message on her father's phone that read, "get on your knees and give me head, bitch."

"I showed my father the text message and asked him what it was. He asked to look at [the] phone, deleted the message, handed it back, and said there were no messages like that on his phone."

Bob Bashara, sitting twenty feet away, dropped his jaw slightly and stared at his daughter. He had sent her a birthday card just a few months before, but since he was arrested, Jessica had never visited him in prison and he received no responses to his letters.

Bashara arrived each day, ankles in shackles, wearing a short-sleeved military green smock and pants—as the garb looked more like hospital wear than prison garments; from the waist up, he looked like he was ready to work in the operating room rather than listen to a litany of his own bad behavior until you saw the "Wayne County Jail Prisoner" emblazoned on the back. To cap off the look, Bashara wore plastic puke green sandals with no socks.

The shackles gave him a doddering walk, and he was naturally stooped, a bad back affliction that had grown worse as his six-foot-four-inch frame aged. He had lost fifty-five pounds since being in prison, and his newly svelte shape was flattering, but Bashara, with thinning hair askew and a pasty, pockmarked complexion, was destined to look older than his fifty-five years.

Jessica's twenty-seven minutes on the stand was a torturous affair for him, but the bad dream kept rolling.

Rachel Gillett, his former lover, told the world that Bob Bashara could not achieve an erection.

Tibaudo, the man Bashara asked to help him put out a hit on Joe Gentz, called him crazy.

Nancy Bashara, his seventy-nine-year-old mother, told the court that she found a gun that belonged to her son in a bank safe-deposit box, contrary to what Bashara had told the media.

The weapon, which had been held for over a year by Bashara's first lawyer, David Griem, was retrieved shortly before the hearing by law enforcement.

The prosecution called twenty-one witnesses to the stand over five days in order to ensure the trial moved forward.

If the district attorney's office failed to convince Judge Kenneth King that it had a strong case, it risked having the whole thing thrown out.

Bob's friend through the lifestyle, Rick Falcinelli, told the court that Bashara had asked him to set up a new identity on his behalf on a BDSM website in the summer of 2012, while Bashara was in jail.

The eye candy of the day was Janet Leehmann, the Portland, Oregon, woman that Rachel and Bob were hoping to begin their new threesome life together with. Leehmann, her hair dyed white and stylish black-framed glasses parked on the bridge of her nose, took the stand wearing a tight, short red dress, with a black suit coat, bright red fingernail polish, a silver ring with an "O" on it on her left hand, first digit, and a gold ring on her right ring finger.

She told of Bob's visit to her home in Bend, Oregon, and how awkward it was. They didn't have sex because, she said, "it doesn't work." The few spectators in the courtroom gallery wore puzzled looks at her referral to Bashara's impotence.

Even Bashara's prison mates got into the testimony. Larry Ellington, who shared a cell with Bashara at Oaks Correctional Facility, told the court that Bashara asked him about having Gentz and two others killed.

Once, he said, a jailhouse card game was disrupted when Bashara got angry and called Ellington "Buckwheat" in reference to the character on the popular *Little Rascals* films from the pre–World War II era.

Ellington understandably took it poorly.

Bashara did himself no favors, making faces and what

he thought were subtle gestures. When Falcinelli took the stand, Bashara winked at him, as in a "Hey, pal" gesture.

Bob smiled at Rachel Gillett, clad in a modest blue blouse and white skirt, as she sat on the stand. He nodded yes when she said something he liked. He frowned when she said something that could incriminate him. He was again Master Bob, if for only a brief moment.

"I knew what he was doing," Gillett says. "He was right in front of me; he was using body language."

As day four began with Gillett on the stand, Judge King started out with a statement.

"I want to point out that I have seen what may appear to be, and I say may appear to be, nonverbal communication from the defendant to the witness, things like hand over heart type of deal," King said. "I just say appear. I want to caution there is going to be no such thing tolerated in this courtroom."

Bashara attempted to respond.

"Yes, sir, I have skin rash on my chest and it itches," he said.

"Again, there is to be no nonverbal communication with this witness or any witness or you will be removed from the courtroom," King said, not buying it.

"Yes, sir," Bashara said, looking down.

On the Saturday after the hearing, Bashara called me.

"There were so many lies in that hearing I needed hip waders," Bashara said, mangling the deep bullshit metaphor. "This is a conspiracy against me. My mom, my children, my cousin, my aunt. It was unbelievable, people lying under oath. The guy giving me cocaine? Absolutely false."

Why would they collectively gather to create a big lie? I asked.

"People all have different reasons," he said. "I'm not going to go into that."

Ellington, his cellie, for example: "That was a made-up bullshit thing."

Bashara talked about how good it was to see some of the people, including his daughter and his mom.

And Rachel, well, he felt sorry for her.

"She's really put on some weight. She doesn't look good," he said. "But if you talk to her, tell her I said, 'Hi.'"

The parade of witnesses delivered impactful statements that made Bashara into a monster.

Judge King likened the entire episode, from the alleged arranging of the murder of Jane to the various players and other moving parts, to a movie and noted the abundance of witnesses, many pulled from the ranks of lowlifes and scum that peopled the world of Bashara.

"This is way too bizarre," King said. "After hearing all the evidence, we probably could have just skipped the exam and gone straight to trial. There's been overwhelming evidence to substantiate each of the charges. This is one of the most unusual cases I've ever had because of the bizarre things surrounding this case."

There would be a trial, although most people had already convicted Bashara over those five autumn days.

"Mr. Bashara, get your hand off your hip," blared Judge Vonda Evans as he stood in her courtroom. He was watching an animated conversation between the judge and his most recent lawyer, Mark Procida. He was initially supported with two other lawyers, but one had dropped out.

It was January 2014, and the system was falling apart. As Bashara's fortunes had fallen, his money taken away by family and the legal system, his legal representation changed to Procida, a court-appointed veteran.

And now Bashara was in the courtroom with Procida trying to sort out what kind of representation he would have for the trial, which was scheduled for March.

Evans turned to Bashara.

"How many times have you seen Mr. Procida?" since December 9, his last hearing.

"I've seen Mr. Procida one time," Bashara said.

"I'm not happy," Evans said to Procida. "This is a very big case. Either you're going to do this efficiently, or you're not going to do it. I know the defendant doesn't want to hear this, but if there's a conviction, there's a good issue for ineffective counsel. He has to have the level of representation afforded to him under the Constitution."

Evans asked Bashara to give her a list of attorney candidates. He'd already tried a local whiz, David Cripps, who asked for $90,000 just to take the case. It already looked to be a lengthy trial, and evidence was still coming in. The state was not going to rest on the laurels of Gentz.

So Evans floated the idea of appointing a team at the federal rate of $125 an hour with the cap of $200,000.

Both sums were paltry in the free market, where decent defense attorneys can get $500 an hour.

Michigan is one of the few states in the U.S. where the

county has to pay the full amount for court-appointed defense lawyers. Wayne County ranks among the lowest in the state for payment to appointed lawyers. Further, the deck was stacked in favor of the power Wayne County prosecutor's office.

In February, Evans announced she had made an arrangement with Cripps to take the case for the federal rate, along with two co-counselors.

The trial was tentatively moved to summer.

In March, Cripps was removed from the case. Another local defender, Lillian Diallo, was added.

Diallo officed in downtown Detroit on Cadillac Square. She stayed close to the Wayne County courts, where for fifteen years she almost exclusively represented bad dudes and dudettes, often appointed and sometimes retained. Diallo advertised herself as the go-to for folks who are facing some hard time.

"If you've been accused or charged with a state or federal criminal offense, the clock is ticking," her foreboding website message read. "Every day you wait, the greater your exposure to a criminal conviction. Make no mistake about it: the police and prosecutors aren't waiting. They're preparing to convict you."

She listed, without naming the defendant, a series of cases in which she had succeeded in keeping the accused out of jail. Cases included murder dismissals and not guilty verdicts.

In an April hearing, still trying to resolve the issue of Bashara's defense, Evans declared that she was having a hard time finding a solid team for him.

"Are you all right?" she asked Bashara. He had stood by and watched the parade of conversation about who would take his life in their hands, a life he found was now worth about $200,000.

"No, I'm not all right, your honor. This is ridiculous," he replied.

A week later, Michael McCarthy was named to the case, joining Diallo.

"Mr. McCarthy has been a lawyer for over thirty years," Evans told Bashara after announcing McCarthy's appointment. "He's done a lot of high-profile cases, more or less in Oakland County. You will be very satisfied with his representation as I know you have been with Miss Diallo's. I want you to know he is more than capable and more than willing to take your case."

McCarthy was just finishing his representation of a young man named Mitchell Young who had earned himself as much public outrage as Bashara.

Young entered the home of a suburban couple in April 2012, accompanied by one of the couple's sons, and clubbed the father to death with a baseball bat and severely beat his wife and another son. It was unwinnable in a county that prides itself on having little patience with the violence of its southern cousin county; McCarthy produced no defense witnesses, instead offering that his client was responding to threats from his partner in the crime. The jury didn't buy it and took ninety minutes to convict him of first-degree murder.

After the trial, Young followed the lead of millions of guilty killers and blamed his defense.

Bashara was a fresh start. McCarthy knew his father. At least that was something.

Diallo and McCarthy would take it from there, heading into a trial on October 7, 2014.

The delay gave more and more time to the state, which kept its team busy as the months wore on. More witnesses, more tests, more statements; the bumbling system was a godsend to the prosecution.

Of course the state always has the edge. Actually, it has the entire ledge, as the imbalance in a criminal case is an obstacle from the outset.

The accused is not the government, and he or she has no endless supply of money to build a case. The power, as always, begins and ends with the government.

But the delay was creating a dearth of news regarding the lurid Bashara case. The circus of the September hearings left a news gap where bondage and murder should be.

Katie Koppin ran into the circus sensationalism of the local media when she granted an interview to WDIV, the NBC affiliate. Koppin visited Bashara when she could, as it was her line of work—she was a prison chaplain. WDIV personality Hank Winchester, who had done the best hard news work in the case early on, teased the interview as "a new woman in Bob Bashara's life?" which mortified Koppin, a twenty-eight-year-old woman who was a more regular visitor to three female convicts in another prison.

"I was horrified to see how Hank twisted things, especially in the teasers," Koppin says. "It was my own fault for trusting him that he would do the story how he said he would, but I think those who know me will not be swayed. Shame on me for trusting him."

Detroit television was caught in sweeps, and without a trial that it was sure it could elevate to ratings nirvana, it had to take what it could get. Anything Bashara was fair game.

Koppin was lucky to be on the outside, though. Inside, a number of witnesses complained of being bullied by the prosecution, including Rachel Gillett, who was treated more like a criminal than someone who could help prosecutors nail down the case.

"Lisa Lindsey would scream at me if I didn't follow the prosecution line that said it was the lifestyle that led to the murder," Gillett says.

Two weeks before the trial was to begin, Leehmann went to the circuit court in Deschutes County, Oregon, where she lived, and filed a motion to quash her subpoena to testify.

"Prior to her testimony at the preliminary hearing, she was informed by Lisa Lindsey, prosecuting attorney for Wayne County, that the State would work to keep Ms. Leehmann's sexual interests out of the preliminary hearing," Leehmann's petition read. "While testifying, under oath, the State brought to the attention of everyone the type of sexual relationship Ms. Leehmann had with Robert Bashara."

Since the murder of Jane Bashara, Leehmann's father had died and her son was in a serious accident that resulted in broken bones. She was also working full-time and had quite simply run out of steam for the case, especially considering she would be flown into Detroit for four days to live on a $20 a day per diem, which is what the court provided.

She asked that she at least be allowed to testify via closed-circuit camera to lessen her travel time and days away from work. She also couldn't resist making public the way prosecutors had treated her in light of her sexual preferences.

"Ms. Leehmann went out of her way to assist the State of Michigan in the prosecution of this case. By doing so, she has been harassed and placed in fear of her life. She has moved as a result of these fears. The State of Michigan does not only want her to testify about what happened but the State seems bent on turning her into a sexual deviant . . . Ms. Leehmann is not a criminal, but the State insists on turning her into one."

The petition was denied.

15

Jane Was the "Golden Goose"

Almost every big trial in Detroit begins with the promise of a "media frenzy," a laughable notion given the city's depleted corporate news landscape under which billion-dollar corporations spend as little as possible on personnel and marketing to maximize their profits.

The local news promised just such a frenzy, but predictably, the first day of Bob Bashara's trial played to a half-full courtroom in the Frank Murphy Hall of Justice, on the downtown's east side.

There was no overflow, no need for closed-circuit viewing. Just seven or eight madly tweeting scribes and a couple of TV and radio reporters. Two cameras on tripods were allowed to record the opening statements, but the trial itself, in keeping with the state's rabid determination to keep the public out of the public's business, would not be allowed for transmission.

Wayne County, like its marquee city of Detroit, is plagued by scandal, avarice, and corruption. On any given day, it's not hard to find someone in the higher ranks of government carrying on in an unethical and, on occasion, illegal fashion. Even the judicial system there is not immune. In fact, if George Bashara were alive today, he would not only be anguished by the situation of his son, but also by the conduct of some of his colleagues.

As the Bashara case wound its way toward trial, Wayne County judge Wade McCree was suspended in March 2014 for hearing the child support case of a woman McCree was sleeping with. The investigation started when McCree texted a topless selfie to a court bailiff. When asked by a reporter about it, McCree said, "There is no shame in my game." He was suspended by the state supreme court but filed papers to run for reelection anyway, given the locals' tendency to reward bad behavior.

Another judge, Michigan Supreme Court justice Diane Hathaway, the daughter of a Detroit cop, was sentenced by a federal judge to one year in prison in May 2013 for working a scam in which she transferred properties out of her name to qualify to make a short sale on her $1.4 million home not far from the Bashara house in Grosse Pointe Park. Hathaway, a former Wayne County judge, was looking to ditch the $600,000 she owed on the home by pretending to be in financial trouble. Even the judge who initially heard Bashara's case, Wayne County Circuit judge Bruce Morrow, was suspended for sixty days in June 2014 after the state supreme court reviewed ten instances of misconduct from the bench (finding him guilty on eight of them), including Morrow's refusal to lock up a defendant awaiting sentencing for first-degree sexual assault on a minor, as required by law, and shaking hands with a defendant in open court.

Judge Vonda Evans, though, simply had a large personality with an attitude of rectitude. She was a social butterfly who wasn't afraid of a camera, with sometimes troubling results. Check the picture of her with rapper Young Jeezy and former Detroit City Council member and convicted felon Monica Conyers.

Jeezy, street shorthand for his real name of Jay Wayne Jenkins, has been in and out of trouble with the law for a series of offenses both social and violent, including the alleged beating of his son. Conyers was convicted in a federal case in March 2010 of bribery in a $1.2 billion transportation deal and served a thirty-seven-month sentence for bribery at a federal women's prison camp in Alderson, West Virginia.

A poor choice of company for someone charged with protecting the public. Yet, Evans presented as a devout Christian, sporting a Twitter account on which she professed primarily spiritual messages.

"When u do Gods work u don't need mans approval! Man will praise u today and crucify u tomorrow," she tweeted on April 15, shortly after she had appointed yet another attorney to the defense team.

In 2011, Evans taped a pilot for a courtroom reality show called *Domestic Justice*. The program was never picked up. Evans soldiered on with her publicity-seeking ways, holding a fiftieth birthday party two weeks before the trial at the PV Lounge, a small, tony downtown dance bar where running up a $100 bar tab gets you a booth and bottles of Moët are sold for up to $150.

Evans also had a rather significant lapse of judgment when a man convicted of sexually assaulting a minor had his bond continued after his conviction. Evans released him, with no objection from the prosecutor, as it was another six weeks before sentencing.

He fled to the streets.

But Evans's ruling conflicted with Michigan's penal code. According to state statute, "A defendant convicted of sexual assault of a minor . . . shall be detained and shall not be admitted to bail."

Evans said she was unfamiliar with the law.

Above her chamber throne is a print of the popular black-and-white Brian Forbes shot *Choices*, which shows a handgun and a dozen loose $100 bills folded together on top of a Bible.

It was into this cauldron of ineptitude that the Bashara trial waded in October 2014. The jury selection took three days, a quick one considering most of the region had at least heard of the case.

The pool of 150 called were split into three groups of 50 and questioned. They would then be broken into groups of 18 or so, and both sides would talk with them.

Each juror was given a four-page questionnaire that included queries both perfunctory—"Have you formed

any preliminary opinions about this case?"—and precise.
Jurors were asked:

- Some people have a very strong reaction to people who are not faithful to their spouses; how do you feel? If so explain.

- Do you think that most people do have a breaking point—where they could be provoked into violent behavior?

- Would a criminal defendant's participation in an open marriage or in an alternative sexual lifestyle affect your ability to determine the facts of the case brought against him in a fair and impartial manner? If so explain.

- Would knowledge of a criminal defendant's marital infidelity affect your ability to accept the legal principle that he is presumed to be innocent of the crime unless and until the prosecutor proves his guilt beyond a reasonable doubt? If so explain.

The legal teams introduced themselves and ran through the list of witnesses, including Joe Gentz, law enforcement officers and agents, and friends and family of both Jane and Bob.

The names of the witnesses were read off, and jurors were asked to call out if they knew any of them. One juror stood up, then another and another. Next came the standard questions: Have you ever served on a jury? Was it civil or criminal? Have you ever been convicted of a felony?

With that, another juror walked—she had a robbery rap.

Another question came, loaded considering the location was the nation's most violent city: Have you or anyone you know ever been a victim of a violent crime? It elicited a litany of street crime. Two women said they had been raped, one man had been carjacked, and another had been mugged. One person's cousin had been murdered. Another's mother had been killed. It was a tough city and a hard place to find someone who hadn't been touched by crime. Still another began to cry at the question, as she explained her cousin was murdered by her husband.

They were all dismissed with a "Thank you" from Judge Evans.

A guy said he was with a religious order. "Thank you."

One said he heard a lot about the case from the media and could not be impartial. No one had to ask which side he was on. "Thank you."

Despite the drama, the jury was seated in three days, a relatively quick process for such a well-documented case.

The demographic breakdown for the panel of sixteen— which would be broken down to twelve for deliberation, at the conclusion of the trial—was six white males, five black males, four black females, and one white woman. It was the defense's jury, with just one white female, who could possibly relate to Jane Bashara, especially given her upper forties age range.

* * *

A look at the witness list indicated something was not quite right, though. Joe Gentz was listed as a witness for the defense, and he was scheduled to testify on day one of the trial.

It was easy to see why the defense would be eager to put Gentz on the stand. He was the one who pointed the finger at Bashara with five or six different versions of the murder. Was there a gun? He said there was at one point, then at another he avoided giving a direct answer. Who let him in the house? Where did he murder Jane?

You could see the victory dance by McCarthy and Diallo on that first night of testimony.

But on October 10, four days before the opening arguments were to be delivered and Gentz was to be sworn in, he declared he wanted a better deal in exchange for his testimony.

He had been schooled by some of his new associates in prison, and they told him he could get a better deal. He should be getting a reduced sentence if he's going to get up there, they told him.

He'd seen his lawyer John Holler III seven times in the preceding months, and each time, Holler saw Gentz constructing a new reality, one in which he would go free soon. Gentz feared Bashara, he told Holler, and wanted to be out of prison now that Bashara was in. He was told by his jailhouse lawyers that he should demand reduced time up front in exchange for his testimony.

"If you choose not to testify, the plea deal can be rescinded," he told Gentz. "It goes away."

"I won't testify unless they give me a promise," Gentz told him.

On prison visits from his brother, Kevin, Joe Gentz said the same thing.

"These guys don't know the law," Kevin said. "Just go with the deal you got."

But the deal was that he would be charged with second-degree murder rather than first on the condition that he tell jurors exactly what he told investigators. And what his prison pals didn't tell him is that by vacating his plea deal, prosecutors could charge him with first-degree murder, negating the gift of his seventeen to twenty-eight years.

But Gentz had some bargaining heft, and even some legal wiggle room, thanks to the overzealousness of a local detective when he first confessed back in January 2012.

The detective was Michael Narduzzi of the Grosse Pointe Park Police, who had never before handled a murder. He was interviewing Gentz when, in response to a question from Narduzzi, Gentz abruptly said the magic words: "I want a lawyer."

The words normally and lawfully end all questioning, as they should in keeping with Miranda rights. Gentz was clearly voluntarily talking that day in January. But Miranda is there for anyone undergoing police questioning, and the detective should have walked out of the room.

Instead, Narduzzi did not, and he later admitted Gentz incriminated himself after asking for counsel.

It was one of those things that could rear its head in a filing down the line, something no one on the prosecution side would want to chance. Gentz had an advantage, despite what his lawyer felt was a stupid move.

It would not be the last time Narduzzi's inexperience with murder would become an impediment to the case. He was doing his best, but the leap from the minors to the major leagues can humble even the most ambitious players. And he was about to get a big dose of humble.

Investigators were still seething about the announcement that Bashara was a suspect three days after the murder by Grosse Pointe Park chief David Hiller. Basic cop procedure, as well as common sense, says you don't tip off your quarry like that.

Maybe Gentz's jailhouse lawyers were onto something. Gentz was struck from the witness list. He'd be sitting this one out. And be dealt with later.

The eighth-floor courtroom was half full on opening day, its four wooden pews mostly occupied by numerous local media, several of whom had followed the case since Jane was found dead.

During her forty-five-minute opening statement, assistant prosecutor Lisa Lindsey at one point walked behind Bashara, who was seated between his lawyers, Lillian Diallo and Michael McCarthy.

"He knew exactly what happened to his wife," Lindsey said, her hair in a ball the size of a softball on the top of her head, adding some height to her five-foot-nothing frame, clad in a black double-breasted blouse and skirt.

"He told two people that this was the last Christmas with his wife on Middlesex."

She used a video presentation of TV interviews Bashara did to show conflicting statements Bashara had made regarding the extent of his acquaintance with Joe Gentz; in one he says Gentz had never met Jane although he went by Middlesex to do some work in the backyard. In another clip, he tells a reporter that Jane had brought him and Gentz some iced tea as they worked in the backyard to prepare it for winter.

At one point during Lindsey's presentation, Diallo tenderly put her hand on Bashara's back. It was a reassuring gesture, some human warmth in a place that was feeling very cold to Bashara.

Lindsey continued to wind through the witnesses she planned to call and what they would tell the jurors, and she flashed a photo of Bashara and Rachel Gillett on the wide screen, both of them beaming, a couple happy to be together.

Diallo began by repeating what Bashara had stated to several people over the past year.

"This is the day Mr. Bashara has been waiting for," she said. He would finally get a chance to tell his version of the story. She said straight up that Gentz was the confessed killer of Jane Bashara, which was why he was in prison serving a seventeen-to-twenty-eight-year sentence.

Diallo then brought up the BDSM lifestyle, which Lindsey continued to push as a motive for the murder, for Bashara forcing Gentz to kill Jane at gunpoint.

"This lifestyle had nothing to do with a homicide,"

Diallo said simply. As for the attempt to have Gentz killed in prison, Diallo said it was not to prevent him from testifying against Bashara, but "this was the confessed murderer of his wife of twenty-six years."

"You are never going to hear Bob Bashara say to anyone, 'I want my wife killed,'" Diallo said, coming down hard on the last word of the sentence so it sounded like a thud.

It was a brief opening, fifteen minutes. The burden was on the prosecution; there was no reason to drag it out. Her point was simple—Bob Bashara did not cause the death of his wife.

A witness list of 300 people betrays a long and often arduous trial. It means there is plenty of room for redundant testimony in an attempt to drive home a message on one side or the other.

Without Gentz to spell out exactly what the prosecution wanted to put across, Lindsey and Moran were bent on pushing both aberrant sex and a desire to be with another woman as the pure motive. The conspiracy and the witness tampering were also-rans in the charges. They needed the murder charge to stick.

The defense had to ensure witnesses had no credibility. That would be difficult with family members on both sides, as they both held their hearts in their hands. Both families were emotionally crippled by the murder.

The people who would talk of the conspiracy were another matter. Some of them were surviving on disability, some lived life on another margin, and others were just plain rough around the edges, and in the middle, too, for that matter.

There is that moment at the break of an anticipated event that crackles with excitement. It starts maybe with the first punch of a schoolyard fight, where two kids are settling a score. It's also the first pitch of a baseball game, the staging lights at a drag race or the gun starting a long running competition.

The crackle was there for the opening witness at 2:12 P.M. on October 14.

Enter Robert Godard, an employee of a local school district. Godard took the witness stand and looked at Bashara through tinted glasses and a bemused expression. Squat and muscular, he wore a black short-sleeved polo shirt that showed off thick forearms and spoke in a deep voice.

Immediately, assistant prosecutor Lindsey led him into the lifestyle. And just as immediately, Diallo objected for the defense, claiming the lifestyle was irrelevant.

Judge Evans overruled her, making it clear that sex was going to be part of the proceedings.

Godard said that he'd known Bashara for eighteen years and that he got turned on to the BDSM scene through Bashara "quite a few years ago."

"What is it? What is the BDSM?" Evans asked.

"Heh, good question. It's very hard to explain," Godard said.

"Does that stand for bondage, discipline, and sadomasochism?" Lindsey asked.

"Yes," Godard said.

"Do you have people defined as submissive people and dominant people?" Lindsey said.

"Yes," he replied.

Godard said that Bashara was open about his relationship with Gillett and told him she was his slave and was going to be his new girl.

He then was asked about a 2011 lunch with Bashara at which he was asked if he knew anyone who could "rough up" a tenant Bashara was having trouble with.

"I told him 'no,' that I didn't know anyone," Godard said.

"How about Jane? How did she and Bashara get along?"

"They were not doing well as a couple," Godard said. "Bob was a little upset that his wife would not participate in the lifestyle.

"After his kids were out of school, he was going to leave her and make his life with Rachel," Godard said. "There was a house they were going to be purchasing somewhere in Grosse Pointe, and they were going to make a life together and live in that house."

On cross-examination, Diallo noted that Godard had golfed with Bob and Jane as recently as 2011, the year before Jane's death, showing that they were a couple and acting as such.

Godard said, under questioning, that he also attended Jessica Bashara's high school graduation in 2010.

It was an effort to humanize Bashara in the face of a lifestyle that was foreign to the jurors. She had no way to dance around Bashara's alleged query regarding the beating of a problem tenant.

So it would go, over and over: Bashara soliciting a beating for someone. Bashara with Gillett, planning to buy a new house together. Bashara bad.

The witness parade kept coming, a barrage of testimony talking of adultery, deceit, and thuggery all capped with heartbreaking stories of the night Jane disappeared turning into the morning Jane was found dead.

It was only day two when the crime scene photos were shown, Jane's bruised face and twisted body lodged in the backseat of her vehicle.

One cop, Detroit Police Department investigator Donald Olsen, said he went to Middlesex at 10:45 A.M. on January 25 to tell the family that Jane's body had been found.

Olsen said it was ten minutes before Bashara asked what happened to his wife.

Lindsey stopped him there and on the video screen showed a tape of Bashara describing to a journalist his reaction to being told Jane was dead.

"I fell to my knees," Bashara told the NBC reporter in 2012.

"Did you see him fall to his knees?" Lindsey asked.

"Not that I saw," Olsen said.

After the first week of trial, Diallo turned to Bashara as they wrapped for the day.

"I don't think the jury likes you," she said. "I can see it in their eyes."

Paul Monroe, a former tenant of Bashara's, was a reluctant witness. The longtime convict stayed away from cops the best he could, a smart move for a guy who moves some blow once in a while.

He took the stand and told jurors that he sold two ounces of cocaine to his former landlord, who did finger bumps and confessed to him that he had his wife killed. Monroe sat in the witness chair and barely budged.

He'd testified in the preliminary hearing a year before that he gave the cocaine to Bashara. No one gives someone cocaine, except maybe in Hollywood and the music industry, and even then there are going to be some tentacles down the line.

"Did you sell it or give it?" McCarthy asked Monroe during cross-examination. Monroe didn't budge but simply said he didn't understand the question. Monroe was a pro at handling questioners trying to corner him.

Some people could flash back to the preliminary hearing when defense attorney Mark Procida questioned why he would give cocaine to Bashara.

"Sometimes people do that," Monroe had said.

Now, Monroe said he was being straight because "it's best to be open" and, since then, God told him to tell the truth.

"Or is it because you've been assured that this is a murder case and not a drug case?" McCarthy asked.

Monroe went on to tell the jury how Bashara paid him $89 and promised to fix $11,000 in parking tickets for him if he would call in a fake tip. To make the bogus and illegal call more enticing to Monroe, Bashara suggested he implicate his ex-girlfriend, April Montgomery, and the man she left him for, Charles Wilson.

Monroe made a number of calls.

"You knew for a fact that wasn't true," McCarthy said.

"It was dishonest," Monroe said.

"It was dishonest . . . You were lying."

"Of course."

"Your word is questionable, correct?"

"Yes."

Phone records, though, connected Monroe and Bashara on the day of the alleged cocaine transaction. And why would those two ever talk, the jury was left to ponder.

Monroe was followed as a witness by Julie Rowe, Jane's youngest sister, who almost stormed to the stand. Rowe was blamed by Bashara and some of his relatives for the divide between the families. Rowe was in her mid-forties and immediately a feisty witness with her mocking of Bashara when he called her to tell her Jane was missing.

"What do you mean she's missing?" Rowe recounted saying. "Did you have a fight?"

After Jane's body was found, Bashara called her back.

"They killed our Jane," Rowe repeated Bashara as saying, drawing the words out in a tasteless, angry parody.

While Rowe had been interviewed twice by police during the investigations, she never mentioned that there were any problems in the marriage.

But now, Rowe testified that Jane was unhappy with her life and had pondered then dismissed the idea of splitting with Bashara.

"She said that if she got a divorce, she would lose her house, at least half her 401(k), end up a fifty-five-year-old single woman living in a condo with no retirement, no savings, and bad credit," Rowe said.

After looking over transcripts of her interviews with police, Diallo said, "You've never said anything about this [divorce] until today."

"I had dozens of conversations with a multitude of law enforcement agents," Rowe said. "I don't recall who I told what to."

But she had never told anyone about Jane's fears of divorce until that day.

As Lindsey tried to salvage the situation, she then said the divorce speculation had been revealed in an interview between Rowe and prosecutors a few days before; again, that was news to Diallo, who should have been apprised of the new turn as part of evidence.

The kids testified on October 23, day four of the trial. Their statements were neither incendiary nor particularly illuminating or damning in themselves. But the fact that they took the stand and talked, albeit under subpoena, spoke to the shunning of the defendant.

Both said that their father denied having an affair, and Jessica said, "My father only gave more information in response to me finding out new information."

He was incredibly frank with his daughter, she said. When she discovered he was surfing pornography on the Web, she says, "He told me that he was on pornographic websites because he had been experiencing erectile dysfunction and he wanted to know if the problem was with him or my mother."

While she refused to return her father's beseeching look from the defense table, Jessica gave him some emotional leeway.

"He did see [my mother] as being very critical of him. Overly critical. I believe it was in respect to work as a salesman and with the rental properties."

Rob Bashara was less composed than his sister. Clad in black dress pants and a white dress shirt, he grasped the fingers of his right hand with his left—known as an "anxiety hold" in some shrink circles—as he listened to the prosecution play back a recording of a jailhouse visit with his father shortly after Bashara's arrest.

"I want to tell you I need your and Jessie's support," Bashara told his son.

Rob is clearly uninterested on the recording, mumbling a tentative "yea."

"Even Aunt Gramma and Aunt Julie," Bashara said.

Several other recorded clips were played, all revolving around Bashara urging his son to help rally support and bring both families together to help him.

As for the money that was derived from Jane's death, Rob Bashara said he received the proceeds from a life insurance policy on Jane for $90,000. He said he distributed the money: $15,000 to himself, $20,000 to his sister, and, at his father's request, $55,000 to his grandmother.

Jane's 401(k), which had $794,535 in it at the end of 2011, had not yet been distributed.

He sounded clearly dispassionate talking about the money.

Like Jessica, he sounded simply unhappy when he said Jane and Bob were in counseling for a troubled marriage.

A little over three weeks into the trial, Bashara keeled over in his jail cell while pulling on his dress socks for his court appearance.

He was found on the floor, disoriented. He said his right kidney was hurting him. It landed him in the hospital for an examination, too sick to attend his trial for three days.

Bashara, clutching a now familiar brown accordion file and a just as familiar black suit and tie, limped tenderly when he returned to the courtroom.

"How are you feeling?" Judge Evans asked.

"Uh, I'm ok your honor."

"If there's anything you need, or you need to take a break, you tell me," she said.

Back after a five-day break, jurors were treated to an hour of Steve Tibaudo singing to the radio, pet talking to his dog, and farting, thanks to the wire he was wearing to record Bashara soliciting the murder of Gentz. Judge Evans wanted the whole thing played for the jury.

In other parts of the lengthy recording, Bob urges Tibaudo, who keeps saying he is having stomach problems, to get his gallbladder removed.

"You don't need it for anything," Bashara says. "You gotta get that thing out."

The two carried on with verbal jousts, then dropped their voices when the hit on Gentz came up. The recording captured Bashara catching Tibaudo calling Detective Matouk on the phone.

"I'm calling a broad here," Tibaudo explained. He made up a name, Timmy Mac, to explain the entry of Matouk in his phone.

On cross-exam, Diallo hammered Tibaudo with thinly veiled dislike.

"Are you the go-to guy to have someone taken care of?" she asked.

"No."

"Did he ask you to go kill his wife?"

"No."

Diallo asked if he had introduced Bashara to Gentz, who once worked for Tibaudo.

"Yes."

"Did you know he was a homicidal maniac?"

In the very next breath, Diallo apologized up and down to the judge.

"I am so sorry, so sorry," she said, halfway sincere but obviously pleased her message got out there.

Judge Evans had the outburst struck, but the jurors heard it, which was the intent.

It took a while, but the first hearty, credible punch to Bashara's contention of innocence, came from a fiftyish real estate agent named Kathy Young, who spoke with a smoker's throat and an air of certainty.

It was the twelfth day of testimony, and jurors had yet to hear a solid, unchallenged statement or detail that would place motive squarely on Bashara.

Young's story was solid. In August 2011, Rachel Gillett

and Bashara met with Young to go over a list of possible homes for purchase.

They didn't represent themselves as boyfriend-girlfriend, she said, but they were certainly making the buy as a couple.

They put in an offer on one house, which was bought before they could get much done. A second house, a small, modern wood-frame house, was exactly what they were looking for, and Bob gave her a $2,500 personal check as earnest money, which would go toward the purchase if the inspection went alright.

Bob and Rachel were walking through the house, on Bishop Road, about two miles from the Middlesex home. "There was a room in the basement of the house on Bishop," Young said. "When we opened the door, Bob said, 'This would make a great punishment room.'"

"He also mentioned to Rachel that the basement would be suitable for a dungeon," Young said, as jurors moved in their seats a bit, suddenly interested in what had started as another variation of "Bob cheated on his wife" testimony. "And they looked at one of the showers in a bathroom, and he said something about how it would fit a lot of people."

There was more. He mentioned to Young, "You seem to be a very submissive person."

"My response was, 'You don't know me very well.'"

The application to purchase, though, needed to be altered after a couple days, when Bob called.

"He asked me to remove Rachel's name because he said the Pointes is a small place and he said he was either

recently divorced or going through a divorce and didn't
need that getting out there."

In fact, she said, on several occasions, Bashara represented himself as divorced, at one point telling her he had
been divorced since July.

The house-hunting process went on, she told the jury,
into the fall. On October 1, he had a meeting scheduled
with Young to see a place at 9:45 A.M. Young was running
late, and she texted Bob.

"Make that 10:45, sorry," she wrote.

"Bitch. n.p.," he responded, meaning "no problem."

Bashara was hitting on her, BDSM-style. It didn't go
over the head of the jury.

Finally, the biggest blow to Bashara was when Young
said that he had finally agreed on the home at 1011 Kensington. The closing was set for January 27, three days after
Jane's murder.

It was an image that was hard to shake, this man telling
everyone he was divorced when he was married to a woman
who would end up dead. And the strange factor never left
the scene; the "bitch" text was blown up and projected
onto the video screens, including the main screen in the
courtroom. It jumped out in its lifestyle reference.

For the first time, Bashara glanced at McCarthy with
a touch of wild fear, looking hemmed in.

No one had stung before, but the jury stared at Young
as she testified, clearly sorting out what she was telling
them. Bashara was taking his girlfriend around, talking
about a future within the lifestyle as if there would be no

impediments. Exactly what Lindsey and Moran of the prosecution were insisting.

There had been hints, innuendo, and even some direct hits on Bashara's reputation, but Young had the goods, which took a quick turn into the weird. Young was the last witness on day twelve, and the courtroom emptied with jurors taking that lurid testimony home to chew on.

After three weeks of testimony from cops, convicts, and Grosse Pointers, Therese Giffin was a hard-looking visual departure. The lanky woman from the suburbs of Chicago was more what people would connect to anything alternative, with blaring white skin and hair dyed just as white. For her appearance she wore a purple jacket, black skirt, and thick black horn-rimmed glasses. She acknowledged that she was a devotee of the lifestyle and she had been granted immunity from charges of obstruction of justice in exchange for her testimony.

Almost immediately it was established that she gave investigators false information—hence the obstruction of justice allegation—when they caught up to her in April 2012. She claimed to be embarrassed at the time by her connection to the murder and to the lifestyle, but she also said she was asked by Bashara to give false information to David Griem, who was representing Bashara at that time.

Giffin said Bashara and Gillett were together when she met them and she sought to connect with them as a partner, sometimes communicating via her email handle of obedient_slave220@yahoo.com.

Whenever Bashara had relationship problems with Rachel, Giffin would be his shoulder to cry on, she told the jury, and he told her he loved Rachel on numerous occasions.

Her testimony devolved into a sad tale of a love triangle: Bashara in love with Rachel, Giffin longing for Bashara, and Rachel trying to rid herself of anyone connected to the whole mess by moving to an undisclosed place.

So in love, in fact, was Giffin that she obeyed Bashara when he asked her to post erroneous information online hinting that Jane had a boyfriend.

In the weeks following Jane's murder, he was particularly attuned to a site called *The Hinky Meter*, a clearinghouse for armchair housewives-cum-detectives that opined on numerous criminal cases. In the days after Jane's murder, the site turned into a particularly vehement vocal force against Bashara, and he was afraid the cops were monitoring the site and taking it seriously.

Some of the information it was delivering was correct albeit hardly new, including the affair with Gillett and the lifestyle. But other allegations were simply posting half-baked theories on the murder implicating Bashara.

So he asked Giffin to go on there and post items "to make Jane not look so good," Giffin testified.

To do so, she created a geographically correct handle, "Across the Lake."

Giffin posted something to indicate "that [Jane] possibly had a boyfriend who could have killed her," Giffin said.

"Why would you help him?" Judge Evans asked Giffin.

"I believed he was innocent," she said.

On cross-examination, McCarthy stressed that the posting on *The Hinky Meter*, the false information she provided to David Griem "were all your decisions, right?" He was ensuring the jury knew that Bashara was not the one hinting online that his wife had a boyfriend or lying to David Griem.

It was a Band-Aid on another severe wound, though. The jury heard that Giffin, Bashara, and Gillett were all enmeshed in a somewhat dubious ethical stew of lifestyle and deceit.

Soon, the trial became known for the frequent disruptions and slow progress. There were two-hour lunch breaks, ninety-minute delays to the start of testimony, and frequent early dismissals of the jury.

Visitors went by the courtroom to watch the action and were often bored and confused by the sitting around, with both defense and prosecution filing through papers and talking while the bailiffs obediently stood around.

There were a few spectators, a sprinkling of Grosse Pointers and crime fans. Some made the eighth-floor courtroom a regular stop, arriving early and leaving late to make sure they caught all of the action.

On the morning of Monday, November 17, the prosecution waived twenty-seven witnesses, an agreeable move to push the proceedings along. Some of those were cops, some more key, including ex-mistress Venita Porter and Suzanne Bashara, Bob's stepmother.

It had been seven weeks since jury selection, and the trial showed no signs ending.

Later that day, Larry Ellington, who was Bashara's cellmate for several weeks at Oaks Correctional Facility in summer 2013, took the stand.

While his testimony was a rehash of the accusations from the preliminary hearing a little over a year before, he had an odd request: that his name and face not be used in news reports. What was odder still was that the media heeded the request.

Ellington complained that he had received threats in prison after testifying in the preliminary examination. Even in the morally challenged world of convicts, a snitch is often in for some bad times.

Assistant prosecutor Robert Moran was eager enough for Ellington's testimony to advocate for such an abridgment of the First Amendment, noting that "inmates tend to watch a lot of news."

Later, during a break, Moran was talking to Ellington and reassured him again that his name and photo would not be used, and said of the media, "If they do it, they're in big trouble."

Bashara attorney Lillian Diallo said, "I believe the name is fair game, and I think you'll have some issues down the line."

Ellington, with his identity obediently protected, told jurors a long story of his time in a cell with Bashara. The detail was impressive and showed what most everyone knew—Bob Bashara rarely shut his mouth.

Ellington said he was told about Bashara's kids, of the

"poisoning" of Jessica's mind by Julie Rowe after the murder, and that he and Jane had not had sex in several years. He also said Bashara told him he had four slaves.

"Isn't that illegal?" Ellington, who is black, said he asked, drawing laughter from the jury.

"These are women who need more guidance in life," Ellington said Bashara explained.

On cross-examination, McCarthy had Ellington explain just why he wanted to conceal his identity in giving the testimony.

"I had issues when I got back last time. I was threatened. I had a fight," Ellington explained. He was eventually transferred.

The standard line given to an inmate who offers evidence is "no promises." But McCarthy pointed out that down the line he can present a letter from prosecutor Moran showing that he cooperated when asking for parole or a sentence reduction. McCarthy also noted that when Ellington was cellmates with Bashara, both were level four offenders, the second highest one can get in terms of oversight.

Today, McCarthy noted, Ellington was a level two offender in a lower level prison.

Steve Virgona knew Joe Gentz for fifteen years before losing track of him in the eighties and nineties when Gentz moved around the country, serving time as a ship hand in the Gulf of Mexico and working some menial jobs in Maryland while married to a local girl.

The two reconnected in the early 2000s in the Detroit area and became friends in 2010 when their daughters attended the same school. They would meet, with several others, at local eateries for coffee and talk.

Virgona told the court the story in a cool, moderate, "I've been here before" voice. He was nicely turned out, with a tie and a well-groomed mustache. He also looked like a cop.

He recounted a period of months before the murder, in the fall of 2011, about the same time Gentz was moving to a new apartment on Wayburn in Grosse Pointe Park, which Bashara had arranged.

The two met at a McDonald's in Detroit, sitting in Virgona's white van. The talk turned to money, as neither was flush.

"Steve, you need some money," Gentz said.

"What for?" Virgona asked.

"You need money for your family," Gentz assured him. And he knew how he could get it: a hit-and-run on someone, for which he would be paid.

It would be worth $10,000, Gentz told him. Virgona wanted nothing to do with it, and it dropped.

A couple of weeks later, Gentz again pushed the idea. Now he floated cash, a Cadillac, maybe a truck, all in payment for the hit-and-run, in which a car he would drive would ram another, ideally injuring or killing the other driver.

Virgona moved forward, and the jury was tight, listening, focused.

In December 2011, Gentz was in Virgona's van talking with Bashara on the phone.

After Gentz hung up, he explained to Virgona, "This guy Bob wants a hit-and-run on his wife, an insurance job," Virgona related. "He wants his wife knocked off."

Bob's wife, Jane, was a CEO, Gentz told him, and she drove home via the highway and exited on Jefferson, which is the closest exit to get to the Bashara home on Middlesex. Gentz was looking for a heavy-duty vehicle to run into hers.

"Joe, this is leading to murder?" Virgona said he asked.

"Yes."

"I want nothing to do with this," Virgona said he replied.

When Jane's death was announced, Virgona said he told a colleague, "I think I know who did this."

Through the testimony, it was clear that Virgona had a front-row seat to the events leading to the murder, even though he made sure to keep his distance from his new-found old friend, who was clearly moving in the direction of committing a homicide.

It was Virgona who took Gentz into the Grosse Pointe Park police department to turn himself in, and it was Virgona who picked up Gentz when he was cut loose three days later.

But if Virgona had been told that Bashara was seeking a person to kill his wife, why did he never tell anyone?

"He knew that Joe was easily influenced," says Joanne Gentz, Joe's mother. She remains unconvinced that the Virgona version of the story is the truth.

Virgona repeated much of what Gentz had already told police about the night of the murder, the murder in the garage at Middlesex, movement of the body, and the fact that "Bob had threatened to kill him if he didn't do as he was asked."

It also appeared it was Virgona who kept calling the media, alerting them to wherever Gentz would be.

He admitted calling a local reporter before he went down to the Detroit police department in May 2012 to make a statement, ensuring he got some space in the day's media reports as the Bashara story was developing quickly.

His activity was contradictory of a claim on the witness stand during the trial that because of a leak in the Detroit Police Department he inexplicably had inside knowledge that "my life was in danger."

It was looking like Virgona was not just a friend of Gentz nor was he simply a bystander. Among his many scattered statements was his notion that he "didn't want to say too much to a police officer without a lawyer." But no one questioned him as to why, if all was as he presented it, he would need legal counsel. Was he connected to the murder?

Records show the Virgona name as the owner of a house at 19181 Annott, a block away from 19451 Annott, where Jane's body was found in the alley, and 19154 Dresden, barely a quarter mile from the alley.

Records show the Annott Avenue house had been passed around the Virgona family since the eighties. The county foreclosed on the house in 2008. While police said Gentz had grown up in the area and therefore that was the reason the body was dumped there, Gentz actually grew up in Warren, six miles north and another world away from that location.

Virgona also said he had talked about the case with detectives in Macomb County, with "people I knew," although he declined to say how he knew them when Diallo pressed him.

Virgona also said, "I put some guys away," referring to providing information to law enforcement, hinting that he may be an informant. The Detroit Police Department claimed it had no recordings of any interviews with Virgona despite his insistence that he sat down with a detective on January 31, 2012, after Gentz had turned himself in.

On cross-exam, Diallo pressed on with that, mentioning some names of people who had records of drug dealing and other crimes. Virgona said he knew nothing of any of them.

By the end of his testimony, the more alert trial watchers were convinced Virgona was either an agent of the police who was escaping a deep look because of his status as a narc or was a cop wannabe with a serious ego problem.

Either way, his credibility was weak. And no one mentioned the proximity of a house with his name on the title to the place where Jane's body was dropped.

When it came time for the defense to bring witnesses, the tank was empty. And it was the prosecution that would retain center stage.

The defense called a bartender at a place called My Dad's Place, who told jurors that Gentz and a fellow named JJ would come in and drink, but never spoke of Bashara.

Lois Valente, the ex-wife of one of Bashara's civil

attorneys who helped him with legal issues regarding property management, had known Jane for twenty-two years, and they talked. A lot.

Valente said Jane had told her in 2010 that "Bob was getting into some weird stuff," and that "he had gone to a key party in Livonia and wanted Jane to go with him."

"I asked Jane what a key party was," she said. Jane explained that it's a gathering where attendees throw their keys into a bowl and then, after all the keys are gathered and tossed around, each person draws a key and has sex with the person whose key they draw.

It was not a heavy hit, but it was titillating enough to keep the jurors listening. Valente and Jane had lunch around January 15, 2012, nine days before Jane was murdered, and Jane told her she and Bob planned to go to a time-share in the Dominican Republic in the spring.

It wasn't much of a help to the defense. There was a feeling of "that's all you've got?" to it.

But the prosecution was awaiting the defense strategy to show a flawed investigation.

In the months that turned into years after Jane's murder, the prosecutor's office and the Detroit Police Department took some public punches for the time it took to bring the Bashara case to trial. Both agencies were maligned as word of multiple mistakes was passed around in discussions of the case.

The delay in charges gave ample time for speculation as to the degree of screwups. Most fingers pointed to the Grosse Pointe Park Police Department, immersed in its first homicide in two decades.

Detective Michael Narduzzi of the Grosse Pointe Park Police took the stand. He identified himself as "co-officer in charge" of the Bashara investigation.

It became immediately apparent that he would be a target; his inexperience was assailed from the start by Lillian Diallo.

"Did you request the clothing of Jane Bashara before it was released to the funeral home?" she asked. "We have no idea today of the evidentiary value of those clothes."

Narduzzi, tall, thin, with close-cropped black-and-white hair, sitting straight, simply answered, "No, I did not."

"Can we agree that would have evidentiary value?"

"Yes."

The prosecution had contended throughout the trial that Bashara was paying Gentz a sum between $2,000 and $10,000 to kill Jane. Now the defense flashed a screen grab of Gentz's bank account showing a $5,000 deposit on January 20, 2012, four days before the murder. The check showed returned on January 24, 2012.

"That check was not from Bashara, was it?" Diallo asked.

"I don't believe so," Narduzzi said. "It came from his stepmom, Letty Gentz."

Indeed, the bad check came from Letty Gentz, who had died on the fourteenth of that month. Was this the money Gentz had told everyone he anticipated?

Diallo asked about the Mercedes in which Jane was found. The rear hatch had smears on it, as if someone had opened and closed it. But it was never checked, never printed, and never photographed.

Why was that? Diallo asked. Narduzzi said he didn't feel it had any value as evidence.

Judge Evans looked surprised.

"Why didn't you look at it?" she said.

"I'm not experienced in this, ma'am," Narduzzi said. He had been a cop for nineteen years, and this was his first murder case as officer in charge.

"Nothing like this has ever happened on your watch, has it?" Diallo asked.

"No, ma'am," he said.

She pushed on, talking about JJ, a man who often accompanied Gentz on his drinking rounds. Little was known about JJ, but a drinking buddy of the confessed slayer would surely be high on the list of people to interview.

Narduzzi said he tried to grill JJ, but he was "very paranoid," and Narduzzi couldn't get a statement from him. JJ was never served a subpoena.

"Did you get information that JJ and Gentz were together on any of the critical dates in this case?" Diallo asked.

"Yes," Narduzzi said.

"What did you do?" Judge Evans interjected. She was getting upset by the shoddy investigation that was being exposed.

"I sought him out . . . He denied all knowledge of anything," Narduzzi said.

What kind of car did JJ drive? Diallo asked.

"I don't believe I asked him that," Narduzzi said.

And so it went until it became crystal clear that Narduzzi had no business being part of a murder investigation.

Then Lisa Lindsey took over on cross-examination.

Narduzzi and another Grosse Pointe Park officer, Captain David Loch, were supposed to have led the inquiry. Narduzzi, in fact, was brought on to help Loch after the captain failed to meet a deadline to produce an investigative report to the Wayne County Prosecutor's Office. He had produced less than twenty pages of a report that should have been at least one hundred pages.

"Let's talk about the inexperience of your department," Lindsey said. "Did you ask for help?"

"No."

"You were in meetings where it was talked about to seek help from other departments—Did you do that?"

"No."

"Did we call you and Captain Loch to the prosecutor's office and did we introduce you to [Michigan State Police detectives] and tell you to get their help?"

"Yes."

"Did you fully utilize all of their services?"

"Probably not, ma'am, no."

After a couple of months, other agencies had to step in and take more responsibility when it became clear that not only were the officers from Grosse Pointe Park woefully inept, they were also reluctant to seek help from agencies with more experience.

The prosecutor's office had asked the officers to come down to their office twice a week to get some schooling on murder investigations. The officers refused.

The reason for the delay in charges was becoming apparent. Some witnesses had to be interviewed again. In some cases, the Grosse Pointe Park officers simply gave witnesses a list of twenty of the exact same written questions to answer.

Lindsey asked of Gillett's first visit to the Grosse Pointe Park police office a day after the murder. Gillett had come in early in the morning, and she was told to come back.

"I believe it was six in the morning and we got in a little later," Narduzzi explained. It was clear that despite all of his admitted screwups and ineptitude, he still didn't get it.

"I know you got to be embarrassed," Lindsey said.

It was a public flogging that would embarrass and humiliate anyone, any professional, but Narduzzi never flinched. Lindsey was clearly harboring some deep dislike for his lack of ability and refusal to take guidance.

By the time Grosse Pointe Park Police's Captain Loch took the stand, Lindsey had exhausted her anger and frustration.

Loch admitted that he'd never investigated a murder in his twenty-eight years with the department. That was apparently supposed to explain why he waited until just weeks ago, while the trial was in progress, to hand evidence to prosecutors that a forensic analysis of leaves on the socks Jane was wearing when her body was found did not match leaf material collected from the garage, where she was murdered.

Such evidence could be considered by some as vaguely exculpatory, and he'd had the evidence for at least two years.

"I made a terrible mistake in not turning that over to the prosecution team in a timely manner," Loch said. "That was my responsibility, and I clearly just dropped the ball in not turning that over in a timely fashion."

Loch also acknowledged that he failed to submit for forensic analysis the coat Jane was wearing when she was found and also waited too long to obtain security camera footage of the alley behind Bashara's Mack Avenue property, where Bashara said he was working the night of the murder.

By the time Loch thought to retrieve it, that evening's footage had been taped over as part of the re-record loop that most security camera setups have.

Lindsey mustered up enough anger to note the same tardy report she had referenced when grilling Narduzzi.

"You held on to a report for thirty days before you turned it over to the prosecution," Lindsey said, stating more than asking.

"Yes."

"That is in keeping with your pattern of not turning things over in a timely fashion."

"Yes."

Her attack was more the domain of the defense, which sought to poke holes in the case. Lindsey did a solid job of that.

She had enough confidence in what she had presented that on this last day, she could finally deliver a beating to someone whom she apparently despised. All trial long, Narduzzi and Loch sat behind the prosecution's courtroom table, fetching witnesses, carrying paper, and acting as servants. They carried out the tasks with grim faces. Could they know what was coming?

Regardless, the verbal dressing-down was their thanks.

*　*　*

Bob Bashara strode into the courtroom on December 10, 2014, and greeted his lawyer Michael McCarthy with a warm handshake and a serious look. He then turned to Lillian Diallo and smiled warmly, also shaking her hand.

He was prepared as he would ever be for the end of the trial and its closing arguments. He set his brown folder of papers down in front of him on the defense table and took his chair between his two lawyers, the same chair he had used for the entire trial, all 74 witnesses and 460 exhibits, much of which amounted to a complete degradation of the way he carried out his life.

The courtroom was jammed, every spot on the wooden benches filled with people sitting knee to knee. Among the crowd were various members of Jane's family, including her mother, who had attended infrequently because of the graphic testimony regarding her daughter's demise.

Bashara had nary a friend in the gallery.

"Every criminal conspiracy basically begins with words," Lindsey said as she began her closing argument. "The defendant created out of his words a whole other reality. This reality was different than the reality he had with Jane Bashara. It was a reality different from his financial struggles. It was a reality where he did not feel his wife was overly critical of him. It was a reality he created with his words of a man who was not emasculated, as he explained to Janet Leehmann that his wife made him feel emasculated. With his words, he named himself Master Bob and therein created another world. In this world, [he said] 'soon you will feel my strength and passion.' That's not a man who has erectile dysfunction. And when those two worlds collided, [Jane Bashara] ended up dead."

It was a masterful opening, crafted as only a seasoned prosecutor can.

Lindsey, sprinkling her presentation with Bible quotes, outlined Bashara's life in a fine house in Grosse Pointe Park, enjoying frequent vacations to sunny climates with plenty of time to devote to community activities, including service as president of the local Rotary Club.

"The other world he spent in the lifestyle with a mistress, a secretary at Wayne State University named Rachel Gillett, with whom he was 'obsessed,'" Lindsey said.

She contended that Bashara intentionally misled police in the days after Jane's body was found by not telling them of his lifestyle and his affair with Gillett, which had been going on for four years.

She showed jurors emails that they had seen over the previous weeks, including the one in which he told Gillett that he was "ready to make a life-changing event," and that he said he would lose money if he divorced his wife, but he would rather live in a one-room shack and be happy than be rich and unhappy.

Lindsey repeated frequently the fact that much of the case hinged on Bashara's lies—to police, to his friends and associates, and to his family—"which can be taken as circumstantial guilt."

She noted that Bashara had written $7,821 in checks to Gillett in 2011; Lindsey said he couldn't afford a wife and mistress.

"The words 'till death do us part' meant one thing to Jane Bashara and another to the defendant," she said. She ended her hour-long presentation citing Proverbs 18:21: "The tongue has the power of life and death, and those who love it will eat its fruit."

Michael McCarthy presented first for the defense's closing argument, stating up front that Bashara "has been waiting for this for almost nine weeks. His time of vindication.

"Since that day nearly three years ago, there's been a cloud over the head of Mr. Bashara and there's been a target on his back," McCarthy said.

McCarthy immediately recalled the previous week's testimony that the investigation into the defendant had been flawed from the start, with misplaced evidence and poorly executed witness interviews.

He cited several theories the prosecution was pushing and attempted to discredit them all.

One was that Bashara wanted to have Gentz hit because Gentz could finger him for arranging Jane's death.

"I'm not justifying what Bob did, but what's important is his motivation for committing that crime," McCarthy said. "He knows Joe Gentz killed Jane Bashara. He wanted revenge, and Joe Gentz could frame Bob Bashara to get a good deal for himself. He ended up making a deal: He committed first-degree murder but got a deal for second."

Another defense notion, McCarthy said, is that Bashara wanted his wife dead so that he could pursue a life with Gillett and the lifestyle.

"It's a smoke screen. It is salacious," McCarthy said.

"The reason we have so much interest in this case is because of sex. The reason the media has followed this is the literal sex appeal. The average person doesn't have much knowledge about"—and here he slipped, saying—"BSDM, BMSD, BDSM; I'll get that right sometime and it will roll off my tongue, but it certainly has given this story life for three years.

"Bob had no desire to see Jane die; he had lived a double life since 2004.

"He had gone out with Gillett since 2008, and whatever he did, she kept coming back to him," McCarthy said. "There was no indication that anything was going to change. Bashara placated her with tales of divorce and a house for Gillett and him to live in. But he had no intention of following through on any of those promises."

McCarthy no doubt thought back to the testimony of Kathy Young, the Realtor who said Bashara and Gillett were ready to move into the house on Kensington. The Realtors that testified, he said, "had a good reason not to like [Bashara]. He wasted their time; they had a legitimate beef. No closing no payday."

The third motive McCarthy poked at was the nearly $800,000 Jane had in her 401(k) account.

McCarthy said Bashara was giving Gillett "a lot of baloney."

"He wouldn't kill Jane and then show up with a sack of money on Friday," McCarthy said. "It's just not gonna happen."

Besides, he said, Bashara earned less than $20,000 in 2011, while Jane made $94,787 plus her pension.

"He's got it good, and she's the person who's giving it to him. Hard figures make it clear she was the breadwinner. Why would he want her dead?"

Jane, he said, was the "golden goose."

In their pursuit of Bashara, the cops and prosecutor's office ignored other potential suspects while allowing others to possibly commit crimes with impunity.

"They want him, why? He lied when he voluntarily goes to the police?" McCarthy said. "He doesn't tell them about BDSM or his affair with Rachel Gillett? Is this consciousness of guilt? Or is that because he's embarrassed? He knows he didn't commit this crime, but he's got some skeletons in his closet. Now he's got this huge problem that he didn't create."

McCarthy named several witnesses who were either of dubious credibility or should have been looked at more stringently as suspects or both: Paul Monroe, the man who called in false tips; Robert Fick, the handyman; Darryl Bradford, a confederate of Monroe's; Therese Giffin, Bashara's lifestyle friend from Chicago who lied to police; Nancy Bashara and Stephanie Samuel, Bashara's mother and cousin, who handled the gun; Steve Virgona, who made several odd statements regarding the murder and Joe Gentz on the stand; and Larry Ellington, the stool pigeon inmate.

After outlining this cast, Diallo took over to deliver more of the defense closing, a rare tag-team move.

"I have spent one fifth of a year with you, and I told you there were three things in this case that were not going to be true," Diallo said. "I told you BDSM was not going to be a motive for murder. We heard it from Jane's friend who spoke about a key party in 2009. That means Mrs. Bashara had some knowledge.

"I am telling you that Rachel Gillett, that was not going to be anybody's motive for murder. Leave, come back, leave, come back. He could not have Rachel without having Jane to provide the money and comfort he had grown accustomed to."

Diallo's three things fell apart midway, but she forged on.

"Women talking about being flogged, everything in the world that has nothing to do with this case."

She noted that when it came to discussing such things in court during the trial, "I had to hand that off to Mr. McCarthy. It's embarrassing and humiliating and beneath the dignity of a courtroom. That has nothing to do with Mrs. Bashara dying, but we had to listen to it."

Diallo then struck at the politics, making sure jurors were aware that "there were meetings with the head prosecutor" about getting Bashara: "Justice for Jane should not mean injustice for Bob."

She then posited that the murder did not happen in the garage.

"Who said it happened at the house?" Diallo asked. She noted the newly revealed testimony—the analysis that Grosse Pointe Park captain David Loch muffed and failed to submit—that the leaves on Jane's socks did not match leaves in the Bashara garage.

She began lobbing bombs, hitting here and there.

"Guess who never got on that witness stand and looked Bob Bashara and you in the face?" she said. "Joseph Gentz."

Lindsey was off her seat with an objection before Diallo started pronouncing the "G" in "Gentz."

"He has the right to remain silent," Lindsey said.

The motion was sustained, but the jury heard it anyway.

Diallo was becoming more animated by the minute, banging on a wooden podium that sat between the defense and prosecution tables, waving her hands and raising her voice.

She started in on Virgona and how, despite the fact that Virgona had involved himself in the case, investigators never sought his phone records to see if he had contact with Gentz on the night of Jane's murder.

She noted that police went first to Virgona, "but they kinda glossed that over."

Diallo also pointed out that Virgona "was the first person to put Bob Bashara's name into this equation. Why?"

She had no answer, just a question, which is what the jury should not have in any finding of guilt.

Then it was back to Gentz and the $5,000 deposit into his account from his stepmother, which was cancelled on January 24, 2012, the same day Jane was murdered and shortly before Gentz's next child custody hearing.

"How about this theory?" Diallo said. "What if Mrs. Bashara is leaving the house as Joe Gentz is coming up to the house, and where is JJ by the way?" referring to Gentz's friend who refused to be interviewed by the cops. "They didn't investigate that because his name isn't Bob Bashara."

She touched on the grilling of Narduzzi, remarkable, she said, because "normally, it's the defense's job to point out that the investigation is bad. A bad investigation is the death knell for a prosecution. Would you have listened to us if we told you that this investigation was messed up? Would you have listened to us if we had told you that you went after Bob Bashara to the exclusion of all others? What the hell do you mean that you are police officers with guns and badges and because someone is uncooperative, they don't get interviewed anymore?" referring to JJ and Narduzzi's failure to execute.

She was coming down a little now but had a clincher. At the time, protests from the failure of a grand jury to indict a New York Police Department officer for the chokehold death of Eric Garner, a street vendor, were raging. Garner was heard to utter "I can't breathe" as his last words while the prohibited tactic was used on him.

Diallo tapped into the news and the power of police.

"We have a situation going on all over this country that tells you they know their power. I don't know what went on with this because I didn't see it. But I know what went on with 'I can't breathe,'" she said, poking her right index finger into the air on each of the last three words.

"And still you walk, still you're out there. Because you know why? They know their power. They can get up there and say whatever they want. If that's what they're so inclined to, then that's fine."

She said that some of the officers in Detroit are the "best you're ever gonna find. But when they set their sights on you, hey, guess what?"

She held up her hands in the surrender position.

"I can't breathe."

The courtroom was dead silent for five long seconds

as Diallo walked back to the defense table. Judge Evans called for a break.

The jury began deliberating at 2:45 P.M. on December 11, a Thursday. They had heard the last of the prosecution's relentless assault on the character of Bashara.

Assistant prosecutor Robert Moran gave a parting shot before ending the completion of his side's closing argument.

"He took his daughter on national TV and put his arm around (her) and used her as a prop to say, 'I'm not having an affair. I absolutely have nothing to do with this,'" Moran said. His words came in a flurry, as if he had more to say than he had time. There was so much to tell.

"He used his daughter. He used his son. He used his mother. He didn't care who he used to do what he wanted, to do his bidding. He claims that he loved his wife and that he wanted to be with his wife. What kind of man uses his own wife? What kind of man has his girlfriend pick up his wife's car for him? What kind of man has two women come over to the marital bed and have sex with them while his wife's out of town? A man who loves his wife? A man who wants to stay married to his wife? Is that what a man does? Is that what a man does to a woman that he loves, a woman he wants to be with? No, it isn't. It's the ultimate act of betrayal."

He outlined for the jury the charges, sipping water from a blue plastic cup in between salvos.

Aiding and abetting, he said, "is if he does something before or to assist during the crime."

Conspiracy and solicitation "are different than first-degree murder . . . They require him to conspire to get someone to do something. They do not require anyone to die or be hurt.

"First-degree murder requires someone to die. So the defendant is guilty of solicitation, conspiracy, and he's also guilty of first-degree murder because he assisted, aided, and abetted the commission of that crime."

It was well spelled out. Just to make sure, Moran addressed doubts that some jurors might have about just where Bashara was when Jane was killed. They had heard repeatedly about Bashara's carefully constructed story of being at the property on Mack, ten minutes away, when Jane was murdered at around 7:30 P.M. on January 24, 2012. Gentz, while he didn't testify, had told police in one of his six accounts of the murder that Bashara was present, holding a gun on him, when he killed Jane by smashing his boot into her throat. No doubt some jurors had heard that story somewhere, although not in the courtroom.

To convict on first-degree murder, Moran said, "you don't have to believe that he's in the garage at the time of that crime. He doesn't have to be in that garage. As long as he did something to encourage Joe Gentz to commit that crime."

Still, Moran said he was convinced that Bashara was in the garage "because the DNA doesn't lie. I submit to you that he had that gun because he tried to hide it . . . The fact that he lied about that gun, that fact in and of itself, and the gun was recovered, and the gun was said to be used by him to get Joe Gentz to commit this crime, that's enough to convict him right there."

In succession, as he spoke, images flashed onto the courtroom's video screen: Bob and Jane's black-and-white wedding photo, the two smiling as Jane clutched a bouquet of flowers, then Bob and Rachel, cheek to cheek, smiling, and finally, Jane stuffed into the backseat of her Mercedes.

The jury left without a hint of emotion, walking single file into the jury room as they had for almost two months. Sometimes they had done so with an adventurous jaunt, but this time it was a solemn march.

The sixteen members became the twelve to deliberate, with three women and nine men serving as jury.

They talked and pored over evidence for a while on Thursday before going home. They did mostly preliminary chores, getting themselves in order before hemming and hawing.

Jurors returned Friday and asked for a legal dictionary and a dry-erase board. Judge Evans denied the legal dictionary, saying, "You have what you're going to get. You cannot have outside reference materials."

The jury asked for testimony transcripts for four witnesses: Nancy Bashara; Janet Leehmann, the prospective third party for Bashara's love triangle with Rachel; Courtney Johns, a tenant; and Stephanie Samuel, Bob's cousin.

No, Judge Evans said, "You have to rely on your collective memories. Unlike modern twentieth-century courtrooms that you just push a button and a transcript comes out."

It would take almost a week to get a transcript, she

said. "But if you say, 'Judge, I don't care,' then I have to do it."

She was telling the jury—already having missed work and family for eight weeks—that she would have to stay on duty until her court stenographer could find the time to deliver the transcripts.

Everything was bogging down.

It was Bashara's fifty-seventh birthday. He was smiling as he sat in the witness room awaiting his fate.

The jury wanted to know the definitions of a couple of words used during the trial: "vitriolic" and "exculpatory." The judge allowed it.

The jury left at 3:50 on Friday. It would not deliberate on the weekend.

When the panel returned on Monday, Bashara was not around. Judge Evans, always sensitive to any issues that could send the case to the appellate court on procedural error, declared that the jury could not deliberate without Bashara in the courtroom.

Bashara complained to jail guards that he was not feeling well early on Sunday. As the day progressed, he felt worse, and by Sunday evening, he was taken to Detroit Receiving Hospital for tests.

"Bob Bashara is not medically competent to appear in court at this time," a spokesman for the Wayne County Jail announced.

His ailing health had already held up the trial, with his collapse in October and a medical appointment in November. He had diabetes and kidney problems, as well as macular degeneration.

But no one was publicly saying what his medical problem was. Not even his own family knew. They had not talked with him for a long time.

By Thursday, Bashara was back, and so was the jury.

A question came from the jury room: If the defendant took an action to conspire or solicit to have someone hurt and the victim died, is the defendant guilty of first-degree murder?

The jurors were struggling on the heaviest of the charges.

Later that morning, the courtroom heard raised voices from the jury room. "I'm tired of this. You need to stand up," one of the male jurors yelled. The response was muffled. They went to lunch.

By 1:50 P.M., after deliberating for less than three full days, the jurors had a verdict. At 3 P.M., Judge Evans read the decision.

Count 1—Guilty of Murder—First Degree
Count 2—Guilty of Solicitation to Commit Murder
Count 3—Guilty of Homicide Murder First Degree,
    Premeditated
Count 4—Guilty of Obstruction of Justice
Count 5—Guilty of Witness Intimidation

Jane's mother watched the reading of the verdict on television at home. A clerk in the Wayne County Prosecutor's Office called her to let her know it was coming on.

"We've waited three years. It's been Bob Bashara every day of our life, morning, noon and night," she said. "And

I'm just so relieved that the jury came back. I've been betrayed. I liked Bob. I thought he was an okay husband and father and it was all show-and-tell. He said they had an open marriage. I call it a double life. I was sure he did it, but yet, could they convince the jury that he did it? So, there was doubt and yet there wasn't. I don't know. I thrashed it over both ways for three years almost. There will never be [complete] closure for us. We will always miss her."

Sentencing was set for January 15. Lorraine Engelbrecht had been writing down what she was going to say during the victim's impact statement portion of the proceeding for months.

16

"You Once Said You Were Living the Dream. Now You're Experiencing a Nightmare"

Going to prison forever wasn't an option in Bob Bashara's head. He insisted to anyone who would listen—a list that had dwindled to fellow inmates, jail guards, and his attorneys—that he was not guilty.

He insisted that the jurors who found him guilty, which included two who initially wanted to acquit, had been bombarded by a media and prosecution bent on twisting his fine character into something it was not. He was not a murderer, he said.

He was also a lousy prisoner. Since he was arrested in June 2012, he'd been racking up repeated written violations in the Wayne County Jail.

Stealing food items, talking down to jail employees, and just being a pain in the ass was common behavior for him. In one case, he asked that his cell toilet and sink be cleaned. When it wasn't done to his satisfaction, he demanded the cleanser used to treat it be left with him.

"You did it ass backwards, and I need to do it again," he told a jail trustee.

He also used the phone in his jail cell to run his land-lord business, a violation that cost him phone privileges for a while.

Between the jury verdict and his sentencing, Bashara, convinced that this was all some terrible mistake, composed a series of motions that he presented on his sentencing day, January 15, 2015.

The gallery was mostly full on that Thursday, a crowd that included several members of Jane's family led by the matriarch, Lorraine. Steve Tibaudo and Steve Virgona also stopped by. It was a little reunion of people who helped put Bashara away.

The live online broadcast feed drew over one thousand viewers.

Bashara walked in with a new haircut, short and tight. Black suit, gray tie, white pocket square.

He asked Judge Vonda Evans for a chance to make a statement regarding his legal status. He told the judge that after he was transferred back to Oaks Correctional Facility in December rather than the local jail, he was unable to meet with or make any calls to his defense attorneys until January 8. On that date, Bashara said, he reached Michael McCarthy and asked to file an extension for two to three weeks before sentencing.

Bashara, reading from a prepared statement to Judge Evans, said McCarthy would not file a motion for an extension.

"I have been handicapped by time," he said. "I had

two days of access to the law library at Oaks and had no assistance from my defense attorneys."

He asked Judge Evans to rule on the lack of testimony from Joe Gentz, noting "he was the only one who accused me, yet we didn't object to this and as a result they were used in submission in what I feel was hearsay." He said being unable to face his accuser was unfair.

Bashara said live streaming compromised and allowed witnesses to see other people's testimony with the blow-by-blow texting narrative provided by news outlets.

He concluded by noting that his presentence report, a whopping 125 pages long, didn't include an eight-page report he had composed on the community enhancement efforts of he and his wife.

The judge sighed audibly.

Then Bashara asked the judge to declare a mistrial.

Judge Evans was unimpressed. She denied the request and asked defense lawyer Lillian Diallo to type up Bashara's eight-page addition to the presentence report and get ready for the sentencing.

She knew what she was obligated to do by law and was ready to do it with great relish; Bashara was going to be put away forever. But first, his dead wife's family could tell him what was up in their impact statements.

"Every day I live I want to think about you rotting in jail and someday burning in hell," Jane's mother, Lorraine Engelbrecht, told him in a two-minute address. Bashara faced her from ten feet away. "Why didn't he just go and live his scummy dungeon life and leave my daughter and my grandchildren alone?"

No one with a heart could listen to her anguish and not tear up. Dry eyes were few.

Jane's sister Julie Rowe delivered a longer, eloquent, and painful lecture to Bashara as well.

"Bob lied to all of us," Rowe said, speaking on behalf of the family. At first, she spoke toward the judge, to the right of Bashara. "Bob manipulated all of us. Bob utterly betrayed all of us. Some of us have sought help through counseling, some have found relief through medicine. Some have found comfort in religion and some grieve alone.

"This crime has had an especially debilitating effect on Jane's mother, my mother. My mom's a strong lady, but she has struggled to keep her chin up. This is not only because of the brutal murder and loss of Jane, but from the deep betrayal, lengthy investigation, and the never-ending drama that Bob and his team have heaped on her.

"This crime and investigation along with my father's death from Alzheimer's complications in March 2014 has been a lot for my mom to deal with. Bob broke her heart and rubbed salt in her wounds."

She then turned to Bashara.

"You've devastated your children's and my family's lives by your stupid, cowardly, foolish acts. You've broke my mother's heart a thousand times over. She loved and trusted you more than anyone else in our family.

"I will go on and we as a family will go on. I will be watching over Jessica and Robert, loving them and sharing their life experiences . . . I will hold [your] grandchildren in my arms. I will come and go as I please. I will be free with Jane's spirit by my side as I live life to the fullest. All of it will be all the more sweet knowing that you are uncomfortable, miserable, alone in a prison where you belong for the rest of your pathetic life."

Bashara then got his turn.

"I will continue to [say] again and again and again, I am innocent, that I had nothing to do with my wife's death—terrible, terrible death—and that I will continue to appeal this sentence brought by this prosecution and witnesses that lied, misstated the truth, and painted a different picture than what was true."

Bashara contended that the prosecution used the media to attack him and, as a result, "turned everyone against me."

Pulling a tattered yellow piece of paper from a brown file folder, Bashara read from a letter he said he got from a state inmate who was in the same prison block as Joe Gentz.

"A few times he would change up his story about buying a car and say a guy named Bashara was not paying him to kill his wife and he lied to get less time off his sentence," Bashara said, reading the letter.

Finally, Bashara compared himself to Job, saying, "I will admit clearly that I am nowhere near as blameless as Job was before the Lord.

"I have done things in my life that I look back and am not 100 percent proud of, but I had absolutely nothing to do with my wife's death."

Judge Evans took her own turn to deliver a speech,

reading from notes. She began by noting the advantage Bashara had begun life with.

"You were a product of privilege, a privileged life. Your mother was wealthy; your father was a prominent court of appeals judge."

Judge Evans said that his parents' divorce began his undoing, as the women in his life waited on him and ensured his life went smoothly.

His mother, Evans said, "was your safety net."

"You were the life of the party, the mayor of Middlesex," Evan said. "While your wife was working, you and your friend were at Lochmoor . . . smoking weed and doing cocaine. And when he asked you how life was, you said, 'Living the dream.'"

On the BDSM lifestyle, Evans said it allowed Bashara "to sharpen your manipulative skills."

"What I learned about that lifestyle from this trial was this: the lifestyle is nonconventional, but it's predicated on consensual exchange of power between the dominant, the master, and the submissive, the slave. You managed to manipulate that consensual lifestyle into a tool that was your arsenal to prey on vulnerable women. Your philosophy was simple: What better way to personally destroy their dignity and respect? This is not what the lifestyle is about. But you manipulated it. And you used it to torture your victims mentally and physically.

"The only person you ever loved was yourself. Just like a predator you used social media, the BDSM lifestyle, your family, your friends, to lure your victims with lies about who you were and what you wanted."

She pronounced the fullest of sentences on all five counts, ensuring that, barring a successful appeal, Bashara would never be a free man again.

"You once said you were living the dream," Evans said as she concluded. "Now you're experiencing a nightmare."

Lisa Lindsey and Robert Moran watched the final chapter in their crusade to take down Bashara with dignity. There was no gloating, just grim faces. They declined to be interviewed for this book. Fair enough. But they had to be gratified, and there had to be some behind-the-doors celebration. Their hard work, despite the fumbling of some investigators and the complaints about mistreatment by Lindsey from some of the witnesses, delivered justice and hopefully brought a sliver of solace to Jane's survivors.

In a county burdened by a legacy mismanagement and an office dealing with 1,200 murders between 2012 and 2014, the prosecution team pushed for this verdict relentlessly.

In the end, they are the pros that make the system work.

AFTERMATH

A little over two weeks after he was sentenced, Bashara sent me an email, dated February 2, 2015:

> *Godd day to you and may our Lord Jesus Christ bles you yours and our friend.*
>
> *I wtire you this once, realizing that your "intentions" in communicating were not sincere, but for personal gain. i would have thought that as an' investigate reporter" (your title, not mine), you would have been more attentive to the sham and circus of a trial that was put on, clerly showing the corrut ways they operate. This must not matter to you, so do as you planned and write what you will, on the lies, flse theories and corruption that is lawenforcement and Wayne Couty prosecution. Any accounts based on what was prsented will be both*

false and liabelious, and certainly without my permis-
sion. You and your friend should treat carefully. Know
that I will never stop, never give up, until i am vindi-
cated, as before you is an innocent man.

So I bid you well and hope that if you dig, like I have, you
will uncover the truth. Has it occured to anyone, that fter
2 1/2 years of shooting his mouth off with lies, he now
alledgely does not want to take the stand ??

does this not cause anyone to wonder ?? This is the core
of the matter. i will continue to ask the Lord to bless all
whom are in our lives. be well and know I am a true
friend of those woh sincerely care about me.

od bless

RB

I didn't expect to hear from him again. I wrote him
back, asking some questions. I asked about the repeated
phone calls between him and Gentz in that month leading
up to Jane's murder. And as I looked at my notes, I saw
that he told me at one point he had not talked with Gentz
for some time before the murder. He came back February 6.

I am going to reply, contrary to my earlier words and
replying . . . if you wish me to, you will need to put 10 to
20 on my jpay, so I can afford stamps . . . while I will not
get specific, you are mistaken as to my words . . . I never
said I did not talk to that evil man much, i id say that

we had just met and I knew little of him, much to my lifelong regret. As for the calls, their supposed expert, looked only at what they wanted him to analysis, but as Paul Harvey used to say, there is the rest of the story . . . there is, upon a more details lok, much to reveal . . . such as . . . 65 to 70% of all those calls were under 25 to 35 seconds, hence never connecting, one area that my legel tem never brought out, contrary to my insitence, as you are orrect, there was discourse between them and then them nd myself, and hence my filing the motin I did . . . which should have been done earlie . . . so you will soon see alot more, as DV may have said, as to the real truth in all this . . . so for now that is all I will say, and hope that you, le so many do not hurt yourselves jumping to the false theories and conclusions they presented . . . like I am vain because I had a vaniety plte. . . . which my dear mother gave me . . . of that there was martial iscourse . . . not one person, in my family, hers or our many friends said they wutnessed ANY discours, another misleading and false seniero they presented. . . . so I bid you well and ask or Lord to bless all we know . . .

Next, I asked about who he suspected of the murder. If it's not Bob, who, then? He had also asked me to put some money on his JPay account in order to continue the emails. JPay is the service that allows both phone calls and emails between inmates and the public. It's a sleazy business akin to the private prison operators and has taken my money on more than one occasion via bureaucratic screwups, disorganization, and conflicting policies. I was told that I could not put email money into an inmate's account. Case closed. But I got one more email on February 17.

> *I would have to have you place monies on my account, then I would be able to buy stamps, so until such time this will be my last message.*
>
> *Know what you said is exactly the type of investigation i had hoped my legal team would have done and yet here you know this . . . I believe that sv is directly involved, so more on that, but know i will not openly discuss any more of this case, as i know that i will be granted a new trial so will save all of this for that . . . as for the calls, again, of those, check out how many actually connected . . . very few . . . he was late on his rent, would not remove the power or pay the bill, and wanted money from me . . . something i was not going to lend him . . . ever . . . so any calls were for those purposes only . . . I bid you well and will look for any money you wish to send, or a visit should you wish to do so . . . beyond that, I ask our Lord, to bless all those you know . . .*

So I was left with an inmate insisting he had been railroaded. Like almost anyone convicted of such a crime, he is appealing.

The old adage about truth is that there are three versions: yours, mine, and the real truth.

Stick with that and you can be suitably dubious, sometimes skeptical, and occasionally cynical. You'll also be well served when it comes to the ever-present question of

"What happened?" with regard to an incident, accident, or disaster.

In telling this story, I stuck as closely with the law enforcement line as I could, for that is, for better or worse, the most accurate account of events regarding a crime. The prosecution did a fine job and while some of the cops involved were painted as bumbling, in the end, the case was made and a conviction was obtained. I did not write this, however, with the cooperation of any law enforcement agency. Joe Gentz's account was what convicted Bashara, and it's also the one used by the prosecution.

The government has tools that no one else has, from subpoena power to access to the highest of tech. The verdict comes from the system that we hold dear. The system doesn't always work, but as they say, it's the best one we have. In this case, Bashara was convicted soundly, with vast amounts of testimony.

There were arguments from the defense that any number of other possible assailants or assistants in the homicide were not properly investigated; in particular a guy known to most as JJ. I was told at one point that this mysterious guy had more knowledge of the case than anyone knows. But he was never hauled in and properly questioned. JJ is not guilty, though; Bob Bashara is, according to the law. The legal system that delivered that verdict is the same one we rely on every day to keep us safe and to mete out justice. So the story that got Bashara convicted is the one that I follow and deliver, for the most part, here.

I drew liberally from documents in constructing the murder of Jane Bashara. The defense of Bob Bashara made an excellent case for someone other than the defendant as the culprit, but the abundance of evidence ensured he would not prevail.

I also relied on the excellent coverage of the case by the Detroit area newspapers and broadcast outlets. While the media landscape today demands loud and sordid events to drive eyeballs, the collective reporting was professional and reliable.

The thanks list: David Patterson, Small Mouse, Karyn Brown, Julie M., Mike Mouyianis, and Andrea Annis.

APPENDIX

TIMELINE

2012

January 24—Bob Bashara reports his wife, Jane Bashara, missing to the Grosse Pointe Department of Public Safety.

January 25—Jane Bashara's body is found in her SUV in an alley in Detroit.

January 27—Police call Bob Bashara a person of interest.

January 31—Joseph Gentz walks into the Grosse Pointe Park Department of Public Safety and tells police he killed Jane Bashara at Bob Bashara's behest.

February 3—Gentz is released from custody without being charged.

March 2—Gentz is arrested and charged with first-degree murder in connection with the killing.

March 5—Gentz is arraigned on charges of first-degree murder and conspiracy.

June 25—Bob Bashara is arrested and accused of attempting to have Gentz killed.

June 27—Bashara is arraigned on a charge of solicitation to commit murder in the Gentz case.

October 11—Bashara pleads guilty to solicitation to murder Gentz, but he never said why he wanted Gentz dead. Prosecutors have said it was to silence the potential witness against him.

December 10—Bashara is sentenced to eighty months to twenty years in prison.

December 21—Gentz pleads guilty to second-degree murder and tells the court Bashara offered him money to kill his wife.

2013

February 19—Gentz is sentenced to seventeen to twenty-eight years in prison for Jane Bashara's death.

April 17—Bob Bashara is charged in his wife's murder.

September 9–13—Preliminary hearing for Bashara. Judge decides there is enough evidence to move to a trial.

2014

March 3—Trial to begin; postponed.

October 7—Jury selection begins.

December 4—Defense rests.

December 10—Closing arguments.

December 18—Bashara is found guilty on all counts.

2015

January 15—Bashara is sentenced to life in prison.